Direction and Socio-spatial Theory

The embodied directedness of human practice has long been neglected in critical socio-spatial theory, in favor of analyses focused upon distance and proximity. This book illustrates the absence of a sense for direction in much theoretical discourse and lays important groundwork for redressing this lacuna in socio-spatial theory.

Many accounts of the social world are incomplete, or are increasingly out of step with recent developments of neoliberal capitalism. Not least through new technological mediations of production and consumption, the much-discussed waning of the importance of physical distance has been matched by the increasing centrality of turning from one thing to another as a basic way in which lives are structured and occupied. A sensibility for embodied processes of turning, and for phenomena of direction more generally, is urgently needed. Chapters develop wide-ranging and original engagements with the arguments of Sara Ahmed, Jonathan Beller, Edmund Husserl, Martin Heidegger, Virginia Held, Bernard Stiegler, Theodore Schatzki, Rahel Jaeggi, Hartmut Rosa and David Harvey.

This book reinterprets practice, embodiment, alienation, reification, social reproduction and ethical responsibility from a directional perspective. It will be a valuable new resource and reference for political and social geography students, as well as sociologists and anthropologists.

Matthew G. Hannah holds the Chair in Cultural Geography at the University of Bayreuth, Germany. His research has addressed relations between constructions of space, power and state knowledge, as well as various aspects of social theory and historical geography. His previous books include *Governmentality and the Mastery of Territory in Nineteenth Century America* (2000) and *Dark Territory in the Information Age: Learning from the West German Census Controversies of the 1980s* (2010).

Routledge Research in Place, Space and Politics

Series editors

Professor Clive Barnett, *University of Exeter, UK*

This series offers a forum for original and innovative research that explores the changing geographies of political life. The series engages with a series of key debates about innovative political forms and addresses key concepts of political analysis such as scale, territory and public space. It brings into focus emerging interdisciplinary conversations about the spaces through which power is exercised, legitimized and contested. Titles within the series range from empirical investigations to theoretical engagements and authors comprise of scholars working in overlapping fields including political geography, political theory, development studies, political sociology, international relations and urban politics.

Un-making Environmental Activism
Beyond Modern/Colonial Binaries in the GMO Controversy
Doerthe Rosenow

The Challenges of Democracy in the War on Terror
The Liberal State before the Advance of Terrorism
Maximiliano E. Korstanje

The Politics of Settler Colonial Spaces
Forging Indigenous Places in Intertwined Worlds
Edited by Nicole Gombay and Marcela Palomino-Schalscha

Direction and Socio-spatial Theory
A Political Economy of Oriented Practice
Matthew G. Hannah

Postsecular Geographies
Re-envisioning Politics, Subjectivity and Ethics
Christopher Baker, Paul Cloke, Callum Sutherland and Andrew Williams

For more information about this series, please visit: www.routledge.com/series/PSP

Direction and Socio-spatial Theory

A Political Economy of Oriented Practice

Matthew G. Hannah

Routledge
Taylor & Francis Group

LONDON AND NEW YORK

First published 2019
by Routledge
2 Park Square, Milton Park, Abingdon, Oxon OX14 4RN

and by Routledge
52 Vanderbilt Avenue, New York, NY 10017

First issued in paperback 2020

Routledge is an imprint of the Taylor & Francis Group, an informa business

British Library Cataloguing-in-Publication Data
A catalogue record for this book is available from the British Library

Library of Congress Cataloging-in-Publication Data
A catalog record has been requested for this book

ISBN 13: 978-0-367-58317-0 (pbk)
ISBN 13: 978-1-138-06104-0 (hbk)

Typeset in Times New Roman
by Taylor & Francis Books

For Ulf Strohmayer
Ardent scholar of the world, intellectual
inspiration, and dear friend.

in memoriam:
John L. Hannah, 1928–2015
Claudia P. Hannah, 1929–2017
John B. Hannah, 1964–2016
Christa Scheld Ricken, 1938–2014

Contents

Figures

Preface

This book is best thought of as an extended essay, with the accent on the older sense of "essay" as "attempt". It is the outgrowth of a long-running but at first sporadic engagement with issues that Ulf Strohmayer and I first briefly touched upon in a 1992 paper on Marxist responses to poststructuralist writings (Strohmayer and Hannah, 1992). What already dimly flickered through the speculative conclusions we offered in that paper was a sense that the compatibility or incompatibility of different political, theoretical or philosophical persuasions is not only a matter of principle but perhaps at an even more fundamental level, of where we direct our critical practice. This theme was picked up again a few years later in a paper that took the work of Roy Bhaskar as an occasion to suggest that critical realism and "skepticism" are in fact not incompatible when viewed from a directional perspective (Hannah, 1999).

After that, the issue went back into hibernation for over a decade, to be awakened from its slumber only very gradually by a range of different experiences in reading, publishing, teaching and the informal exchanges both inside and outside university settings. Probably the most pervasive of these experiences was that of the arrival and intensification of neoliberal New Public Management techniques and the corporatization of the universities at which I have worked. It is commonplace to object to the intensified "time pressures" academics are now forced to deal with as a result of neoliberalization (Berg and Seeber, 2016). These "time pressures" are more precisely understood as pressures on our embodied directed practice, that is, the problem is not simply temporal but spatiotemporal.

As Stefan Collini nicely puts it, "Writing is a complex activity, and quite a lot happens along the way, including discovering what we really think" (Collini, 2016, ix). This has certainly been the case with the present book: the argument has shifted and changed the entire time in response to reading, mulling over new ideas, and listening to reactions from colleagues. It has been very path-dependent. This path-dependency only intensified after the necessary moment of fixation mandated by writing a book proposal. Thus, although the end result still broadly resembles the original plan, much of the structure and detail has changed. Among the many omissions, incompletenesses and non-engagements that constitute so many open flanks of the argument, a number are probably worth mentioning.

First, the path-dependency noted above has led me to and through a sequence of engagements that could very well have been quite different. The argument travels widely over a number of different fields and engages with an eclectic range of perspectives and authors. It unfolds as a conversation with various perspectives and insights. But this conversation could have been carried out with a cast of writers diverging significantly from those whose work I in fact read. I have no great defense to offer for these particular conversation partners other than that they each in turn seemed of burning relevance for an issue I was trying to figure out. At the same time, the way these positions are interpreted or contextualized is colored most strongly by debates and developments within my own field of human geography. Had I been a sociologist of space, for example, my argument and the literature I cite would undoubtedly have been different. I hope this disciplinary bent does not interfere too much with the usefulness of the argument for the many non-geographers interested in socio-spatial theory. In thematic terms, the most grave silences may be the only glancing engagement with poststructuralist, post- and decolonial thought, with non-Western, especially Buddhist discourses surrounding attention and attentiveness, and the decision not to offer an extended discussion of the senses of time and temporality I rely upon. All of these are vast topics, and none could be adequately discussed given all the other things it seemed more important to say.

Many other silences will be conspicuous as well. Some of these have to do with linguistic specificity. I have drawn upon works available in English and in German, a capacious but still arbitrarily limited pool of insights. Among German-language theoretical perspectives, the most glaring gap is probably the absence of an engagement with Niklas Luhmann's systems theory, which would undoubtedly have a lot to say especially about problems relating to the selectivity of our relations with the world. Finally, as hinted at already above, some readers will be puzzled by the very marginal presence of Foucauldian terminology and methodology. To all but the last of these non-engagements I can only plead directional finitude: to incorporate these perspectives, the book would have had to wait another few years. Foucauldian ideas on the modern Western episteme do play a role in framing the book in the Introduction, brief reference is made to his ideas on governmentality in Chapter 1 and then at somewhat more length in Chapter 7. Ultimately, Foucault's own directed practice, and the collective practices of all those who have taken up and extended his insights, can be described within the framework developed here. The reverse is also true, of course, but my feeling is that socio-spatial theory is less in need of yet another Foucauldian analysis than of a redirection toward a political economy of orientation.

A third point is worth foregrounding. The conversation that constitutes the book's main thread is relatively "coarse-grained" or "chunky". I usually dwell for some pages upon the approach of a particular author before moving on to the next step in the argument. This is a result of my strong preference for engaging with book-length arguments as opposed to academic articles. If the approach in this book sometimes inadequately reflects the contexts of the literatures on which it draws, it at least strives to be fair to the specific contributions engaged within these literatures. The result may seem "whiggishly" focused upon individual authors, possibly an unexpected stylistic approach coming from someone whose previous work has been so centrally indebted to the genealogical injunctions of Foucault. The point, though, is not to do justice to the authors but to their extended arguments, a unit of discourse I believe has been given short shrift in academic debate of recent decades. Sometimes, though, repeated citations of authors do not necessarily add up to a coherent account of their positions. This is probably most evident in the way ideas of Edmund Husserl repeatedly "pop up" but fail to "add up". Unlike the use made of the arguments of Bernard Stiegler, Sara Ahmed or Theodore Schatzki, with whom I basically agree, Husserl is a strange case. Like many previous commentators (including Ahmed and Stiegler, but also others who have seen themselves as furthering his project, such as Maurice Merleau-Ponty and Aron Gurwitsch), I have discovered many interesting and original treatments of different topics in his sprawling work. In this book, the key Husserlian notions I draw upon are his early thoughts on attention (Chapter 2), some aspects of his account of synthetic consciousness (Chapter 5) and his path-breaking reflections upon retention and memory (Chapter 6). Nevertheless, this is in no sense a "Husserlian" argument. In any event, this coarse-grained, conversational aspect is the second main sense in which the present work should be understood as an essay.

A final note on the "mood" of the book is in order. Compared with much of the literature in human geography drawing in some manner upon cultural theory, this book is not particularly "affirmative" (Harrison, 2015). It does not discover behind or to the side of the phenomena of power, alienation and reification it discusses a robust set of new possibilities for emancipation or authentic life. This is not to say that it rules such possibilities out. In fact the argument reinforces many more familiar left-progressive political positions. But it is not constructed on the principle that one may only offer a critical analysis if one can simultaneously offer a commensurable – or even stronger – dose of hope and optimism. It is not a pure example of what the geographer Paul Harrison calls "thinking like a loser", but it is in any case decidedly not an example of thinking, reading or writing "for victory" (Harrison, 2015, 3). I can neither claim unassailable mastery over the literatures I have wound my way through nor offer a new way of surmounting the difficulties I use these literatures to theorize, beyond giving a new inflection to some relatively well-known political positions in the Conclusion.

References

Berg, M. and Seeber, B. (2016). *The Slow Professor: Challenging the Culture of Speed in the Academy.* Toronto: University of Toronto Press

Collini, S. (2016). Foreword. In M. Berg and B. Seeber, *The Slow Professor: Challenging the Culture of Speed in the Academy*. Toronto: University of Toronto Press, pp. ix–xiii.

Hannah, M. (1999). Skeptical realism: from either/or to both-and. *Environment and Planning D: Society and Space, 17*, pp. 17–34.

Harrison, P. (2015). After affirmation, or, being a loser: on vitalism, sacrifice and cinders. *GeoHumanities, 1*(2), pp. 285–306.

Strohmayer, U. and Hannah, M. (1992). Domesticating Postmodernism. *Antipode, 24* (*1*), pp. 29–55.

Acknowledgements

This book has benefited from countless interactions and discussions over the years, only some of them explicitly connected to the topic. To thank everyone by name who in one way or another helped move the ideas along would be impossible. Restricting the list to people and events directly connected, I am, first, grateful for invitations to speak about various aspects of the theme. Thanks go to David Clarke and Marcus Doel at Swansea University, colloquium organizers at the Goethe-Universität Frankfurt, Don Mitchell for the invitation to participate in the conference on the occasion of his receiving the Anders Retzius Medal in Stockholm, Detlef Müller-Mahn along with the editorial board of the *Geographische Zeitschrift* for inviting me to give the GZ Lecture in Berlin, and Jessica Pykett and J.D. Dewsbury for the invitation to participate in a workshop on neuroliberalism and psychopolitics at the University of Bristol. I learned valuable things from the audiences and participants at all of these events. Individuals who have commented at greater length, made crucial recommendations for reading along the way, or just said something that suddenly shifted the kaleidoscope include Matthew Crawford, Florian Dünckmann, Iris Dzudzek, Jan Hutta, David Jansson, Tom Mels, Peter Merriman, Antje Ricken, Theodore Schatzki, Ulf Strohmayer and Mark Whitehead. Florian Dünckmann, Iris Dzudzek, Jan Hutta, Theodore Schatzki and Ulf Strohmayer also read and commented very perceptively on different parts of the manuscript. I am grateful to the University of Bayreuth for the research semester during which a good part of the writing was done. The editorial staff at Routledge have been very helpful. Lastly, the deepest and most comprehensive thanks go to Antje Ricken for her love, friendship, support and patience.

Introduction

Every social practice is directed, and when we are engaged in something, we cannot be engaged in other things simultaneously. Apart from a very modest and not easily expandable capability of multi-tasking – actually, task-switching – when it comes to more focused practices requiring some concentration, being occupied with one matter means not being occupied with others. True, not all practices and not all states of human being are directed in this exclusive way. Our lived bodies are constantly engaged in non-conscious passive monitoring of ourselves and our environments, and much of our activity plays out on a substrate of relatively automatic, unreflected "doings and sayings" (Schatzki, 1996). We can be suffused with desire, paralyzed by fear, absorbed in atmospheres, and much else besides. But focused, directed attention and directed practices are clearly central to social life. This seems to be a simple, well-understood circumstance, "terrifyingly banal", as Tim Freytag puts it (Freytag, 2015, 253). And yet, although everyone is happy to admit *that* it is an important and ubiquitous feature of social life, a systematic understanding of *how* it shapes the social world has yet to be attempted. This book seeks to sketch at least some of the rudiments of a theory of directed practice encompassing the processes through which our directed engagements move as well as the effects of their directedness. The phrase "rudiments of a theory" is chosen advisedly. The argument is not complete; many threads are left hanging. Despite what at first sight appears to be a "terrifying banality", the question of the directedness of attention and practice reveals itself upon closer inspection to be "discouragingly complex" (Freytag, 2015, 253). This is why the book is best described as an "essay". Its main ambition is not to set out an ironclad theoretical edifice but rather to *cultivate a sensibility* for the issue of direction, and in so doing to try to nudge the "style of thought" (Fleck, 1981) typical of much socio-spatial theory in a different direction. Doing so, I hope, will help draw attention to the importance of direction in human geography, sociologies of space and related fields.

There are three main claims to be defended in what follows. First, the fact that embodied human beings are fundamentally limited and finite in our powers of active, directed engagement with the world is more important in explaining social processes than previously assumed. Second, in reducing the significance of physical *distance* as an organizing principle of social practice, recent changes in the dynamics of capitalism have correspondingly increased the importance for practice of *directional change or turning*, especially in the Global North. Thus there is at least the potential for a clash or contradiction between intensifying demands upon our directed engagement and our finite embodied capabilities. Third, the style of thought shaping socio-spatial theory has long been focused upon phenomena of distance, separation and proximity, paying scant attention to the inherent directedness of practice. Therefore, if socio-spatial theory is to adapt to its changing context, it will have to reconsider and supplement distance-based accounts of the world with theorizations of direction across a range of traditional thematics. These three general claims will be advanced in an integrated way in the course of the book. Some of the more specific claims that will be developed along the way are as follows:

- The directedness of attention and the directedness of embodied practice are closely, if complexly, related. Attention can be particularly important in helping to explain switching between practices.
- The distinctive significance of the directedness of practice can often be most sharply discerned in a dynamic register, that is, in processes of turning toward and away from matters of concern.
- Embodied human being-in-the-world, understood relationally and non-dualistically, is characterized by "directional asymmetry". We are constantly "open" to appeals, desires, impulses and solicitations from all directions, both internal and external, but largely only able to act in a sustained and deliberate way in a directionally limited fashion.
- Much socio-spatial and cultural theory operates on the basis of what can be termed a "petri-dish" model of human agency. This model assumes that social actors have a potentially active, creative or destabilizing relation to our social environments in all literal and metaphorical directions at once. It thus obscures both sides of our directional asymmetry.
- Coupled with the petri-dish model is what Sara Ahmed calls "the phenomenology of the 'I can'" (Ahmed, 2006, 138), a common tendency to foreground possibilities for active engagement at the expense of the inherently limited character of our actual engagements in the here and now.
- Neglecting directional aspects of practice in these ways, much socio-spatial and cultural theory interprets a wide range of phenomena and processes, for example, alienation and reification, largely in terms of distance and separation, and thus does not do full justice to their complexity.
- Accounts of social reproduction are likewise often incomplete – they tend to grasp the relative stability of social systems exclusively through analyses of past, present or future active engagements, coupled with "unacknowledged conditions" and "unintended consequences" (e.g. Giddens, 1984), rather than through the effects of non-engagements as such. They thus miss the importance of what I call the "social dark matter" behind our backs that accompanies everything we do.

- The more complete picture entailed by taking account of directional dimensions of socio-spatial processes makes it possible to recognize an important, hitherto insufficiently appreciated species of power relation, which I term "occupation". Understanding how occupation interacts with more familiar types of power relation treated in the critical literature can improve our grasp of a number of political and ethical phenomena.
- An important tension highlighted by the notion of occupation concerns the extent to which increasingly sophisticated exploitation by capitalist actors of our constitutive openness to appeal is pre-empting the relations of care and solidarity, as well as "resonance" (Rosa, 2016), for which our openness and answerability is likewise a precondition.

Direction, interpellation and the analytic of finitude

Processes of turning will be an important focus of the argument. For many readers, a focus upon turning may call to mind Louis Althusser's 1969 essay "Ideology and ideological state apparatuses", which theorizes the process of the "hailing" or "interpellation" of subjects and illustrates it with a brief scenario of a person responding to a call from a police officer (Althusser, 1971). The aim of the present book is likewise to argue that turning is central to social and political processes, but in a way markedly different from that described by Althusser. Turning to respond to the officer's call does have to do with assuming a subjectivity in relation to the state. But it also raises much more mundane, practical questions. What was the individual hailed by a police officer doing beforehand? What matters of concern did he or she have to drop in order to turn in response to the officer's hailing? What did the officer set aside in focusing upon the hailed individual? What larger effects did these changes of direction entail in the lives of those involved and in other lives touched by them? More fundamentally, what is it about human relations to the world that allows hailing to take place and to find an answer? To ask and then pursue such questions, I treat individual, embodied human beings provisionally as separable local centers of thoughts, feelings, affects and actions, always embedded in and co-determined to one degree or another by external factors.

This approach cuts against the grain of much critical work. Such work has turned up many crucial insights regarding the relationality, contingency and derivativeness of human "subjects", none of which I would contest. But the starting point for the argument here is that the subjecthood accreted through complex processes of interpellation and subject-formation – whether for those in more privileged or for those in more marginalized positions – acquires a weight and durability which means subjectivity is not reinterpellated from the ground up with every new passing encounter or hailing. As concrete individual subjects we do not live our lives as though we are recreated or reassembled in a nominalistic fashion from moment to moment. Even if "life-changing" events and the performance of new subjectivities are of course possible at any given moment, for the vast majority of people, they are not actually experienced at every moment. Part of this everyday inertia is attributable to our corporeal materiality. Despite the exhaustively rehearsed dangers of stabilizing the figure of "the" human subject, I think doing so in a specific, carefully circumscribed sense still has something useful to teach us.

In taking this path I explicitly place the argument presented in this book *within* the framework of what Foucault termed the "analytic of finitude" (Foucault, 1970, 312ff). In his archaeology of the human sciences, Foucault argued that the modern episteme emerging at the end of the European 18th century for the first time placed the figure of the finite human being itself at the center of scholarly investigations of those realms conditioning and limiting human possibilities: biological life, economic systems and language. Human being became the reference point and principle of explanation for the very conditions that limit human possibilities.

> The mode of being of life, and even that which determines the fact that life cannot exist without prescribing its forms for me, are given to me, fundamentally, by my body; the mode of being of production, the weight of its determinations upon my existence, are given to me by my desire; and the mode of being of language, the whole backwash of history to which words lend their glow at the instant they are pronounced [...] are given to me only along the slender chain of my speaking thought.
>
> Foucault, 1970, 314–315

The analytic of finitude refers to a "doubling" of the role of the human within the emerging human sciences: both as limited individual and collective being and as the source of the limitations placed upon it, both as actor and knower and as object or product of action and knowledge. The human being becomes "a strange empirico-transcendental doublet, since [it] is a being such that knowledge will be attained in [it] of what renders all knowledge possible" (Foucault, 1970, 318). The great Kantian problematic of human access to knowledge of reality as such is but the most prominent manifestation of a wider pattern that encompasses not just philosophical reflection but many other disciplines as well. The newly conceived human sciences at once trace the limits of human knowledge and action and hold out the hope that by studying humanity in its empirical positivity, these limits might progressively be overcome.

Foucault famously suggested, though, that the modern episteme would soon be coming to an end. The modern "counter-sciences" of psychoanalysis, ethnology and linguistics, along with new approaches in historiography, had been pushing the study of human finitude ever more radically in a direction which seemed increasingly likely to dissolve "the human" itself as the anchor point and reference for the analytic of finitude. In the closing pages of *The Order of Things*, Foucault notes that "man [*sic*] is neither the oldest nor the most constant problem that has been posed for human knowledge", rather merely one "which began a century and a half ago and is now perhaps drawing to a close" (Foucault, 1970, 386). Humanity as the founding principle of knowledge is "an invention of recent date [and] one perhaps nearing its end". If this happens, he writes in the book's famous final sentence, "one can certainly wager that man [*sic*] would be erased, like a face drawn in the sand at the edge of the sea" (Foucault, 1970, 387).

To situate the current argument it is helpful to distinguish two general strands in the critiques of the human that have emerged within and have come to challenge the terms of the analytic of finitude. These two strands correspond roughly to the two halves of the "doublet" noted by Foucault. The first might be described as a tradition of questioning the modern human subject of knowledge and action, whether in terms of its rationality (Freud, Lacan), the historical and geographical conditions of its agency (Marx, the Frankfurt School, Foucault), its mediation through language and culture (Levi-Strauss, the Frankfurt School, Derrida, Lyotard), its entanglement in power relations (Nietzsche, Althusser, Foucault), its construction through practices (Bourdieu), or various combinations of these. Much of what is now considered mainstream social theory (Giddens, Taylor, Schütz and many others) has been in part a series of attempts to respond to such critiques in defense of the ongoing relevance of the human subject. The second strand of challenges to the analytic of finitude often draws upon the first but focuses more strongly upon the processes through which definitions of the modern knowing and acting subject have been constructed through the exclusion, othering and oppression of various contrasting figures. Women (Gilman, de Beauvoir, Friedan), racialized and colonized groups (Davis, Fanon, Said, Spivak, Bhabha, Subaltern Studies), sexual minorities (Foucault, Butler, Sedgwick), the disabled (Shakespeare, Oliver), and other "others", in chronicling their long struggles against oppression and in validating their own independent historical agency, have robbed the modern subject of its former luster and legitimacy by exposing the injustices upon which it has been built. This second strand has also made clear that construction of the same and of the other have always gone hand in hand.

All of this work has rightly complicated the definitional politics of "the human" immensely, revealing "the human" as a long-running site of struggle. However, I don't believe we have actually left the analytic of finitude behind, not least because struggle itself, whether understood in terms of social movement theory or accounts of performativity, continues to be theorized in a way that implicitly presupposes some basic notion of embodied human agency. Foucault himself, writing in the mid-1960s, certainly portrayed the dismantling of the analytic of finitude as an event or a result still to be realized. He frankly acknowledged that "the thought of finitude laid down by the Kantian critique as philosophy's task – all that still forms the immediate space of our reflection. We think in that area" (Foucault, 1970, 384). In the Preface to the English edition of *The Order of Things*, he made it clear that the point of the study was not to deny the role of human beings and their activities as constitutive factors either in social life or in the history of the human sciences (Foucault, 1970, xiii–xiv). *The Order of Things*, in other words, is a work within the analytic of finitude. Foucault's last works in the 1980s on subjective self-formation are perhaps the strongest evidence that the dissolution of the subject announced in the earlier works remained only a partial accomplishment (see for example Foucault, 2005).

This is the starting point for the present book. Its argument is situated largely within the first of the two strands of the analytic of finitude: it remains focused primarily upon the figure of the modern human subject, upon the "same" rather than the "other", while of course acknowledging the ultimate inseparability of the two issues. Kirsten Simonsen offers a subtle argument about the continuing relevance of the notion of human subjectivity even in the aftermath of "anti-humanism" and "posthumanism" (Simonsen, 2013; see also Dörfler and Rothfuß, 2018). Outlining a "practice-oriented re-reading of phenomenology" indebted to Merleau-Ponty, she seeks elements of a "residual" or "renewed" humanism stripped of the "theological, rationalist and Eurocentric presuppositions" that render previous humanisms unusable for critical thought in the early 21st century (Simonsen, 2013, 12, 10). Theodore Schatzki, whose theory of practice is central to the present work, likewise sees a "residual humanism" as unavoidable even in the wake of poststructuralist critiques of the human (Schatzki, 2002). The argument developed in the chapters to follow is broadly aligned with these perspectives. But if the humanism advanced here is likewise "residual", what exactly is "left over" of human existence and effectivity that could possibly form the basis for an argument about the socio-spatial world? The full sense of the answer offered here will only emerge in the course of the chapters to follow. But a first approximation would run something like this: however relational, ontogenetically and phylogenetically derivative, differentially positioned or performative we are, human beings are not simply featureless knots or bundles of external determinations or fleeting stabilizations. Nor are we merely some kind of deceptively stable-looking but actually effervescent foam thrown up by performative events. We inherit generically human biological features, acquire and develop specific embodied properties – some likewise universal to the species – that we need to understand in order to understand social reality. These properties shape intentional relations with the world in fundamental ways regardless of our positionality. A relational perspective that pays no attention whatsoever to the generic characteristics of the relata (in this case, embodied human subject and external world) is incomplete. It is from this perspective that the importance of the inherent directedness of embodied human practice can be most easily perceived.

It seems telling to me that critiques of the centrality of human beings to social explanation have continued unabated for over fifty years now. The suspicion of a growing frustration with the inability of all this critique definitively to vanquish the figure of the human being at the center of the analytic of finitude is heightened by the sheer frequency of such exhortations. Karen

Barad, to take just one example, urges critical scholars to dislodge "unwanted remnants" of humanism and anthropocentrism from science studies and other critical fields (Barad, 2007, 27). This impatience and frustration is perhaps nowhere more strongly suggested than in Alain Badiou's repeated screeds against Kant. Badiou's neoplatonist perspective could hardly differ more strongly from Barad's (Badiou, 2005, 2009). Yet, like Barad, he expresses a fervent wish to have done with the "remnants" of humanism. Kant is portrayed as "the inventor of the disastrous theme of our 'finitude'. The solemn and sanctimonious declaration that we can have no knowledge of this or that ... render[s] impracticable all of Plato's shining promises – this was the task of the obsessive from Königsberg, our first *professor*" (Badiou, 2009, 535). Badiou goes on to describe Kant as a philosopher "whose intentions repel, whose style disheartens, whose institutional and ideological effects are appalling, but from whom there simultaneously emanates a kind of sepulchral greatness" (Badiou, 2009, 536). These are only two – somewhat arbitrarily chosen – examples of frustration with the peskiness of the figure of the human subject, but they conjure up the famous line spoken by Queen Gertrude in Shakespeare's *Hamlet*: "The lady protests too much, methinks" (Shakespeare, 2008, 261). This line, as the *Oxford Dictionary of Reference and Allusion* notes, is often invoked, as I am invoking it here, "when someone denies something very strongly, which suggests that they may in fact be hiding the truth" (Delahunty and Dignen, 2012, 238). I don't claim Barad, Badiou or any other modern critical scholars are in any sense deliberately "hiding the truth" about the continued centrality of finite human subjectivity. However, their ongoing inability finally to banish the figure of the human, and their shared frustration with the apparent resilience of this figure, speak in favor of seeing these efforts as a symptom of something else more fundamental.

Within the analytic of finitude, my argument is both a quasi-anthropological argument about fundamental features of human being-in-the-world and an historical or genealogical argument about the ways in which recent developments in technologically mediated neoliberal capitalism in the twenty first century Global North are now straining these features of human being. The two baseline perspectives are given alternating priority at different stages of the argument. This introduction and Chapter 1 frame the issues in longer and more recent historical contexts, Chapters 2 through 4 address the generically human aspects of directed practice, and then Chapters 5 through 7 return to and deepen the account of historical-geographical change. Chapter 8 and the Conclusion both summarize the argument and address the question of what is to be done if its claims are to be accepted. The overall point to emerge out of this arc from genealogy to ontology and back again is that the ontology and the genealogy actually presuppose each other. The directed character of practice is only becoming so important in 21st century capitalism because it is a non-contingent feature of embodied human beings. And the irreducibility of our directional embodiment is becoming clearer now in scholarly and public debates in large part due to the novel strains placed upon it by the temporal-spatial dynamics of capitalism.

The second strand of thought that has emerged to challenge the analytic of finitude, namely the genealogy of exclusion, othering and hierarchical difference (whether in terms of race, class, gender, sexuality or other categories), is largely left aside in what follows. The genealogy of dividing practices and exclusions is a worthy and an urgent project, of course. Without an account of how the interpellation of subjects is bound up with the production of power-laden difference, the story is fundamentally incomplete. To take just two examples that would fit well with my concerns, the literatures of critical whiteness and masculinity studies, focusing as they do upon previously unmarked social categories, have clear connections with cultural relations of visibility and invisibility, or better, obtrusiveness and unobtrusiveness, crucial for the directedness of attention (Garner, 2007; Gilroy, 2002; Adams and Savran, 2002; Roediger, 2007; Kimmel, 2012). But doing justice to genealogies of difference while at the same time developing the political economy to follow would require an even more complex triangulation between accounts of directed features of human embodiment, the historical geography of capitalism and the complex inscriptions, exclusions, dividing practices and struggles around the formation and contestation of social group identities. This would be too much to tackle in one volume. Nevertheless, I will occasionally flag places at which genealogies of difference and group identity would intersect with the partial theme of the historical dynamics of capitalism that is the chosen focus here.

There are two important exceptions to the general neglect of critical genealogies of difference, namely, a repeated engagement with the feminist ethics of care, and the framing of some core argument through concepts emerging from critical disability studies. However, in both cases I focus not so much on critical genealogies of difference as on what these perspectives tell us about the nature of embodied human beings more generally. A fundamental inspiration for me in trying to balance ontological with genealogical arguments, and in trying to understand the directionality of practice, has been the discourse of critical disability studies. Perhaps more than any other critical discourse of recent decades, critical disability scholars and activists have had to confront, and have creatively debated, the relation between physical embodiment and socio-material context. The central and most profound critical insight emerging from activism and academic or policy debates around disability since the 1970s is that "disability" is a contingent and contextual social relation between bodies/minds and material and immaterial environments (Oliver and Barnes, 2012). Whether a person is "disabled" or not, or to what degree, depends not as such on the "impairments" that may happen to be part of their embodiment but on the relation between impairments and the physical, social and cultural surroundings in which the disabled lead their lives. "Disablement" is always relative to contingent norms of "ability" manifested in built environments, customs, systems of mobility and communication, and cultural expectations. This fundamental and powerful insight was originally dubbed the "social model" of disability, a per-spective consciously set in opposition to the previously hegemonic "medical model", which saw disability as exclusively a pathology of individual bodies. The social model is rooted in Marxist political economy, and accordingly traces the social construction of modern disability especially to the historical emergence and consolidation of capitalism (Shakespeare, 2006; Oliver and Barnes, 2012, 7ff). The development of capitalism went hand-in-hand, in this view, with the construction of norms of individual human abilities suitable for integration into the burgeoning system of industrial production. Those falling outside the scope of these norms have been categorized as "handicapped" or "disabled" in a classic process of othering historically intertwined with processes of othering relating to race, ethnicity, gender and age. Various objections have been raised – and continue to be raised – against the social model, for example against the naturalization of "impairment", or against the lingering hierarchical interpreta-tion of physical difference (Shakespeare, 2006, 200ff.; Goodley, 2014, 6–7, 100; Hall and Wilton, 2017, 728). Despite these objections, however, and despite the ongoing discursive struggle over the significance of the social model, none of the participants in the debates of critical disability studies simply reject the social model outright or advocate returning to a naturalized, individualized, medical model of disability. Working within a relational approach to disability, human geographers have been among those critical scholars researching the specific ways in which built environments, cultures of space-time and issues of belonging or not-belonging in specific places shape experiences of being dis-abled and are performatively shaped by the creative engagements of the dis-abled (e.g., Chouinard, 1997; Butler and Parr, 1999; Hall and Wilton, 2017).

The crucial point disability studies offers to the present argument is that the contingency of the condition of ability or disability with respect to the physi-cal, social and cultural trappings of human life is *a general feature of the human condition*. As Dan Goodley puts it, disability is not just about a specific disadvantaged group but also "an invitation to think again about the human" (Goodley, 2014, 13; see also Finkelstein, 2004). For, as feminist care ethics also recognizes, even "abled" individuals are never abled throughout their lives: infancy, illness, injury and advanced age are all phases in which one's embo-died capabilities are not adequate to successful, independent negotiation of everyday environments, social norms and expectations (Tronto, 1993; Held, 2006; Noddings, 2013). The contingency and episodic character of our "able-ment" and "disablement" interacts in complex ways with other systematic forms of privilege or with dimensions of injustice and marginalization such as racism to produce variegated kinds and degrees of intersectional ablement/ disablement. Depending on how we are situated in this multidimensional sense, there will be many different ways in which "our *incompatibilities* with life" as much as our compatibilities "define us" (Harrison, 2015, 8–9). Critical disability studies and feminist care ethics thus provide a crucial complication of "the phenomenology of the 'I can'", a phrase I will return to repeatedly throughout the pages to follow (Ahmed, 2006, 138).

Direction and socio-spatial theory

Human geographers might be expected to have a lot to say about the role of direction in maintaining or transforming social orders. In his classic 1963 paper, John Nystuen placed the concept of direction at the very top of his list of core concepts of geography, discussing it even before distance (Nystuen, 1996). But unlike distance – for example, in work on the globalization of the capitalist space-economy – direction was not subsequently taken up into general treatments of the socio-spatial structures and processes of modern societies. There have been some strands of behavioral geography and geographies of spatial perception explicitly addressing the role of directional orientation in spatial way-finding and other perceptual processes (Downs and Stea, 1977), as well as treatments of direction of the visual gaze in studies of visualization techniques relating to map design (MacEachren, 1995). Humanistic geography of the 1970s and 1980s addressed the theme of direction repeatedly, for example in Seamon's discussion of "choreographies of place" (Seamon, 2015) and Tuan's work on bodily orientation and the cultural significance of different directions in *Space and Place* (Tuan, 1987). Seamon's work probably provides the most detailed and useful treatment of direction in a sense akin to the one I want to develop, and some of his insights will be taken up in Chapter 2. Yet although both Seamon and Tuan suggested changes to how socio-spatial structures should be conceived and organized, neither was primarily interested in connecting their insights with critical, systematic theoretical analyses of social relations. Direction as pointing is a recurring motif in the writings of Gunnar Olsson (1991) and lurks near the surface of a number of interventions in non-representational theory, though it is rarely explicitly examined (Thrift, 2007; Anderson and Harrison, 2010; Ash and Simpson, 2016; Dewsbury, 2015). The time-geographies of Parkes and Thrift (1980), Hägerstrand (1967; 1996) and Pred (1977, 1981, 1984) incorporated issues of directional movement, but privileged distance over direction in outlining socio-spatial constraints and possibilities. More recent developments (Adams, 1995; Kwan, 2002; Miller, 2005; Couclelis, 2009) have updated and elaborated time-geographic methods, but direction remains a largely implicit and underdeveloped concept in this area as well. In part, the intention of the present study is to revive an interest in direction within human geography and related fields, and in particular to mobilize and supplement forms of graphical presentation associated with time-geography (see Chapter 8).

The "socio-spatial theory" mentioned in the title can be thought of as the wider interdisciplinary frame for this book. My reading of it is centered upon human geography due to my own training, but the aim is to speak to sociology, cultural theory and cultural studies as well. Socio-spatial theory was always a rather amorphous category, even as exemplified in the landmark volume *Social Relations and Spatial Structures* (Gregory and Urry, 1985), which probably represented the high point of its coherence as a concept. The subsequent suffusion of social and geographical research with concepts and sensibilities of cultural theory, the "spatial turn" in cultural theory itself (Bachmann-Medick, 2006, 285ff), and the development of sociologies of space (Löw, 2016; Schroer, 2006) have all contributed to an efflorescence of spatial thought in a variety of different directions that is as impossible to summarize as it is fruitful. Yet in this wider context as well, at least until very recently, there is a relative neglect of direction and related concepts. Regions and regionalization (Giddens, 1984; Werlen, 1997, 1999; Paasi 2009), territoriality (Sack, 2009), place (Cresswell, 2014; Löw, 2010), spatial arrangements (Löw, 2016), networks (Castells, 1996), scale (Herod 2010), and mobilities (Cresswell, 2006; Urry, 2007) have all come to the fore at one time or another over the last thirty years as fundamental spatial organizing principles (Jessop, Brenner and Jones, 2008). Closely connected work on the material/economic (Lefebvre, 1991; Harvey, 1991; Smith, 2008) and cultural production of space (Soja, 2011; Gregory, 1994) has helped ensure that these organizing principles not be misunderstood as static structures independent of practice, struggle and ongoing transformation. Some of this scholarship has tackled issues that could form part of the context for the directedness of practice (e.g. Giddens and Werlen on "front" and "back" regions, or mobilities research), but theory-building that focuses primarily and systematically on the phenomenon of directed practice itself is still lacking. A major assertion supported in the chapters to follow is that socio-spatial theory has habitually focused in its typical style of thought (Fleck, 1981) upon *distance or separation and proximity* to a far more extensive degree than upon matters of *direction* or *orientation*. (I will use these last two terms interchangeably throughout the pages to follow.)

Positionality and direction

The inherent directedness of attention and practice may appear to be accounted for by considerations of positionality (Dzudzek, 2015, 248–249). The orientation or direction we take towards some matter of concern is indeed closely related to the social, cultural, political or economic "position" from which we address it. The selectivity of what becomes visible or invisible from particular positions or within particular "thought collectives" is likewise a familiar theme in critical scholarship (see Haraway, 1988; Fleck, 1981). My argument is that the directedness of practice is not adequately accounted for by positionality, however important the latter is in framing the former. I will discuss this point further in the course of the book. For now, it is important to reflect upon my own positionality, even if it does not fully account for the details of the argument to follow. A good overall characterization of this positionality might be that of a privileged critical human geographer. I suggest this description because it already contains a basic tension. On the one hand I am multiply privileged as an occupant of a number of dominant "unmarked categories" (white, male, heterosexual, abled – at least at the time of this writing), and as someone with the increasingly rare privilege of a secure job. This already shapes the entire argument in a profound way. Precisely because of the fact that I am not typically personally confronted with racism, sexism, homophobia, ableism, poverty and other obvious forms of oppression and injustice, the forms of power discussed here, which, from a subaltern perspective might appear to be "luxury problems" or "problems of the Global North", have stood out clearly for me on the basis of a stronger "felt relevance" than might otherwise have been the case. Thus one danger inherent in the position from which I begin is what Bourdieu called a "scholastic" theory that generalizes the position of the academic, an approach born of a privileged "distance from necessity" (Bourdieu, 1990, 14). I would not dispute this reading. Despite the marks of scholastic theory, though, I would ask the reader to have some patience before concluding that this starting point necessarily dooms the entire argument.

One reason to urge patience is the second dimension of positionality mentioned above. Although positionally privileged, I am, on the other hand, also positioned as a critical human geographer working in the earlier 21st century. I may originally have had little compelling biographical reason to engage with analyses of oppression, exploitation, injustice and the like, or indeed to question many of the ruling ideas of racist, sexist, capitalist life in the Global North. But my education and research – and in no small part, the example set by a series of smart, engaged and patient colleagues I have had the good fortune to work with – have comprehensively denaturalized for me the entire range of cultural-discursive, social, economic and political contexts within which I occupy a relatively privileged position. Thus, like many colleagues, I am at least latently aware that everyday assumptions about the subject, autonomy, dualisms of various sorts, exclusion, unexamined essentialisms, and many other seemingly stable and unpolitical anchors of "common sense" understandings of the world, are in fact power-laden and in principle should be called into question. This situation, an awareness of the comprehensive possibility of revealing the purportedly necessary as contingent and power-laden, forms the second half of my positioned starting point.

For many critical scholars, this kind of double positionality generates a permanent tension. The problem can be simply stated, and is in fact a specific version of the problem with which I opened this introduction: nobody, also no critical scholar, can avoid relying, in the flow of embodied practice, upon myriad dualisms, hypostatizations, reifications, and naturalizing assumptions about aspects of the world. And not just some few dualisms and reifications, but many. Here, too, as suggested in the opening paragraphs above, we may believe that we already understand this. The standard response is then more or less, "Yes, of course! So we need to be more reflexive or vigilant about which hypostatizations and reifications we rely upon, so as to minimize their negative effects." It is my conviction that this response fails to grasp the reason for the problem. The reason is not primarily epistemological but practical and directional – having to do with the inherent directedness of embodied practice. Thus it is a problem that cannot be eliminated, even gradually; at best, we can learn better ways of redistributing its effects. The politics of knowledge, to put it simply, is circumscribed by an underlying politics of directionality. Our directional asymmetry and the directedness of human practice condition what we can know and do, on the one hand, but also what we can critique and undo, on the other. The same is true of the argument in this book. Through its selective exclusions – for example, of discussions of race, postcolonial theory or Eastern practices of attention – the present argument exemplifies the very political economy of orientation that is its subject. But this reflexive "consistency" does not confer directional "emancipation" from the analytic of finitude. The directedness of human practice is not something that can be "overcome" once we recognize it. Nevertheless, recognition can help us gain clarity about a dimension of political economy that I submit is growing increasingly relevant in the early 21st century Global North.

Structure of the argument

Part I of the book lays out the basic blend of political economic, phenomenological and practice-theoretic perspectives from which the phenomenon of directed practice is to be approached. The starting point for the longer argument is a range of recent analyses of attention. Attention has been portrayed as a hitherto unrecognized but important founding concept of European cultural modernity (Crary, 1999), a scarce resource coming under increasing pressure from information overload in the context of neoliberal capitalism (Rau, 2010; Han, 2014; Wu, 2016), a newly important and increasingly measurable form of currency (Franck, 1998, 2005), or a hitherto unremarked basis for uncompensated exploitation of consumers (Beller, 2006). It also plays a crucial, underlying role in new theorizations of "neuroliberalism" (Whitehead, et al., 2018) and power relations in gaming interfaces (Ash, 2012, 2015). Chapter 1 summarizes some of these writings on the economy and political economy of attention, focusing especially on the work of Bernard Stiegler (1998, 2010). Together these approaches suggest the central significance of the fact that active, focused attention is exclusive and that human beings do not possess a significantly expandable capability of multi-tasking, facts clearly established in experimental psychological research (Styles, 2006; Gazzaley and Rosen, 2016). These writings also point toward the importance of attention in orienting practice more generally, but theorize neither practice nor its historical context in adequate depth.

Characteristic for this literature on the commodification of attention is a relative lack of attention to the phenomenon of attention itself. In recent political economies attention is largely understood as directed or focused. While directed and selective attention plays a central role in the entire argument here, it is not the only form of attention. Chapter 2 seeks to paint a more detailed and differentiated picture of attention, and thus makes the first move from a genealogical to an ontological perspective. It traces the development of more substantial phenomenological accounts of attention in the writings of James (1950), Husserl (1991, 2012), Gurwitsch (1964, 1966), Merleau-Ponty (1962), Waldenfels (2004) and Wehrle (2013). These accounts expand the category of attention to include a range of more passive and unfocused modes that are likewise crucial for the argument to follow. Chapter 3 is intended to bring the sensitivity for directional issues gleaned from the literature on attention to bear upon theories of practice, simultaneously extending the range of directional analysis beyond the sphere of explicit awareness and sharpening those elements of practice theory concerned with the directionality of practice. The very detailed practice theory elaborated by Theodore Schatzki (1996, 2002, 2010) will be the main focus here, though it will be supplemented with insights from Bourdieu (1977, 1990) and Crawford (2015) among others. The chapter will issue in a more detailed account of the directedness of practice as intimately bound up with the dynamics of attention. Chapter 3 completes the first part of the book.

Part II is intended to describe in more depth the embodied intentional relations between subjects and world that forms the ground of the directedness of practice. Because the foregoing chapters will have taken the reader through a fairly involved trajectory of argument, it is worth pausing to frame Part II in a separate Introduction. This will briefly explore the notion of directionality as it is developed in Martin Heidegger's work, as a way of sharpening the contours of the alternative concept of directed practice developed in the present work. Heidegger's account of direction and distance in *Being and Time* is exemplary of the general neglect of directional issues in socio-spatial theory. The individual chapters in Part II are all intended to begin to redress this neglect by explicating the phenomenon of turning as a hitherto under-appreciated feature of the subject-world relations that subtend social activity. Chapter 4 confronts some of the questions about the nature and status of subjectivity raised by the first three chapters. Grounding some of the claims of Chapters 2 and 3, it anchors the ontological or quasi-anthropological side of the overall argument. The argument is oriented around key insights from, queer theory (Ahmed, 2006; Wills, 2008), the paleontological thought of Leroi-Gourhan (Leroi-Gourhan, 1993), and some strands of Marxist, feminist and non-representational human geography (Fracchia, 2005; Harvey, 1998, 2014; Orzeck, 2007; Simonsen, 2013; Harrison, 2008, 2015). Out of these perspectives a description of the "directional asymmetry" of embodied human being as the core of "the timespace of human activity" (Schatzki, 2010) is assembled. In the process, the petri-dish model of subjectivity underlying much social theory is called into question. Chapter 4 also includes a rudimentary attempt to illustrate directional asymmetry in graphic terms. I use graphical figures in Chapters 4, 5, 6 and 8 to enhance the sensibility for directional issues, the thought-style, which the book seeks to cultivate. The graphics are not able to depict the argument with complete precision but instead are intended as suggestive aids that in turn point toward connections that may not always be made as clear merely by narrative argument (Krämer, 2016). They lend the argument a kind of geometrical literalness which may suggest the reductiveness of the quantitative revolution (Couclelis, 2009). This is deliberate: I do actually want to argue that in our fascination with more affective, virtual and intangible features of embodied existence, we have lost track of the importance of corporeal organization in socio-spatial theory.

Chapter 5 turns from the corporeal organization and embodied directionality of subjects to a discussion of how the nature of subject-world experiential relations can be reconceived in "rotational" terms. Here recent writings on resonance (Rosa, 2016) and alienation (Jaeggi, 2014) are taken up and adapted in order to sketch an approach to more or less successful forms of subject-world relations. The concept of "montage" borrowed from some theorizations of the political economy of attention in Chapter 1 (Beller, 2006; Stiegler, 2010) is brought into articulation with the question of alienation through Lefebvre's concept of "rhythmanalysis" (Lefebvre, 2004). Chapter 6 completes the three-chapter trajectory from "subject" to "world" by taking up the question of how directionality affects our understanding of matters beyond the embodied subject, the things and objects of the material world. It supplements familiar critiques of reification by identifying two additional kinds of stabilization attendant upon states and processes of *turning away*. Critiques of reification (Lukács, 1971; Bewes, 2002) are recast using Sara Ahmed's "queer phenomenological" approach (Ahmed, 2006), the ideas of Husserl on retention and memory, and those of Schatzki on the segmentation of practical life. Husserl's graphic representations of time and memory are revived and adapted to illustrate this central step in the argument (Husserl, 1991).

Part III explores theoretical and practical implications of the foregoing argument and develops a composite graphical representation of the directedness of practice. Chapter 7 outlines the "political economy of orientation" announced in the book's subtitle. First a conception of power as "occupation" is sketched. This in turn forms the basis for some rudiments of an expanded political economy that both builds upon Harvey's notion of the body as an "accumulation strategy" (Harvey, 1998; Orzeck, 2007) and balances this with a discussion of feminist care ethics (Held, 2006). Here as well the dialectical historical process is at last specified in which recent stages of time-space compression and social acceleration have not only reduced the importance of distance but at the same time enhanced the importance of direction and turning in social practice. In other words, the struggles over attention discussed in Chapter 1 finally receive a fuller contextualization. The arc of the argument from an historical-genealogical mode to an ontological mode and back again is thus completed. Chapter 7 finally also spells out the dynamics of what I call "reproduction by neglect".

Chapter 8 draws together most of the graphical elements developed throughout the previous chapters, first, to offer a series of graphic depictions of different configurations of "social dark matter", and second, to suggest an elaborated version of time-geography's daily- and life-path diagrams that can do more justice to the dynamics of turning. Hägerstrand's (1996) and Pred's (1977, 1984) suite of time-space constraints are brought into conversation with the incipient directional dimensions of Adams's (1995) enhanced life-path diagrams and Couclelis's arguments about some of the increasingly obsolete assumptions of early time-geographic studies. The graphic construct developed by articulating directional graphemes with pre-existing conventions of visual representation provides a heuristic device that at once crystalizes the sensibility the argument seeks to cultivate and suggests visually how a political economy of directed practice engenders social reproduction and transformation. The Conclusion reviews the key points and considers possible implications of the argument by addressing ethical and political questions of responsibility from a directional perspective. In many ways, the argument reinforces already well-established progressive political positions by deepening or enriching existing justifications for holding such positions. In illustrating a novel style of thought, it does suggest some different emphases for progressive politics and ethics.

References

Adams, P.C. (1995). A reconsideration of personal boundaries in space-time. *Annals of the Association of American Geographers*, 85(2), pp. 267–285.

Adams, R. and Savran, D., eds., (2002). *The Masculinity Studies Reader*. Oxford: Wiley.

Ahmed, S. (2006). *Queer Phenomenology: Orientations, Objects, Others*. Durham, NC: Duke University Press.

Althusser, L. (1971). Ideology and ideological state apparatuses. In: L. Althusser, *Lenin and Philosophy and Other Essays*. Trans. B. Brewster. London: New Left Books, pp. 127–186.

Anderson, B. and Harrison, P., eds. (2010). *Taking Place: Non-Representational Theories and Geography*. Farnham: Ashgate.

Ash, J. (2012). Attention, videogames and the retentional economies of affective amplification. *Theory, Culture & Society*, 29(6), pp. 3–26.

Ash, J. (2015). *The Interface Envelope: Gaming, Technology, Power*. London: Bloomsbury Academic.

Ash, J. and Simpson, P. (2016). Geography and post-phenomenology. *Progress in Human Geography*, 40(1), pp. 48–66.

Bachmann-Medick, D. (2006). *Cultural Turns: Neuorientierungen in den Kulturwissenschaften*. Reinbek bei Hamburg: Rowohlt.

Badiou, A. (2005). *Being and Event*. Trans. O. Feltham. London: Continuum.

Badiou, A. (2009). *Logics of Worlds: Being and Event II*. Trans. A. Toscano. London: Continuum.

Barad, K. (2007). *Meeting the Universe Halfway: Quantum Physics and the Entanglement of Matter and Meaning*. Durham, NC: Duke University Press.

Beller, J. (2006). *The Cinematic Mode of Production: Attention Economy and the Society of the Spectacle*. Dartmouth, NH: Dartmouth College Press.

Bergson, H. (1991). *Matter and Memory*. Brooklyn, NY: Zone Books.

Bewes, T. (2002). *Reification, or the Anxiety of Late Capitalism.* London: Verso.

Bourdieu, P. (1977). *Outline of a Theory of Practice.* Trans. R. Nice. Cambridge: Cambridge University Press.

Bourdieu, P. (1990). *The Logic of Practice.* Trans. R. Nice. Stanford, CA: Stanford University Press.

Butler, R. and Parr, H. (1999). *Mind and Body Spaces: Geographies of Illness, Impairment and Disability.* London: Routledge.

Buttimer, A. (1976). Grasping the dimensions of the life-world. *Annals of the Association of American Geographers,* 66, pp. 277–292.

Castells, M. (1996). *The Rise of the Network Society.* Oxford: Wiley Blackwell.

Chouinard, V. (1997). Making space for disabling difference: challenging ableist geographies. *Environment and Planning D: Society and Space,* 15(4), pp. 279–287.

Couclelis, H. (2009). Rethinking time geography in the information age. *Environment and Planning A,* 41, pp. 1556–1575.

Crary, J. (1999). *Suspensions of Perception: Attention, Spectacle, and Modern Culture.* Cambridge, MA: MIT Press.

Crawford, M. (2015). *The World Beyond Your Head: How to Flourish in an Age of Distraction.* New York: Viking.

Cresswell, T. (2006). *On the Move: Mobility in the Modern Western World.* New York: Routledge.

Cresswell, T. (2014). *Place: An Introduction.* 2nd ed. Oxford: Wiley-Blackwell.

Delahunty, A. and Dignen, S. (2012). *Oxford Dictionary of Reference and Allusion.* 3rd edition. Oxford: Oxford University Press.

Dewsbury, J.D. (2015). Non-representation landscapes and the performative affective forces of habit: from "Live" to "Blank". *Cultural Geographies,* 22(1), pp. 29–47.

Dörfler, T. and Rothfuß, E. (2018). Lebenswelt, Leiblichkeit und Resonanz: Eine raumphänomenologisch-rekonstruktive Perspektive auf Geographien der Alltäglichkeit. *Geographica Helvetica,* 73, pp. 95–107.

Downs, R. and Stea, D. (1977). *Maps in Minds: Reflections on Cognitive Mapping.* New York: Harper & Row.

Dzudzek, I. (2015). Zum Beitrag von Matthew Hannah in der Geographischen Zeitschrift, Heft 3/2015: Zur Aufmerksamkeitspolitik medizingeographischer Forschung. *Geographische Zeitschrift,* 103(4), pp. 245–251.

Finkelstein, V. (2004). Representing disability. In J. Swain, S. French, C. Barnes and C. Thomas, eds. *Disabling Barriers: Enabling Environments.* 2nd ed. London: Sage, pp. 13–20.

Fleck, L. (1981). *Genesis and Development of a Scientific Fact.* Trans. F. Bradley. Chicago, IL: University of Chicago Press.

Foucault, M. (1970). *The Order of Things: An Archaeology of the Human Sciences.* New York: Vintage Books.

Foucault, M. (2005). *The Hermeneutics of the Subject: Lectures at the Collège de France, 1981–1982.* Trans. G. Burchell. New York: Palgrave Macmillan.

Fracchia, J. (2005). Beyond the human-nature debate: human corporeal organization as the "first fact" of historical materialism. *Historical Materialism,* 13, pp. 33–61.

Franck, G. (1998). *Ökonomie der Aufmerksamkeit: Ein Entwurf.* Munich: Carl Hanser Verlag.

Franck, G. (2005). *Mentaler Kapitalismus: Eine Politische Ökonomie des Geistes.* Munich: Carl Hanser Verlag.

Freytag, T. (2015). Überlegungen zu einer geographische Praxis (auch jenseits) der Aufmerksamkeit. *Geographische Zeitschrift*, 103(4), pp. 252–254.

Garner, S. (2007). *Whiteness: An Introduction*. London: Routledge.

Gazzaley, A. and Rosen, L. (2016). *The Distracted Mind: Ancient Brains in a High-Tech World*. Cambridge, MA: MIT Press.

Giddens, A. (1984). *The Constitution of Society*. London: Polity Press.

Gilroy, P. (2002). *There Ain't No Black in the Union Jack: The Cultural Politics of Race and Nation*. London: Routledge.

Goldhaber, M. (1997). The attention economy and the net. *First Monday* [online], 2 (4–7), n.p.n. Available at: http://firstmonday.org/article/view/519/440#dep6 [Accessed 20 March 2015].

Goodley, D. (2014). *Dis/Ability Studies: Theorising Disablism and Ableism*. New York: Routledge.

Gregory, D. (1994). *Geographical Imaginations*. Oxford: Wiley-Blackwell.

Gregory, D. and Urry, J. (1985). *Social Relations and Spatial Structures*. London: Palgrave Macmillan.

Gurwitsch, A. (1964). *The Field of Consciousness*. Pittsburgh, PA: Duquesne University Press.

Gurwitsch, A. (1966). Phenomenology of thematics and of the pure ego: studies of the relation between Gestalt Theory and phenomenology. In: A. Gurwitsch, *Studies in Phenomenology and Psychology*. Evanston, IL: Northwestern University Press, pp. 175–286.

Hägerstrand, T. (1967). *Innovation Diffusion as a Spatial Process*. Chicago, IL: University of Chicago Press.

Hägerstrand, T. (1996). Diorama, path and project. In: J. Agnew, D. Livingstone and A. Rodgers, eds. *Human Geography: An Essential Anthology*. Oxford: Blackwell, pp. 650–674.

Hall, E. and Wilton, R. (2017). Towards a relational geography of disability. *Progress in Human Geography*, 41(6), pp. 727–744.

Han, B.-C. (2014): *Psychopolitik: Neoliberalismus und die neuen Machttechniken*. Frankfurt am Main: Fischer Verlag.

Haraway, D. (1988). Situated knowledges: the science question in feminism and the privilege of partial perspective. *Feminist Studies*, 14(3), pp. 575–599.

Harrison, P. (2008). Corporeal remains: vulnerability, proximity, and living on after the end of the world. *Environment and Planning A*, 40(2), pp. 423–445.

Harrison, P. (2015). After affirmation, or, being a loser: on vitalism, sacrifice and cinders. *GeoHumanities*, 1(2), pp. 285–306.

Harvey, D. (1991). *The Condition of Postmodernity*. Oxford: Wiley-Blackwell.

Harvey, D. (1998). The body as an accumulation strategy. *Environment and Planning D: Society and Space*, 16(4), pp. 401–421.

Harvey, D. (2014). *Seventeen Contradictions and the End of Capitalism*. Oxford: Oxford University Press.

Heidegger, M. (1962). *Being and Time*. Trans. J. Macquarrie and E. Robinson. Oxford: Blackwell.

Held, V. (2006). *The Ethics of Care: Personal, Political and Global*. Oxford: Oxford University Press.

Herod, A. (2010). *Scale*. London: Routledge.

Husserl, E. (1991). *On the Phenomenology of the Consciousness of Internal Time (1893–1917)*. Trans. J. Brough. Dordrecht: Springer.

Husserl, E. (2012). *Ideas.* Trans. W.R.B. Gibson. London: Routledge.

Jaeggi, R. (2014). *Alienation.* Trans. A. Smith. New York: Columbia University Press.

James, W. (1950). *The Principles of Psychology.* 2 Volumes. New York: Dover.

Jessop, B., Brenner, N. and Jones, M. (2008). Theorizing sociospatial relations. *Environment and Planning D: Society and Space,* 26, pp. 389–401.

Kimmel, M. (2012). *Manhood in America,* 3rd ed. New York: Oxford University Press.

Krämer, S. (2016). *Figuration, Anschauung, Erkenntnis: Grundlinien einer Diagrammatologie.* Frankfurt am Main: Suhrkamp.

Kwan, M.-P. (2002). Progress Report: Time, information technologies, and the geography of everyday life. *Urban Geography,* 23(5), pp. 471–482.

Lefebvre, H. (1991). *The Production of Space.* Trans. D. Nicholson-Smith. Oxford: Wiley-Blackwell.

Lefebvre, H. (2004). *Rhythmanalysis: Space, Time and Everyday Life.* Trans. S. Elden and G. Moore. London: Continuum.

Leroi-Gourhan, A. (1993). *Gesture and Speech.* Trans. A. Bostock Berger. Cambridge, MA: MIT Press.

Löw, M. (2010). *Soziologie der Städte.* Frankfurt am Main: Suhrkamp.

Löw, M. (2016). *The Sociology of Space: Materiality, Social Structures and Action.* Trans. D. Goodwin. London: Palgrave Macmillan.

Lukács, G. (1971). *History and Class Consciousness: Studies in Marxist Dialectics.* Trans. R. Livingstone. Cambridge, MA: MIT Press.

MacEachren, A. (1995). *How Maps Work: Representation, Visualization and Design.* New York: Guilford Press.

Merleau-Ponty, M. (1962). *Phenomenology of Perception.* Trans. C. Smith. London: Routledge and Kegan Paul.

Miller, H. (2005). A measurement theory for time geography. *Geographical Analysis,* 37, pp. 17–45.

Noddings, N. (2013). *Caring: A Feminine Approach to Ethics and Moral Education.* 2nd ed. Berkeley, CA: University of California Press.

Nystuen, J. (1996). Identification of some fundamental spatial concepts. In: J. Agnew, D. Livingstone, and A. Rogers, eds., *Human Geography: An Essential Anthology.* Oxford: Blackwell, pp. 590–599.

Oliver, M. and Barnes, C. (2012). *The New Politics of Disablement.* London: Palgrave Macmillan.

Olsson, G. (1991). *Lines of Power/Limits of Language.* Minneapolis, MN: University of Minnesota Press.

Orzeck, R. (2007). What does not kill you: historical materialism and the body. *Environment and Planning D: Society and Space,* 25, pp. 496–514.

Paasi, A. (2009). The Resurgence of the "Region" and "Regional Identity": Theoretical Perspectives and Empirical Observations on Regional Dynamics in Europe. *Review of International Studies,* 35, pp. 121–146.

Parkes, D. and Thrift, N. (1980). *Times, Spaces and Places: A Chronogeographic Perspective.* Oxford: John Wiley.

Posner, M. (ed.) (2004). *Cognitive Neuroscience of Attention.* New York: Guilford Press.

Pred, A. (1977). The choreography of existence: comments on Hägerstrand's time-geography and its usefulness. *Economic Geography,* 53(2), pp. 207–221.

Pred, A. (1981). Social reproduction and the time-geography of everyday life. *Geografiska Annaler Series B: Human Geography*, 63(1), pp. 5–22.

Pred, A. (1984). Place as a historically contingent process: structuration and the time-geography of becoming places. *Annals of the Association of American Geographers*, 74(2), pp. 279–297.

Rau, A. (2010). *Psychopolitik: Macht Subjekt und Arbeit in der Neoliberalen Gesellschaft.* Frankfurt am Main: Campus Verlag.

Roediger, D. (2007). *The Wages of Whiteness: Race and the Making of the American Working Class*, 2nd ed. London: Verso.

Rosa, H. (2015). *Social Acceleration: A New Theory of Modernity*. Trans. J. Trejo-Mathys. New York: Columbia University Press.

Rosa, H. (2016). *Resonanz: eine Soziologie der Weltbeziehung*. Frankfurt am Main: Suhrkamp.

Sack, R. (2009). *Human Territoriality: Its Theory and History*. Cambridge: Cambridge University Press.

Schatzki, T. (1996). *Social Practices: A Wittgensteinian Approach to Human Activity and the Social*. Cambridge: Cambridge University Press.

Schatzki, T. (2002). *The Site of the Social: A Philosophical Account of the Constitution of Social Life and Change*. University Park, PA: Penn State Press.

Schatzki, T. (2010). *The Timespace of Human Activity: On Performance, Society, and History as Indeterminate Teleological Events*. Lanham, MD: Lexington Books.

Schroer, M. (2006). *Räume, Orte, Grenzen: auf dem Weg zu einer Soziologie des Raums*. Frankfurt-am-Main: Suhrkamp.

Seamon, D. (2015). *A Geography of the Lifeworld*. London: Routledge.

Shakespeare, T. (2006). The social model of disability. In: L. Davis, ed., *The Disability Studies Reader*, 2nd ed. New York: Routledge, pp. 197–204.

Shakespeare, W. (2008). *Hamlet: The Oxford Shakespeare*. Oxford: Oxford University Press.

Siebers, T. (2006). Disability theory: from social constructionism to the new realism of the body. In: L. Davis, ed., *The Disability Studies Reader*, 2nd ed. New York: Routledge, pp. 173–183.

Simonsen, K. (2013). In quest of a new humanism: embodiment, experience and phenomenology as critical geography. *Progress in Human Geography*, 37(1), pp. 10–26.

Smith, N. (2008). *Uneven Development*. 3rd ed. Athens, GA: University of Georgia Press.

Soja, E. (2011). *Postmodern Geographies*. 2nd ed. London: Verso.

Stiegler, B. (1998). *Technics and Time, 1: The Fault of Epimetheus*. Trans. R. Beardsworth and G. Collins. Stanford, CA: Stanford University Press.

Stiegler, B. (2010). *Taking Care of Youth and the Generations*. Trans. S. Barker. Stanford CA: Stanford University Press.

Styles, E. (2006). *The Psychology of Attention*. 2nd ed. New York: Psychology Press.

Thrift, N. (2007). *Non-Representational Theory: Space | Politics | Affect*. London: Routledge.

Thrift, N. and Pred, A. (1981). Time-geography: a new beginning. *Progress in Human Geography*, 5(2), pp. 277–286.

Tomasello, M. (1999). *The Cultural Origins of Human Cognition*. Cambridge, MA: Harvard University Press.

Tomasello, M. (2014). *A Natural History of Human Thinking*. Cambridge, MA: Harvard University Press.

Tronto, J. (1993). *Moral Boundaries: A Political Argument for an Ethic of Care*. New York: Routledge.

TuanY.-F. (1987). *Space and Place*. Minneapolis, MN: University of Minnesota Press.

Urry, J. (2007). *Mobilities*. Cambridge: Polity Press.

Waldenfels, B. (2004). *Phänomenologie der Aufmerksamkeit*. Frankfurt am Main: Suhrkamp.

Wehrle, M. (2013). *Horizonte der Aufmerksamkeit: Entwurf einer dynamischen Konzeption der Aufmerksamkeit aus phänomenologischer und kognitionspsychologischer Sicht*. Munich: Wilhelm Fink Verlag.

Werlen, B. (1992). *Society, Action and Space: An Alternative Human Geography*. New York: Routledge.

Werlen, B. (1997). *Sozialgeographie alltäglicher Regionalisierungen, Band 2: Globalisierung, Region und Regionalisierung*. Stuttgart: Franz Steiner Verlag.

Werlen, B. (1999). *Sozialgeographie alltäglicher Regionalisierungen, Band 1: Zur Ontologie von Gesellschaft und Raum*. Stuttgart: Franz Steiner Verlag.

Whitehead, M., Jones, R., Lilley, R., Pykett, J. and Howell, R. (2018). *Neuroliberalism: Behavioural Government in the Twenty-First Century*. London: Routledge.

Wills, D. (2008). *Dorsality: Thinking Back through Technology and Politics*. Minneapolis, MN: University of Minnesota Press.

Wu, T. (2016). *The Attention Merchants: The Epic Scramble to Get Inside Our Heads*. New York: Alfred A. Knopf.

Part I
Foundations

1 Political economies of attention

Attention is a name given to a complex set of processes relating embodied human beings – and of course other living things – with their actual or virtual surroundings, as we shall see in Chapter 2. One central feature of attention, however understood, is that in many of its forms it is characterized by selective directedness. This has been the most prominent idea running through over a century of research on attention in phenomenology as in psychology (Styles, 2006; Wehrle, 2013). The discourse on economies of attention that emerged in the 1990s takes this selective directedness as its point of departure and develops a set of conceptual tools with which to begin to grasp the larger effects of the directedness of engaged practice. By tracing some themes in this discourse the present chapter begins to flesh out both what is meant by directional asymmetry and the critique of the centrality of distance in explaining socio-spatial phenomena. Attention has begun to attract the interest of geographers, whether researching principles of urban design (Schmid, 2007), the politics of landscapes (Hannah, 2013), design of video games (Ash, 2012, 2015), or activist geographic information system (GIS – Wilson, 2015). All of this work draws upon the discourses reviewed here, but as yet a more systematic assessment of the spatial politics of attention has been lacking (though see Hannah, 2015).

The discourse on (political) economies of attention is thought-provoking and innovative, particularly in historicizing the problematic of directed attention and in linking it to power relations. A critical overview of this discourse turns up important concepts and insights that will be developed further over the course of the book. Sprawling loosely over a variety of disciplines, it is not tightly organized into a conversation. Nevertheless, for the sake of efficient presentation, I distinguish between three important strands or thematic groupings, while acknowledging that there are overlaps and common themes shared across them. I focus in each case on a small number of authors whose writings raise exemplary points. Broadly speaking, the first strand constructs attention as a limited embodied capacity of human beings, a capacity susceptible to commodification. The second strand treats attention as a vehicle of surplus value creation, and the third focuses more on attention as a contested field of subjectivation. Against the background of these three strands, the work of Bernard Stiegler on attention is introduced in more detail. Stiegler's approach to attention can be read as a partial synthesis of important points from all three strands, and a number of aspects of his thinking will play an important role in shaping the subsequent argument. Although the entire discourse surveyed here strongly implies that there are relatively stable phenomenal features of attention, the arguments put forward in this literature nevertheless leave the details and structure of attentional processes underdiscussed. Again, Chapter 2 will address this silence by turning to phenomenological accounts of attention. This then sets up an encounter with practice theory to be staged in Chapter 3.

Attention as a commodity

The first set of recent writings depicts attention essentially as a commodifiable human capacity around which a market economy has emerged. The basic problem that motivated this strand is one the cognitive scientist Herbert Simon already identified in 1971, namely, that "a wealth of information creates a poverty of attention" (Simon, 1971, 40–41). This idea led Michael Goldhaber to identify the "attention economy" as a new economic form destined to eclipse the material-industrial economy in the same measure as the Web and the Internet become the central platforms for economic activity (Goldhaber, 1997). As Goldhaber himself admits, he was not the first to make this kind of argument, but his version of it proved to resonate strongly. His paper originated as a presentation for a conference at Harvard's Kennedy School of Government in January of 1997 on "The Economics of Digital Information". In his presentation, Goldhaber pointed out that an academic conference like the one where he was speaking is itself a miniature attention economy:

> While you are here, your main concern is how you pay attention and where you pay it, perhaps whether you get enough in return to have a chance at being one of the conference stars, perhaps only through the brilliance of the questions you ask. Even between sessions, the exchange of attention is what mostly tends to occupy people at a conference. Of course, there are material considerations, such as having enough to eat, a comfortable chair, etc. But they tend to be secondary issues, taken for granted, and not occupying much attention. We are living a temporary attention economy in miniature right at this moment.
>
> Goldhaber, 1997

Not coincidentally, another author whose writings would help draw attention to attention in the late 1990s, the Austrian planner, architect and philosopher Georg Franck, likewise modeled his analysis of "the economy of attention" centrally upon the neoliberalized academic world of citation indices, impact factors and reputation (Franck, 1998). "Scholarship", he asserts, "is [little else than] a dance around attention" (Franck, 1998, 37). Franck defines attention [German: *Aufmerksamkeit*] as a combination of the English terms "aware-ness" and "attention" (the latter in the narrower sense studied in psychol-ogy), insisting that he does not reduce it to mere information processing on the model of a computer. Instead, "with *Aufmerksamkeit* both the capacity for selective information processing and the state of conscious presence [*Geistesgegenwart*] are always addressed" (Franck, 1998, 28–30). Never-theless, like Goldhaber, he often treats attention simply as a limited capacity or scarce resource:

> The capacity of our attention for information processing is organically limited. [...] Our intentional consciousness is limited both in terms of the number and complexity of objects on which we can concentrate and in terms of the speed with which we can take up, grasp and order them.
>
> Franck, 1998, 49

Franck argues that as attention has become more measurable and comparable through innovations such as impact factors and citation indices, it has started to take on the full range of functions of an academic currency. Using aca-demic discourse as a touchstone, he explores how phenomena such as repu-tation or stardom can be understood in attentional-economic terms in other areas of professional life as well. His and Goldhaber's portrayal of attention as a commodity in which we can invest, as well as a form of income or profit, can easily be extended to the techniques by which large internet concerns such as Google® and Facebook® track user activities, whether to generate real-time customized advertising markets or to refine search suggestions. The process by which advertisers engage in automatic bidding to place their ads at precisely defined locations on the screens of individually profiled Google® users illustrates very literally how the scarcity of attention can create a com-petitive market (Wu, 2016, 323–324).

Taken as a whole, these and related writings establish a crucial point that plays a key role in this entire study: that however historically contingent as a concept, and however many levels, modalities and dimensions it can be seen to have, in the flow of purposeful activity or practice, *focused attention is selective and exclusive in its effects.* This conclusion has been confirmed again and again in experimental psychology as well as in our naïve everyday experiences (Gazzaley and Rosen, 2016; Styles, 2006; Wehrle, 2013). A crucial point to make here is that this circumstance is not merely an artifact of neo-classical economic epistemology, regardless of how well it has lent itself to incorporation within essentially neoclassical narratives (*contra* Dzudzek, 2015, 246). The scarcity of focused attention was first constructed as an epis-temological object in the decades of intense industrialization around 1900, as Crary shows (Crary, 1999). However, what was then first defined is not merely an epistemological convention but is anchored in an embodied feature of human being-in-the-world, as will be argued at greater length in Chapters 2 and 4. Put differently, I want to argue that the scarcity of focused attention is an important, if hitherto under-appreciated, dimension of the analytic of finitude within which we still find ourselves. Acknowledging that the idea of the scarcity of focused attention has a specific genealogy as a concept does not disqualify an acknowledgement that it also has real bodily referents. And thinking of it as a real form of embodied finitude does not automatically imply buying into the entire edifice of neoclassical economics, *homo œconomicus*, etc. This becomes clearer once we move from the conceptions of Goldhaber and Franck to more political-economic approaches.

Attention as a vehicle of value-creation

The second strand of recent discussions of attention offers a more historical materialist *political* economy of attention. Attention appears here as a vehicle of value creation increasingly appropriated by capital. This strand highlights the genealogy of attention. The aesthetic theorist Jonathan Crary's subtle study *Suspensions of Perception: Attention, Spectacle, and Modern Culture* (Crary, 1999) shows that attention is an historically specific concept that emerged in close connection with the crisis of epistemology – and of the sovereign, self-transparent subject – in late 19th century philosophy, psychology and art. This period was characterized by alarmed reflection on widespread experiences of subjective faculties being overwhelmed by ever-faster, ever-more-complicated sensory and cognitive environments thrown up by industrializing capitalism. The alarm provoked by accelerating industrialization, urbanization and mobility in Europe and North America is well documented (Kern, 2003). Developments in psychoanalytic theory and philosophy gave discursive shape to the felt loss of control. In Crary's account:

> attention emerges as a discursive and practical object at the historical moment when vision and hearing have become progressively severed from the various historical codes and practices that had invested them with a level of certainty, dependability and naturalness. The more the senses are revealed to be inconsistent, conditioned by the body, prey to the threat of distraction and nonproductivity, the more a normative individual is defined in terms of objective and statistical attentional capacities that facilitate the subjects functional compatibility within institutional and technological environments
>
> Crary, 1999, 287

Crary traces the rise and elaboration of the problem of attention in the works of figures as diverse as William James, Edward Muybridge, Edmund Husserl, Georges Seurat, Paul Cezanne and many others. Drawing upon Guy Debord's 1967 argument in *Society of the Spectacle* (Debord, 2009), Crary makes an important claim about what the historical emergence of the problematic of attention implies for modern power relations, both a century ago and today:

> [T]he management of attention, whether through early mass-cultural forms in the late-nineteenth century or later through the television set or the computer monitor [...], has little to do with the visual contents of these screens and for more with a larger strategy of the individual. Spectacle is not primarily concerned with *looking at* images but rather with the construction of conditions that individuate, immobilize, and separate subjects, even within a world in which mobility and circulation are ubiquitous. In this way attention becomes the key to the operation of non-coercive forms of power.
>
> Crary, 1999, 74

Crary sees here a convergence between Debord's diagnosis of the spectacle and Foucault's concern in his studies of discipline: in both cases it is a question of how "docile bodies" are produced (Crary, 1999, 74). The seemingly paradoxical separation effect of strategies of attentional control in the midst of a world characterized by mobility and connection is nowhere more clearly illustrated than in a phenomenon that has only appeared since the publication of Crary's book: people glued to smartphone screens and heedless of the surrounding hustle of city streets, or immersed in gaming worlds and deaf to all else (Ash, 2015). Crary closes the main text of his study by crediting Cézanne in particular for relentlessly attending to "both the ground and the overcoming of the administered perception of spectacular culture, for which attention would be made attentive to everything but itself" (Crary, 1999, 359). In the argument to follow, I will elaborate on Crary's suggestions about how to understand modern, non-coercive power, bringing the individuating and separating effects of attention management into an analysis of "occupation" as a distinct form of power relation that encompasses not only attention but embodied practice more generally.

If Crary's approach updates Debord's "society of the spectacle" and lends the attention economy historical depth, the work of Jonathan Beller can be seen as an elaboration of the basic insights of Walter Benjamin in his 1935 study of "The work of art in the age of mechanical reproducibility" (Benjamin, 2008). Like Benjamin, Beller investigates the impact of cinematic forms of engagement of attention upon social, economic and political consciousness. If Crary chronicled the impacts of the intense phase of industrialization in the decades around 1900, Beller can be seen to do something broadly similar for the current phase. He argues that we now live under a "cinematic mode of production" organizing the consolidated reign of the visual in modern capitalist life. We can understand this mode of production on the basis of an "attention theory of value", which "finds in the notion of 'labor', elaborated in Marx's labor theory of value, the prototype of the newest source of value-production under capitalism today: human attention" (Beller, 2006, 4). Beller later suggests that the labor theory of value can even be understood as a special case of the more general attention theory of value (Beller, 2006, 201). Through the ingenious new methods of attracting and exploiting attention, "the image structures the visible and the invisible, absorbs freeing power, and sucks up solidarity time" (Beller, 2006, 5). We are divided from each other and diverted from projects of solidarity by the new technologies of attention capture. One of the few geographers to follow up on this idea was Heiko Schmid, who applied analysis of visual strategies of attention capture to urban design (Schmid, 2007).

By capturing and managing our attention, "cinema" – by which Beller means not just specific cultural institutions but the increasingly visual mediation of culture in general – "*ceaselessly coordinates global economic forces with the extremely local* (meaning regional, but also interior to particular individuals) *productions of affect, trajectories of desire, and proprioception*" (Beller, 2006, 26). In ways that suggest intriguing extensions of Harvey's sketch of "the body as an accumulation strategy" (Harvey, 1998), Beller puts forward the hypothesis that "from the standpoint of capital, as geographical limitations are in the process of being overcome by capital, capital posits the human body as the next frontier. By colonizing the interstitial activities of bodies, each muscular contraction or each firing neuron is converted into a site of potential productivity" (Beller, 2006, 202). As capital recognizes the enormous potential of mining human attentional capacities, "[t]he increasing efficiency and development of new attention-siphoning technologies becomes [its] central province of endeavor" (Beller, 2006, 206). Tim Wu's documentation of the 20th century quest by US media and advertising industries to squeeze profit from human attention, the "epic scramble to get inside our heads", lends historical detail to Beller's account (Wu, 2016). According to Beller, the cinematic mode of production in effect extends the working day, serving as an important counter-measure to the historical tendency of the rate of profit to fall. "After what is officially known as work, spectator-workers 'lounge' about in front of TV or at the cinema [or now, of course, with their smartphones], producing more of the world, for capital" (Beller, 2006, 204). In a point that harks back to Benjamin, Beller notes that this productive work often takes the form of "montage", the piecing together into a minimally coherent narrative structure of a flood of disconnected images and impressions. This montage work can be seen as a continuation of earlier, more physical forms of industrial labor (Beller, 2006, 39). Christoph Türcke likewise identifies montage as an increasingly central task in everyday environments ever more thickly populated with moments of "picture shock" [*Bildschock*], sudden changes of our sensory fields deliberately designed to grab our attention (Türcke, 2016, 104–105).

In all of this, Beller never loses sight of the fundamentally limited character of embodied attention. One of the most intriguing suggestions he makes comes in a footnote, where he muses on the increasingly intense and thorough occupation of human time under the cinematic mode of production. He suggests that it "should be possible to develop a kind of saturation coefficient to describe the number of sites and the intensities of capital's occupation of the human faculties" (Beller, 2006, 236, note 14). This idea of saturation will be taken up at more length and adapted to a more general notion of embodied practice in Chapter 7, where I try to consolidate an account of "occupation" as a distinct form of power and to identify a new contradiction emerging in 21st century capitalism.

The more historical and political economies of attention in the writings of Crary and Beller place the problematic of attention within the context of the ongoing history and shifting geography of capitalism. The richer picture of attention provided by this historical embedding makes it possible to distinguish between, on the one hand, the relative stability of embodied attention as a feature of basic corporeal organization (Fracchia, 2005) and a quasi-resource of which we undeniably only have a limited "stock", and on the other, the evolving and shifting ways in which this dimension of bodily existence becomes important, is historically shaped and given cultural meaning, and is made relevant to socio-economic processes. Even if, as some authors suggest, attentional capacities, too, evolve or change (Hayles, 2012), there are limits to how quickly and flexibly such change can take place (Gazzaley and Rosen, 2016).

Attention as a field of subjectivation

The third strand of recent critical writings on attention tends to supplement references to the Marxian tradition with stronger doses of Foucault, to focus more upon psychological and neurological power relations, and to frame analysis within an account of the neoliberal present. Attention in this third strand becomes a field of contestation over processes of subjectivation. Here, too, the authors discussed do not constitute a clearly defined and internally referential conversation, and the thematic distinction between this and the second strand is very porous. Further, not all of them even thematize attention directly. But this strand provides some intriguing ways to grasp the political and economic significance of attention that go beyond the portrayal of attention in the previous two strands.

A key framing concept in this third strand is "psychopolitics", a term developed most carefully by Alexandra Rau but picked up as well as by Byung-Chul Han. Following the example of Foucault in his genealogy of "the population", and picking up some insights of Nikolas Rose on the genealogy of techniques of psychological self-development (Rose, 1998), Rau asks how "the psyche" was constructed in Western discourse, and how its identification and description has anchored governmental power relations in Western culture. Rau's focus is upon how the emergence of the psyche and of "homo psychologicus" has interacted with the better-known genealogy of "homo oeconomicus" to shape conditions of labor under neoliberal capitalism:

with the historical rise of "psychopolitics" and a specific homo psychologicus, a social "care of the self" is transported (Foucault), at the center
of which stand the principles of the ability to act [*Handlungsfähigkeit*]
and authenticity – and this [figure] proves amenable to connection with
homo œconomicus, which, programmatically, is supposed to conduct
itself as a business, especially as labor power in the sphere of subjectivized
wage labor but also in other social spheres.

Rau, 2010, 13

One of Rau's central points, however, is that the articulation between homo
psychologicus and homo œconomicus has never been smooth or free of tensions. She argues that although Foucault was right to highlight the importance of psychotechniques, his account remained one-sided. These techniques
have taken on very different valences according to whether they have been
developed and deployed primarily to support "care of the self" or instead to
optimize the entrepreneurial self (Rau, 2010, 15). Rau gives this point
empirical weight, first, through a review of oppositional movements that have
drawn on psychological insights about care of the self, and, at greater length,
by reporting the results on her own interview-based research with workers in
the IT industry.

Although Rau does not elaborate an explicit political economy of attention, one of the major results of her research is, effectively, that this tension
between care of the self and self-optimization in the context of labor expresses
itself as an ongoing struggle for control over the direction of attention, and
indeed, of practice more generally. In the testimony of her research subjects
she discerns a clear orientation toward a form of counter-self-governance she
calls (adapting a phrase from Foucault), the "defense of the self" (Rau, 2010,
324):

> The art of *defense of the self* found here consists in finding activities or
> frames of reference that allow a "switching off". Sports are mentioned in
> this connection, as well as being together with family or friends. Engage-
> ment in a hobby, in organizations or political groups is likewise men-
> tioned. All of these are tactics that allow the forgetting of sources of
> oppression and anxiety, and [allow respondents] to stop thinking further
> about problems of work. Employees try in this way – in part very actively
> and consciously – at the same time to dissolve the obligation or 'chaining'
> of the self (*die Haftbarmachung des Selbst/Selbstverhaftung*) to work and
> to occupy in a new and different way the self-relation with other systems,
> themes and interests.

Rau, 2010, 341–342

A key term in this passage, one which simultaneously acknowledges the finitude and exclusiveness of directed engagement and suggests a bridge between
attention and practice more generally, is "occupation" (see also Rau, 2010, 45).

As mentioned earlier, this term will form the basis for a reconsideration of power relations in Chapter 7.

Although in a far more schematic, aphoristic way, Byung-Chul Han echoes many of Rau's points, and also adopts the concept of "psychopolitics". Like Rau, he offers a constructive critique of Foucault's governmentality approach to power relations:

> Disciplinary power extends beyond the corporeal also into the mental. [...] The *psyche* nevertheless is not the focus of disciplinary power. The *orthopedic* technique of disciplinary power is too blunt to reach and take possession of deeper layers of the psyche with its hidden wishes, needs and desires. [...] Biopolitics is the governing technique of the disciplinary society. However, it is completely inappropriate for the neoliberal regime, which above all exploits the *psyche*.
>
> Han, 2014, 35

Han takes Foucault to task for clinging to the categories of biopolitics in the late 1970s while trying to develop an analysis of neoliberalism. In Han's view, Foucault untimely death in 1984 prevented him from seeing that he needed to drop the biopolitical vocabulary and elaborate a psychopolitics of neoliberalism (Han, 2014, 38).

In a manner that echoes both Rau and Beller, Han understands the goal of neoliberal techniques of rule to be that of occupying and exploiting "not only labor time but the entire person, the entire attention, indeed the entire life" (Han, 2014, 43). An important way in which psychopolitical techniques work toward this goal is in targeting and manipulating pre-reflexive emotion and affect (Han, 2014, 67; cf. Ash, 2012; Thrift and French, 2002). The algorithms deployed in the Big Data systems that form an increasingly important infrastructure for psychopolitics render visible and manipulable what he calls "actomes", "micro-actions" that do not rise to the level of consciousness (Han, 2014, 88). Through subjecting our actomes to exhaustive analysis, Han argues, the psychopolitical techniques enabled by Big Data will gradually uncover our "digital unconscious" (Han, 2014, 89).

Rau and Han maintain a critical distance from psychological discourses that medicalize psychopathologies as purely individual phenomena. But they and other writers in this third strand are not shy about identifying pathologies of attention attributable to neoliberal capitalism and new communication technologies. Key psychopathological issues for some writers in this third strand are Attention Deficit Syndrome (ADS) or Attention Deficit Hyperactivity Disorder (ADHD), as well as "the exhausted subject" (Han, 2015, Ehrenberg, 2016). With some variation in the details, a number of authors argue that these pathologies are collective and social, not just individual. Türcke identifies a "global attentional regime" in which the face-to-face interactions with other human beings necessary for cognitive and social development are increasingly replaced by a focus on the fast-shifting images on screens. Since these images are designed to produce constant "picture-shock" (abrupt transitions between presented images) as a way of holding attention, they train younger generations to forms of behavior – "concentrated dissipation" – which are then pathologized as ADS and ADHD (Türcke, 2016, 105–106, 109). But these individual effects can only appear in the context of what he calls "attention deficit culture" (Türcke, 2016, 108).

A final nexus of argument in which attention can be seen to relate to psychologically focused power relations is exemplified by the work of Mark Whitehead, Rhys Jones, Rachel Lilley, Jessica Pykett and Rachel Howell on emerging forms of "neuroliberalism" (Whitehead, et al., 2018), and of James Ash on "affective amplification" and "envelope power" (Ash, 2012, 2015). Ash's work can be read as a further development and refinement of Beller's account of the ways in which capital increasingly captures and mobilizes attention as a source of profit. Ash charts the efforts of video game designers not only to develop new means of attention capture but to "amplify" "modulate" and increase the "bandwidth" of the affectively laden attention of players (Ash, 2012, 9). Such affective design, Ash argues, has played an important role in the development of what he calls "envelope power", the ongoing "attempt by interface designers and publishers to increase users' capacity to sense difference and use this capacity to alter the relationship between anticipation and memory in order to keep users engaged in the products they sell" (Ash 2015, 140). An important premise of envelope power is that attentional capabilities are indeed capable of a certain degree of enhancement through training.

The term "neuroliberalism" developed by Whitehead, *et al.* is a name for new techniques and rationalities of "behavioral government" related to but different from the more familiar workings of neoliberal governmentality. Unlike in the case of envelope power (Ash, 2015), the accent here is on the limits to the malleability of our cognitive capacities. The new techniques of behavioral government aim not so much at improving people's efficiency or tweaking their capacities as at accepting and working with the fact that "there are significant limits to the human capacity to make information-rich and deliberative decisions" (Whitehead, et al., 2018, 13). It is because we cannot even approximate the presumed emotionless rationality, unlimited calculating capacities and perfect information possessed by *homo œconomicus* that we constantly act according to unreflected, rough-and-ready, often emotionally tinged "heuristics", that is, practical short-cuts that help us make decisions even in the absence of adequate time or information (Whitehead, et al., 2018, 57). These heuristics often work well enough to satisfy us at a subjective level but are not optimal in their outcomes, for example in the myriad decisions we make impacting our health and nutrition. Another symptom of our limited capacities is the fact that unlimited choice is not experienced by everyone as liberating, but often rather as overwhelming and disabling in situations where some choice must be made (Whitehead, et al., 2018, 103; Schwartz, 2005).

Like Alexandra Rau, Whitehead and his colleagues do not address political economies of attention in a sustained, explicit way. But limited attentional capacity is clearly one of the most important general conditions underlying the fact that "a significant portion of our daily behaviors (particularly those associated with habit and routine, but also including complex decision-making) largely elude our self-regulatory grasp and available cognitive capacities" (Whitehead, et al., 2018, 80). Limited ability to sustain focused attention is, as much psychological research has shown, one of the most important limited cognitive capacities (Styles, 2006; Gazzaley and Rosen, 2016). This is what makes the techniques of neuroliberalism interesting in the present context. The concept of "nudge" popularized by Richard Thaler and Cass Sunstein is probably the best-known neuroliberal technique (Thaler and Sunstein, 2009). "Nudges", such as requiring people to opt out of instead of opt into beneficial programs and services, are based upon research in behavioral economics that has identified a host of typical ways in which people make irrational or non-optimal decisions, even in situations where they know and can explain what is best for them. Nudges and other forms of "libertarian paternalism", though, can be seen to hollow out the meaning of our freedom to choose and along with it our responsibility for our actions (Whitehead, et al., 2018, 87–88). Thus whereas we might think of increased demands on our limited attention as analogous to techniques for intensifying its exploitation analyzed by Marx, it is possible to conceive of neuroliberal methods of marginalizing the importance of attention (and other limited cognitive capacities) as analogous to the mechanization of former handicrafts or the more recent replacement of living labor with robots. It is not easy to decide whether over-burdening the attentional capacities of ever more people is worse than rendering these capacities redundant through the outsourcing of decision-making to designed environments. In either case, there are important potential implications for socio-spatial processes. Some of these issues will be taken up in Chapters 4 and 7.

Attention and human evolution

The philosopher Bernard Stiegler, in line with Türcke and other authors discussed above, perceives "a collossal deficit of attention, an immense neglect in the form of a *global attention deficit disorder*, stemming directly from the proliferation of psychotechnologies that no political power can control" (Stiegler, 2010a, 57; see Wilson, 2015 for a geographical discussion of Stiegler). I devote a separate section to Stiegler, first, because his work on attention condenses many points discussed in other strands, second, because he contextualizes the current crisis of attention in terms of longer processes of human evolution, and third, because his perspective on attention exemplifies a particularly interesting mode of argumentation within the analytic of finitude. In laying out his approach, Stiegler is able to connect his analysis to fundamental features of embodiment that will play an important role as the argument unfolds in subsequent chapters.

Like Crary, Beller and Ash, who explicitly draw upon his work, Stiegler frames his global diagnosis, proximally at least, in terms of the historical geography of capitalism. Indeed, he locates the newly intensified exploitation of human attention at the center of his call "for a new critique of political economy", as one of his books is entitled (Stiegler, 2010b). Stiegler concurs with the authors discussed above that human attention has begun to function for capital like a previously unexplored continent at the scale of billions of individual human bodies, whose ruthless mining is now underway. He discerns three limits to capitalism: (1) the tendency of the rate of profit to fall; (2) the destruction by overstimulation of the libidinal energies necessary to fuel constantly increasing consumption; and (3) biological and geophysical limits (Stiegler, 2010a, 47–48). Focusing upon the second of these limits, he argues that the strategy of ever more efficiently capturing libidinal energies by channeling consumer attention is doomed to failure because it tendentially exhausts and numbs, through stimulative overload and the resulting "desublimation", the very libidinal energies it seeks to harness (Stiegler, 2010a, 63, 79–80). The idea behind Beller's pithy assertion that "to look is to labor" (Beller, 2006, 2) is developed by Stiegler into an analysis of the ways in which capturing the attention of consumers leads to the "proletarianization" of human nervous and muscular systems (Stiegler, 2010b, 45). This proletarianization tends, in a dialectical fashion, to produce a disengagement with the consumption processes through which surplus value is realized as profit.

Stiegler's contextualization of the political economy of attention is particularly interesting for the present argument because he provides a way of thinking on timescales that set the current period dominated by the history of capitalism within a much longer anthropological narrative. Stiegler takes as his point of departure the account of "grammatization" sketched by his mentor Derrida, but he historicizes it with reference to the paleontologist André Leroi-Gourhan, Simondon and others. The argument he develops in his three-volume history of *Technics and Time* (Stiegler, 1998; 2009; 2011) recasts the emergence of the human species as a process that from the beginning has been inseparable from the development of "technics", prostheses in the broadest sense with which embodied humans have interacted with their surroundings. *Technics and Time*, then, is an explicit challenge to Heidegger's demotion of the technical to something that stands in the way of our recognition of a supposedly more authentic being-in-the-world properly characteristic of *Dasein*. One important thread running through all three books is a sustained critical engagement with Heidegger's entire approach to understanding the human. The ambition of the trilogy is to rehabilitate, both philosophically and historically, the humanity of technics and the technics inherent to humanity.

Central to Stiegler's account of the history of technics and grammatization is a progressive narrative extending Husserl's insights on the temporality of experience (Husserl, 1991). What we ordinarily think of as "memories" are past experiences that are no longer "live" and thus have to be recalled.

Husserl contrasted these "secondary memories" or "secondary retentions" with "primary retentions", showing that consciousness of the now shades continuously out of a retained consciousness of the just-passed, the latter remaining part of our experience of the now (Husserl, 1991, 25–26, 122). Similarly, future-oriented, anticipatory "protentions" are continuous features of our now-experiences and thus distinct from discrete "expectations" in the usual sense. Through protentions, our lived now leans continuously forward into a sense of the just-to-come (Husserl, 1991, 37–38). The picture of human temporality painted by Husserl would provide a launching point for his student Heidegger's transformative elaboration of the *ek-stases* of *Dasein*'s temporality (Heidegger, 1962).

Stiegler's most important conceptual innovation is to posit the category of "tertiary retentions", a category that encompasses all the ways in which memory takes the form of externalized experience and knowledge (writing, tools and other practical objects, art, etc.). Externalization of memory in these forms can be thought of, according to Stiegler, as a long process of "grammatization", or discretization and fixation of elements of continuous flows of practice. The history of grammatization Stiegler proposes is arresting in its sweep:

> In the course of human history [...] the mnemotechnical retentional layer is transformed, increasing in both complexity and density. It leads, in particular, from the advent of Neolithic sedentarization, to the formation of tertiary retention systems which constitute increasingly analytical recordings of primary and secondary retentional flows or fluxes – such as systems of writing and numeration. It is in this way that the *logos* is constituted: as the discretization of the continuous flow of language, which, spatialized, can be considered analytically. [...] But this discretization also affects gestures. [...] Gesture must be considered here (like speech) as a retentional flow, that is, as a *continuous chain* [...] of gestures, and the learning of a craft [...] consists in producing gestural secondary retentions, whereas the discretization and the spatialized reproduction of the time of gestures constitutes technical automation. [...] This reproducibility results in retentional grains that one can call *grammes*. And this is why we posit that the evolution of tertiary retention, from the Neolithic age until our own, constitutes a process of grammatization.
>
> Stiegler, 2010b, 9–10

This may seem a long way from a political economy of attention, but the connection Stiegler draws is interesting. Insofar as human societies have externalized ever more of their memories through grammatization, and in the process have enveloped ourselves in ever-thicker mantles of tertiary retentions, the process of becoming a social subject has been transformed. Becoming a subject has moved ever further away from any simple matter of "individuation" and has come to constitute what Stiegler calls, echoing Simondon, "transindividuation". Through more or less institutionalized socialization and education, young people are taught how to access and mobilize the tertiary retentions accumulated by their forebears and thus acquire the full complement of capabilities necessary for adult life. "[A]s the internalization of the heritage of previous generations, only possible because of memory's [...] tertiary [...] nature, this transmission itself presupposes a close intergenerational relationship that can be achieved only *as education*" (Stiegler, 2010a, 7). In sustaining education across the generations, transindividuation continuously recreates humanity in a process Stiegler calls "epiphylogenesis", the ongoing regeneration of the human through incorporation of external traces of sedimented human activity and knowledge. But exactly to the degree that such connections with the accumulated experience of previous generations has been externalized in tertiary retentions, modes of access to these external recordings (literacy, numeracy, gestural and manual proficiency, etc.) are not pre-given, innate skills but must also be acquired. "[T]he entire question," Stiegler writes of cultural memory, "is one of knowing the degree to which it is ap-propriable" (Stiegler, 2009, 8). For Stiegler, a core condition of possibility for learning how to access tertiary retentions is *disciplined, sustained attention* (Stiegler, 2010a, 65–66). "[A]ttention emerges from a formational process that is a social organization, constitutive of the transindividual and transindividuation, transindividuation being transmitted as much technically as ethically from generation to generation" (Stiegler, 2010a, 186). The learning of attentional skills takes time, and, once acquired, their exercise continues to take time. This is one way to understand what Fleck portrays as the process of acquisition of a "style of thought" that allows discernment (Fleck, 1981).

Thus the magnitude of the crisis Stiegler perceives begins to become apparent. For him, the deterioration of certain key attentional capabilities among young people, whether attributable to television, as he suggests (writing just a few years ago), or even more acutely now to the Internet, laptops and smartphones, is not just a matter of a pathology of capitalism but threatens future generations' access to the immense accumulation of knowledge and practical experience by human civilization in the broadest sense. The pressure of rhythmic disjuncture placed upon our bodily capabilities by the acceleration of life under capitalism is increasing. This rhythmic pressure, mediated by new prosthetic tools through which our attention is being ever-more-optimally exploited, is at the same time undermining our ability to engage in the continuous process of selection and concentration necessary to deal with it in a productive way. As he puts it elsewhere, we are now plagued by attentional "pollution" (Stiegler, 2011, 217). Thus, not only our continued responsiveness to solicitations of our attention but more broadly, the ongoing "epiphylogenesis" of humanity itself, is threatened.

Interestingly, this line of argument leads Stiegler to offer an extended critique of Foucault's conception of disciplinary power (Stiegler, 2010a, 115–139). The crux of his objection to Foucault's genealogy of discipline is that the latter neglects the salutary effects of bodily discipline in enabling children to develop sustained attention. Stiegler recasts some of Foucault's own concepts to highlight his point: what Foucault had called the "rules of discourse" are interpreted by Stiegler as "the regulated process of connections between psychic, collective and material retentions" (Stiegler, 2010a, 149). Ultimately, says Stiegler, Foucault began to recognize the more enabling and emancipatory functions of (self-)discipline in his last works (Stiegler, 2010a, 155). This more positive evaluation of discipline as a prerequisite for attention leads Stiegler to be highly skeptical as well of the more optimistic diagnosis of what is happening with human attention drawn by digital humanities scholar Katherine Hayles (2012). Hayles argues that the changes now restructuring the attentional habits and capacities of young people can still be integrated into new modes of learning that allow a synthesis between fast-moving, ever-shifting "hyper attention" (akin to what Türcke terms "concentrated dissipation" – Türcke, 2016, 109) and "deep attention", or the capacity to sustain focused concentration on a single activity or theme for a significant length of time (Stiegler, 2010a, 73–80). Hayles acknowledges that "[a]s contemporary environments become more information-intensive, it is no surprise that hyper attention ... is growing and that deep attention ... is diminishing, particularly among young adults and teens" (Hayles, 2012, 69). But she insists that "hyper attention can be seen as a positive adaptation that makes young people better suited to live in the information-intensive environments that are becoming ever more pervasive", because it can "conserve attention by quickly identifying relevant information" (Hayles, 2012, 99, 12).

As will be explained below, my position is closer to that of Stiegler, though with a couple of caveats. On the one hand, it is important to acknowledge the significance of differential social positioning for the question of access. Bringing these two issues together it is possible to ask about differential resources for the cultivation and relatively autonomous use of attention available to different social groups. This connects the issue of attention to more familiar issues of social justice from which a number of writers on the political economies of attention tend to shy away. As mentioned in the Introduction, however, developing this line of thinking is beyond the scope of the present book. A second caveat has to do with Stiegler's characterization of recent changes merely as an atrophying of deep attention in favor of hyper-attention, which is too simple. As James Ash makes clear in his work on gaming interface design, some recent innovations can be seen as *intensifications* of deep attention (Ash, 2012, 2015). In this context the problem is not the depth or focus of attentional engagement *per se* but the extent to which we can retain control over it. There are thus two problems here. One the one hand, experimental psychology has shown that the "occupation" of our attentional capacities by hyper- in place of deep attention is at best a zero-sum game and at worst a general threat to adult human competencies (Styles, 2006; Gazzaley and Rosen, 2016). It is largely (though not exclusively) through a variant of deep attention that we are capable of the kind of focused critical analysis, reflection, and planning that makes other worlds possible as deliberate projects. The second and related problem arises if, as Ash's work suggests, deep attention increasingly only survives in environments designed in such a way that we have little control over when it sets in. In that case deep attention may not be endangered as such but may nevertheless tendentially lose its emancipatory potential as a platform for critical reflection or deliberate projects. If Stiegler, Wu and other commentators are right that recent changes to attention come with a serious, potentially disastrous cost, then it is not too much to speak of a crisis of attention (Jackson, 2009).

What Stiegler shares with a number of other writers on economies of attention is, first of all, a sense of the fundamentally limited character of attention, quite apart from the variety of ways in which it was historically first constructed or in which it has been cultivated, shaped, trained and supplemented with techniques of memory across human geo-history: "attention is always technically assisted by memory aids (since attention is fabricated from retentions), especially as grammatization of secondary retentions into tertiary retentions such as the book, agenda, PDA, GPS, and so on; yet none of these can be 'attentive' in place of consciousness, which *is* attention" (Stiegler, 2010a, 102). Among other things, this perspective places at least some of the neuroliberal techniques discussed by Whitehead and his colleagues into a critical light. If tertiary memories are intended for appropriation and self-development by future generations, the outsourcing of decision-making in expert-designed choice architectures constitutes a form of externalization not oriented toward cultivating human capabilities but rather based upon abandonment of this project. For some neuroliberal programs at least, any further erosion of human attentional capabilities of the sort feared by Stiegler can simply be accommodated by taking ever-larger areas of decision-making out of human hands.

A second point of agreement, between Stiegler, Wu, Han and others, is that what is being eroded, threatened or dissolved in the hyper-mediatized world of 21st century capitalism is sustained, focused or deep attention (Stiegler, 2010a, 73). The rapid and destructive changes wrought by digitally mediated neoliberal capitalist culture in what Wu helpfully calls our "built attentional environment" (Wu, 2016, 225) have rendered deep attention much more difficult to sustain even for those of us still benefiting from forms of education that cultivated it as a capacity. Wu brings the changes discussed above back to the level of everyday experience:

> How often have you sat down with a plan, say, to write an e-mail or buy one thing online, only to find yourself, hours later, wondering what happened? And what are the costs to society of an entire population conditioned to spend so much of their waking lives not in concentration and focus but rather in fragmentary awareness and subject to constant interruption? In this respect our lives have become the very opposite of those cultivated by the monastics, whether in the East or the West, whose aim

was precisely to reap the fruits of deep and concentrated attention. [...]
At stake, then is something akin to how one's life is lived.

Wu, 2016, 343–344

What Stiegler adds fundamentally to the ideas surveyed above is, first, the contextualization of political economies of attention in longer, anthropological terms, and second, a tremendously subtle perspective on how human finitude continues to circumscribe the forms of cultural externalization that have sought to overcome it. Stiegler's conception, borrowed from Leroi-Gourhan, of humans as essentially technical beings portrays human bodies non-dualistically as fundamentally relational and prosthetic. This view accords in many particulars with Michael Tomasello's evolutionary accounts of human cognition and thinking (Tomasello, 1999, 2014). Tomasello argues, drawing on research in paleoanthropology, primate behavior and human early childhood behavior, that it is through processes of shared foci of attention and cooperative projects that most of the uniquely human cognitive and mental attributes have emerged – and emerge in each of us – on the timescales of phylogenesis, human history and individual ontogeny. A central role in these processes is given to the emergence of "joint attention", a way of relating to others that recognizes them as intentional agents like oneself (Tomasello, 1999). Tomasello had hypothesized that it was the emergence of this uniquely human capability that set humans upon our divergent evolutionary path. In a more recent book, Tomasello takes into account new research that has discovered this capability in other primates as well. His revised hypothesis is that the uniquely human arises in recognizing others not only as intentional agents but as "mental agents" (Tomasello, 2014). Joint attention still plays an important preliminary role in the revised version of his argument. But it serves as "common ground" two agents know they share, and the coordinative communication only humans can manage takes place now against the background of the already shared common ground of joint attention (Tomasello, 2014, 55, 68). The leap from joint attention to joint intention (a "we" intention) requires not only common ground but "mutual assumptions of cooperation and relevance" (Tomasello, 2014, 61).

As second-person intentionality becomes generalized in a group into collective intentionality, one crucial step is the evolution of truly cultural learning, which involved two key elements:

> Teaching borrows its basic structure from cooperative communication in which we inform others of things helpfully, and conformity is imitation fortified by the desire to coordinate with the normative expectations of the group. Modern humans did not start from scratch but started from early human cooperation. Human culture is human cooperation writ large.

Tomasello, 2014, 82

Once these practices and attitudes were commonly held, the kind of cultural transmission highlighted by Stiegler became established:

> Individuals thus did not have to invent their own ways of conceptualizing things; they just had to learn those of others, which embodied, as it were, the entire collective intelligence of the entire cultural group over much historical time. Individuals thus "inherited" myriad ways of conceptualizing and perspectivizing the world for others.
>
> Tomasello, 2014, 96

The great merit of Stiegler's argument is to recognize that the success of this intergenerational educational processes is contingent. Crucially, this contingency of cultural transmission depends in part on *relatively constant features of human corporeal organization*. It is only in and through the contingent, contextually determined development of the attentional capabilities of human bodies, understood at least provisionally as having an "inside" separate from the rest of the world, that we gain access to the tertiary memories which allow us fully to "transindividuate". This is utterly central for the argument offered here: *precisely because* individual humans are, on the one hand, derivative products of social learning, and on the other hand, always extend beyond ourselves both individually and collectively through technical (as well as intersubjective) relations, we need to understand the specifics of individual human embodiment. Human embodiment *circumscribes* not only intergenerational learning processes but also, very much in line with the analytic of finitude, the contingency and instability of any particular cultural construction of the human. Chapter 4 will be devoted to a fuller account of human corporeal organization, and this account will form the basis of what I believe needs to be retained in a concept of "the subject".

What can we take from the three strands of discourse on the political economy of attention and from Stiegler's framework? The following points are most crucial for the argument to be developed here:

- Attention is relational, but the embodied human anchor or pole of this relation appears to be finite and limited relative to technical, economic and cultural change.
- The identification and analysis of attention as a site or condensation point for social, economic and cultural problems first occurred and has subsequently been prompted by periods of especially rapid social, economic and technological change.
- The attentional capacities of human beings have been targeted with increasing focus in capitalist strategies for expanding and intensifying the exploitation both of the capabilities of embodied labor and of the libidinal energies and desires of consumers.
- Attentional capabilities are an important theater for tensions and emerging crises or contradictions in the forms of subjectivation characteristic of the most recent, neoliberal phase of capitalism.

• From a longer perspective, attentional capabilities can be seen as a key battleground not merely in the current phase of capitalist development but in the question of what is to become of the human.

If all of this can be accepted at least provisionally, it still does not go very far toward specifying exactly what we should understand by human attention. The writers surveyed – with the chief exception of Crary – largely refrain from systematic, in-depth analyses of attention as a phenomenon, though many do point to its complexity and to the range of ways in which it has been constructed in different contexts (see, for example, Ash, 2012, 2015). They largely agree that attention is relational and that deep attention at least is finite, limited and capable of manipulation. But they do not, for example, explicitly address the directional asymmetry of human embodiment upon which their arguments implicitly rely. Attention in the sense of focused concentration is portrayed as directionally limited. But the very possibility of distracting, interrupting and capturing attention so central to new commercial techniques presupposes a less directionally specific vulnerability or answerability that leaves us exposed to solicitations from anywhere. Chapter 2 begins to build a more substantial sense of directional asymmetry by defining and explaining attention in more phenomenal terms. Doing so will both ground some of the political-economic and historical points gleaned from the literature surveyed above and provide important insights that can be used to supplement existing accounts of practice in Chapter 3.

References

Ash, J. (2012). Attention, videogames and the retentional economies of affective amplification. *Theory, Culture & Society*, 29(6), pp. 3–26.

Ash, J. (2015). *The Interface Envelope: Gaming, Technology, Power*. London: Bloomsbury Academic.

Beller, J. (2006). *The Cinematic Mode of Production: Attention Economy and the Society of the Spectacle*. Dartmouth, NH: Dartmouth College Press.

Benjamin, W. (2008). *The Work of Art in the Age of Mechanical Reproduction*. Trans. J. Underwood. London: Penguin.

Crary, J. (1999). *Suspensions of Perception: Attention, Spectacle, and Modern Culture*. Cambridge, MA: MIT Press.

Debord, G. (2009). *Society of the Spectacle*. Trans. K. Knabb. Eastbourne: Soul Bay Press.

Dzudzek, I. (2015). Zur Aufmerksamkeitspolitik medizingeographischer Forschung. *Geographische Zeitschrift*, 103(4), pp. 245–251.

Ehrenberg, A. (2016). *The Weariness of the Self: Diagnosing the History of Depression in the Contemporary Age*. Trans. E. Caouette, J. Homel, D. Homel, D. Winkler. Montreal: McGill-Queens University Press.

Fleck, L. (1981). *Genesis and Development of a Scientific Fact*. Trans. F. Bradley. Chicago, IL: University of Chicago Press.

Fracchia, J. (2005). Beyond the human-nature debate: human corporeal organization as the "first fact" of historical materialism. *Historical Materialism*, 13, pp. 33–61.

Franck, G. (1998). *Ökonomie der Aufmerksamkeit: Ein Entwurf.* Munich: Carl Hanser Verlag.

Franck, G. (2005). *Mentaler Kapitalismus: Eine Politische Ökonomie des Geistes.* Munich: Carl Hanser Verlag.

Gazzaley, A. and Rosen, L. (2016). *The Distracted Mind: Ancient Brains in a High-Tech World.* Cambridge, MA: MIT Press.

Goldhaber, M. (1997). The attention economy and the net. *First Monday* [online], 2 (4–7), n.p.n. Available at: http://firstmonday.org/article/view/519/440#dep6 [Accessed 20 March 2015].

Han, B.-C. (2014). *Psychopolitik: Neoliberalismus und die neuen Machttechniken.* Frankfurt am Main: Fischer Verlag.

Han, B.-C. (2015). *The Burnout Society.* Trans. E. Butler. Palo Alto, CA: Stanford University Press.

Hannah, M. (2013). Attention and the phenomenological politics of landscape. *Geografiska Annaler, Series B - Human Geography*, 95(3), pp. 235–250.

Hannah, M. (2015). Aufmerksamkeit und geographische Praxis. *Geographische Zeitschrift*, 103(3), pp. 131–150.

Harvey, D. (1998). The body as an accumulation strategy. *Environment and Planning D: Society and Space*, 16(4), pp. 401–421.

Hayles, K. (2012). *How We Think: Digital Media and Contemporary Technogenesis.* Chicago, IL: University of Chicago Press.

Heidegger, M. (1962). *Being and Time.* Trans. J. Macquarrie and E. Robinson. Oxford: Blackwell.

Husserl, E. (1991). *On the Phenomenology of the Consciousness of Internal Time (1893–1917).* Trans. J. B. Brough. Dordrecht: Springer Science-Business Media.

Jackson, M. (2009). *Distracted: The Erosion of Attention and the Coming Dark Age.* New York: Prometheus Books.

Kern, S. (2003). *The Culture of Time and Space, 1880–1918.* Cambridge, MA: Harvard University Press.

Rau, A. (2010). *Psychopolitik: Macht Subjekt und Arbeit in der Neoliberalen Gesellschaft.* Frankfurt am Main: Campus Verlag.

Rose, N. (1998). *Inventing Our Selves. Psychology, Power and Personhood.* Cambridge: Cambridge University Press.

Schmid, H. (2007). Ökonomie der Faszination: Aufmerksamkeitsstrategien und unternehmensorientierte Stadtpolitik. In: C. Bernd, and R. Pütz, eds., *Kulturelle Geographien. Zur Beschäftigung mit Raum und Ort nach dem Cultural Turn.* Bielefeld: Transcript, pp. 289–316.

Schwartz, B. (2005). *The Paradox of Choice: Why More is Less.* New York: Harper Perennial.

Simon, H. (1971). Designing organizations for an information-rich world. In: M. Greenberger, ed., *Computers, Communication and the Public Interest.* Baltimore, MD: Johns Hopkins University Press, pp. 38–72.

Stiegler, B. (1998). *Technics and Time, 1: The Fault of Epimetheus.* Trans. R. Beardsworth and G. Collins. Stanford, CA: Stanford University Press.

Stiegler, B. (2009). *Technics and Time, 2: Disorientation.* Trans. S. Barker. Stanford, CA: Stanford University Press.

Stiegler, B. (2010a). *Taking Care of Youth and the Generations.* Trans. S. Barker. Stanford, CA: Stanford University Press.

Stiegler, B. (2010b). *For a New Critique of Political Economy.* Trans. D. Ross. London: Polity.

Stiegler, B. (2011). *Technics and Time, 3: Cinematic Time and the Question of Malaise.* Trans. S. Barker. Stanford, CA: Stanford University Press.

Styles, E. (2006). *The Psychology of Attention.* 2nd ed. New York: Psychology Press.

Thaler, R. and Sunstein, C. (2009). *Nudge: Improving Decisions About Health, Wealth and Happiness.* New York: Penguin.

Thrift, N. and French, S. (2002). The automatic production of space. *Transactions of the Institute of British Geographers* NS 27(3), pp. 309–335.

Tomasello, M. (1999). *The Cultural Origins of Human Cognition.* Cambridge, MA: Harvard University Press.

Tomasello, M. (2014). *A Natural History of Human Thinking.* Cambridge, MA: Harvard University Press.

Türcke, C. (2016). Aufmerksamkeitsdefizitkultur. In: J. Müller, A. Nießeler, and A. Rauh, eds., *Aufmerksamkeit: Neue Humanwissenschaftliche Perspektiven.* Bielefeld: Transcript, pp. 101–114.

Wehrle, M. (2013). *Horizonte der Aufmerksamkeit: Entwurf einer dynamischen Konzeption der Aufmerksamkeit aus phänomenologischer und kognitionspsychologischer Sicht.* Munich: Wilhelm Fink Verlag.

Whitehead, M., Jones, R., Lilley, R., Pykett, J., and Howell, R. (2018). *Neuroliberalism: Behavioural Government in the Twenty-First Century.* London: Routledge.

Wilson, M. (2015). Paying attention, digital media, and community-based critical GIS. *Cultural Geographies,* 22(1), pp. 177–191.

Wu, T. (2016). *The Attention Merchants: The Epic Scramble to Get Inside Our Heads.* New York: Alfred A. Knopf.

2   Toward a political phenomenology
of attention

Attention first appears as a phenomenon and a high-profile problem for psychology and the newly established discipline of phenomenology in the midst of the crescendo of classical industrial capitalism in the decades surrounding 1900 (Crary, 1999). As in the later wave of interest briefly reviewed in Chapter 1, the first concern addressed a century earlier was the nature of attention as directed and selective, and the underlying anxiety was likewise that of a loss of control over the movement of attention. However, phenomenological and psychological research on attention both led by different paths to a broadening of the category to include various non-focused, passive, routine or automatic attentional phenomena (Wehrle, 2013; Styles, 2006; Posner, 2004). It would turn out to be the interplay between focused, sustained and directed attention and the vagaries and solicitations associated with more background and unreflective forms of attention that attracted most analytical interest. In other words, theorizations of attention already sketch the outlines of the directional asymmetry I will attribute in Chapter 3 to practice in a more general sense. Our active engagements are directionally limited, but our openness or answerability to solicitations and address of all forms is not.

One of the most important accounts of the problem of attention at the height of classical industrialization is to be found in William James's hugely influential 1890 two-volume work *Principles of Psychology* (James, 1950). In this work he drew together the results of early psychological research as it had developed up to that point in Germany, France and the English-speaking world, and subjected all of it to a critical synthesis suffused with highly perceptive and often proto-phenomenological reflections on his own experience. The *Principles* continue to be cited by both phenomenologists and psychologists to the present day. As with many other topics, James addressed attention in such vivid and pithy prose that quotes from it remain standard epigraphs for writings on the subject. Much of what he writes about attention – if we indulge some of his outdated terminology – still seems compelling as a set of common-sense reflections on how we experience attention. For example, James describes the most basic characteristic of attention, its selective directedness, in the following terms: "the mind is at every stage a theatre of simultaneous possibilities. Consciousness consists in the comparison of these with each other, the selection of some, and the suppression of the rest by the rein-forcing and inhibiting agency of attention" (James, 1950, 288). Part of James's continued appeal for phenomenologists is the subtlety of his reflections on his own experience, as when he associates attentional processes with bodily sensations:

> [T]he acts of attending, assenting, negating, making an effort, are felt as movements of something in the head. In many cases it is possible to describe these movements quite exactly. In attending to either an idea or a sensation belonging to a particular sense-sphere, the movement is the adjustment of the sense-organ, felt as it occurs. I cannot think in visual terms, for example, without feeling a fluctuating play of pressures, con-vergences, divergences, and accommodations in my eyeballs. [...] My brain appears to me as if all shot across with lines of direction, of which I have become conscious as my attention has shifted from one sense-organ to another, in passing to successive outer things, or in following trains of varying sense-ideas. When I try to remember or reflect, the movements in question, instead of being directed towards the periphery, seem to come from the periphery inwards and feel like a sort of *withdrawal* from the outer world.
>
> James, 1950, 300

Importantly for many later thinkers, James distinguishes between distinct images or ideas and "that staining, fringe or halo of obscurely felt relation to masses of other imagery about to come, but not yet distinctly in focus" (James, 1950, 478, note), an idea that would be developed by phenomenolo-gists in the 20th century.

One central conviction underlying the present argument is that these dis-tinctions, and James's basic approach to attention more generally, have not lost all meaning, even in the purportedly "post-humanist", "post-subjective" age. Inadequate though his talk of "the mind" is, there is still something to James's ringing declaration of the centrality of attention to the issue of how we live our lives:

> When we reflect that the turnings of our attention form the nucleus of our inner self; when we see [...] that volition is nothing but attention; when we believe that our autonomy in the midst of nature depends on our not being pure effect, but a cause, [...] we must admit that the question whe-ther attention involve such a principle of spiritual activity or not is metaphysical as well as psychological, and is well worthy of all the pains we can bestow on its solution. It is in fact the pivotal question of meta-physics, the very hinge on which our picture of the world shall swing from materialism, fatalism, monism, towards spiritualism, freedom, plural-ism, – or else the other way.
>
> James, 1950, 447–448

As we shall see later on, the experience of having our attention addressed by appeals of various sorts, and the ongoing question of whether and how to respond to these appeals, indeed lies at the core of a political economy arguably even more important than at the time James was writing. Broadly speaking, phenomenological research will serve as the basis for the account of attention developed in what follows. Although insights from the psychology of attention will be drawn upon here and there in the chapters to follow, the non-dualistic and much more nuanced sense of subject-world relations provided by phenomenology is a more fruitful basis for the argument. But it is worth noting, first, that those strands of phenomenology producing the most fruitful work on attention drew explicitly and extensively on the tradition of Gestalt psychology, and second, that cognitive psychological research on attention has, over the course of the twentieth century, undergone a series of shifts broadly parallel to and convergent with those in phenomenology (Wehrle, 2013, 17–18).

A plausible provisional definition of attention is given by Maren Wehrle: it is the "subjective element that in a passive or active way undertakes a differentiation [...] [within the stream of awareness] and at the same time integrates new impressions into the experiential context" (Wehrle, 2013, 25). Differentiation into foreground and background, or selection, and incorporation of newly noticed matters into awareness, are the two main features shared by most accounts. Wehrle's definition may provide a useful initial orientation, but in both psychological and phenomenological traditions, the simple question of what attention is has never been answered in a conclusive way. Here, as in the research surveyed, the term "attention" will be defined only in a relatively general and flexible way, and deployed more as an umbrella term for a coherent bundle of concerns than as a straightforward noun. This bundle of concerns will allow me to suggest changes to practice theory and to critical understandings of power relations.

Husserl and phenomenology

A very brief overview of the project of phenomenology as conceived in the writings of Edmund Husserl, the founder of phenomenology as a self-conscious and distinct philosophical school, is necessary here. Husserl's work on attention was hesitant and incomplete in many ways (Depraz, 2004; Steinbock, 2004; Wehrle, 2013, 36). Hans Blumenberg, one of Husserl's most subtle sympathetic critics, notes the "remarkable tenacity" with which Husserl "passed by" a phenomenology of attention even while lecturing on the topic and episodically returning to it in his writings (Blumenberg, 2007, 192). Despite this foundational hesitancy, though, Husserl's initial forays into the description of attentional phenomena would continue to form the touchstone for much subsequent writing on the subject. These forays took place within the framework of the phenomenological philosophy Husserl made it his life's work to establish. As one of Husserl's most important students, Aron

Gurwitsch, phrased it, "[p]henomenology is [...] a systematic study and theory of subjectivity for the sake of an ultimate clarification and elucidation of objects of any description whatsoever" (Gurwitsch, 1964, 5). Husserl's project is located broadly within the Kantian strictures placed on the possibility of objective knowledge by the mediating role of human faculties. But instead of laying out logical *a priori* conditions of knowledge, Husserl seeks to discover the possibility of objective knowledge starting from within the "natural attitude" in which we largely experience the world and live our lives.

The basic relational connection between subject and object around which Husserl would organize his project was the concept of "intentionality" he adapted from Brentano. Intentionality denotes the "aboutness" of conscious experiences, their referentiality, the fact that they are always experiences of something (Moran, 2005, 5). As Moran paraphrases it, "[i]ntentionality refers to the manner in which objects disclose themselves to awareness as transcending the act of awareness itself" (Moran 2005, 53). Intentionality can thus be understood as a kind of transcendence that remains immanent to the realm of phenomenal knowledge (Husserl, 2012, 112). If objective descriptions of phenomena is the goal and the everyday understanding or "natural attitude" of human beings has to be the starting point, the question is how to conceive philosophical methods capable of reaching it. Another of Husserl's most important innovations was the set of methods he developed for this purpose. These methods, which he developed under the headings of transcendental and phenomenological "reductions", start from everyday, common sense experience and perception, and seek to "reduce" or "bracket" accidental or conjunctural features of involved consciousness and the objects it perceives. For example, the phenomenological reduction *sets aside* existential belief in the world (Gurwitsch 1964, 164). Husserl sought, through processes of reduction, to achieve a purified conception both of the knowing *cogito* and of the object of consciousness, which he designates the "noetic" and "noematic" poles of conscious acts, respectively (Husserl, 2012, 184–185). His transcendental ambitions would be abandoned by his most important inheritors, Heidegger and Merleau-Ponty. But these thinkers would reject Husserl's transcendentalism precisely by radicalizing his basic insight that the analysis of human experience must begin with our embeddedness in the world and our "natural attitude" (cf. Merleau-Ponty, 1962, 71; Strohmayer, 1998, 108–109). For Heidegger, Merleau-Ponty and others, we can never shake off or climb all the way out of this embeddedness.

This thumbnail overview of key features of Husserlian phenomenology allows us to understand why attention was for him at first relatively marginal, more of a persistent irritant than a central question (see Depraz, 2004). Attention had been studied psychologically as a feature of the empirical conscious life of individual minds in terms of "stimulus-response" models, whereas phenomenology sought to divest conscious experience of empirical specifics in order to get at its underlying determinations and to overcome the mechanical dualism of stimulus-response. Husserl had to acknowledge the pervasive role of attention in perception and experience. But it was important for him to portray it as a derivative, contingent aspect of intentionality. The fundamental structures of intentionality, not their momentary alterations in concrete situations, formed his main interest (Wehrle, 2013, 36). Among these fundamental structures of intentionality was what Husserl described as an inherent tendency of consciousness toward "fulfillment", that is, toward ever-deeper and more-complete perception of its objects. The distractibility associated with attention thus constituted a constant threat of "interruption of an intention" (Blumenberg, 2007, 199). There is thus something faintly grudging about Husserl's writings on attention. Nevertheless, these writings contain valuable seeds of insight that would be cultivated by later thinkers. This chapter sketches Husserl's analysis of attention, and then chronicles three modifications of his approach that successively bring us to a conception of attention capable, on the one hand, of grounding the political economies of attention discussed in the previous chapter, and on the other, of enriching Theodore Schatzki's theory of practice in Chapter 3.

Husserl on attention

In his early descriptions of attention in *Logical Investigations*, Husserl treated attention as a "modification" of intentionality, a supplementary highlighting or emphasis of matters within the basic structure of intentional relation to the world (Husserl, 2001, 258ff; Wehrle, 2013, 37). In other words, his interest at first lay squarely upon selective, directed forms of attention. In *Ideas I*, Husserl fleshes out this basic idea to interpret attention as a mediator of actuality and inactuality of perception. Here the state of being "turned toward" something is central:

> In perception [...] I am turned towards the object, to the paper, for instance, I apprehend it as being this here and now. The apprehension is a singling out, every perceived object having a background in experience. Around and about the paper lie books, pencils, ink-well, and so forth, and these in a certain sense are also "perceived", perceptually there, in the "field of intuition"; but whilst I was turned towards the paper there was no turning in their direction, nor any apprehending of them, not even in a secondary sense. They appeared and yet were not singled out, were not posited on their own account. Every perception of a thing has a zone of *background intuitions* (or background awareness) [...] and this also is a "*conscious experience*". [...] What we say applies exclusively to that zone of consciousness which belongs to [...] a perception as "being turned towards an object". [...] But it is here implied that certain modifications of the original experience are possible, which we will refer to as a free turning of the "gaze" – not precisely or not merely of the physical but of the "*mental gaze*" - from the paper at first [singled out] to objects which had already appeared before, of which we had been "implicitly" aware,

and whereof *subsequent* to the directing of one's gaze thither we are explicitly aware, perceiving them "attentively".

Husserl, 2012, 65–66

Implicit in this tableau is first of all an acknowledgement that attention is relational, a matter of differential engagement of living awareness within a field of presented matters and possibilities. There is also here an initial distinction between primary and secondary attention, the first being roughly the active focus of current perception, the second including surrounding perceived matters (thoughts, feelings, objects, other people, etc.) that are present in the perceptual field but not currently the center of concern. Husserl distinguishes these two categories from inattention, the perceptual non-relation to what is not present in the perceptual field (Husserl, 2012, 193; Wehrle, 2013, 38). Finally, Husserl also acknowledges the necessity of understanding attention as a process, a movement. These points will undergo further refinement, especially in the writings of Gurwitsch, but even in Husserl's first formulation, the inseparability of attention and the *field* in which it moves is evident (Gurwitsch, 1964). The field constitutes the basic structure of awareness within which the turnings and dwellings of attention take place.

In line with the relational view, Husserl argues that the directedness of attention is not that of some separable sense or faculty pointed at an external object but of an "attending ray" inseparable from the perceiving "ego" or "cogito" itself: "An attitude which bears the personal ray in itself is thereby an act of the Ego itself. [...] The Ego [...] 'lives' in such acts" (Husserl, 2012, 194–195). This can be read as a specification of what James meant in placing attention at the center of human life. It suggests also in a more concrete sense the kind of immanent transcendence Husserl sought to analyse. In other writings on attention, Husserl would shift from a focus on attentional modifications as achievements of the acting Ego to a more passive account in which attention appears more as a form of affective response, and the Ego as an affectable bodily entity (Wehrle, 2013, 63ff.). This would coincide with a stronger focus upon the paying of attention as a temporal process bound up with retentions and protentions. Thus this second set of themes in Husserl is often designated as a "genetic" account of attention (Wehrle, 2013, 89–90). Here the movements of attention take center stage, whether in "integrating" or "constituting" an object successively through a process of synthesis or in the transition from involved attention to reflection upon involved attention. The issues surrounding the movement of attention are illustrated by Husserl across a number of works. Here two particular treatments are of interest.

The first treatment comes in his lectures on time consciousness, which span the two decades around 1900 (Husserl, 1991). In these lectures he is concerned at a number of different levels with the constitution of unities within the flow of consciousness (whether unity of the sense of time itself or of an object of consciousness that remains stable for us through changing momentary perceptions of it). An important distinction for my purposes here is one

Husserl adopts from Anton Marty and Carl Stumpf, between "attending to" something [*Aufmerken*] and "noticing" it [*Bemerken*]:

> In the ordinary case the fixed point [of attention] – that is, the focal point in the narrowest sense of the word – is at the same time the primarily noticed [*bemerkte*] point; often also the object of an attending [*Aufmerken*], but not always. [...] Not every noticing is linked to attending. Attending is a kind of being-curious [*Gespanntsein*] about the content, to which there clings a certain intention that strives after satisfaction. Noticing is representation [*Vorstellen*] in the strict sense of the word; the simple recording of a content, the simply-being-turned-toward-it.
>
> Husserl, 1991, 150 (translation modified)

This distinction will be important, on the one hand, because it separates the direction of attentional regard more clearly from perceived or experienced contents. This difference needs to be clear if we are to discern the specific form of power relation I term "occupation", a point I return to in Chapter 7. Secondly, the distinction between attending and noticing gives us a framework on which to analyse how the solicitation of attention works as a temporal sequence (see below).

The second relevant treatment of attention as a process is found in *Ideas I* from 1913. If the initial turning of our attention to something can be analysed in terms of attending and noticing, it is also possible to discern a number of stages that continue on from there. As noted above, Husserl was interested in processes of "fulfilling" or "completing" intentional acts of perception through synthesis of individual perceptual moments. Through attending to successive aspects of something, we gradually fulfill the intentional relation to it (Husserl, 2012, 253–254; Gurwitsch, 1964, 287). As a sequential process of synthetic consciousness, Husserl discusses the attentional modifications involved in turning toward and then away from a theme in terms of "grasping", "holding in grasp", "still maintaining in grasp" and "releasing from grasp" (Husserl, 2012, 253–255; Gurwitsch, 1966, 179). The last of these is particularly relevant to the argument in Chapters 5 and 6 about turning away. Gurwitsch discusses the process of releasing from grasp in terms of the tripartite structure of perceptual fields:

> The following possibilities obtain when we turn away from our theme. (1) The theme completely disappears from consciousness. (2) It continues being given, i.e., is co-given, but belongs only to the partial domain other than the thematic field [...]; here the theme is released from grasp. (3) The theme ceases to be the theme and now belongs to the thematic field of the new theme. It is "still in grasp" and still partakes of thematic consciousness.
>
> Gurwitsch, 1966, 230

At both ends of the sequential process of attending, the initial turning to something and eventually turning away from it toward something else, there are fascinating questions both about the finer details behind the "manual" imagery Husserl uses and about the politics that attach to the movement of attention. It would fall to later interpreters of phenomenology to take up these questions, and I will return to them in Chapters 5 and 6.

Subsequent students and interpreters of Husserl, most important among them Maurice Merleau-Ponty and Aron Gurwitsch, would unfold more detailed accounts of the structure and variety of perceptual experience (Merleau-Ponty, 1962; Gurwitsch, 1964, 1966). Both would depart from a strictly Husserlian perspective, but both also believed themselves to be advancing Husserl's overall project through these departures. Gurwitsch would seek to de-center phenomenological accounts of perception away from Husserl's emphasis on the "spontaneity" of the pure, acting ego as the source of perceptual events, giving a much stronger role to structures of the attentional field, and would interpret these structures with the help of key insights from Gestalt psychology. Merleau-Ponty would drop Husserl's transcendental ambitions and abandon his focus on reflective consciousness, re-centering phenomenology toward the lived body. The two worked closely together in Paris and each influenced the other's work. Gurwitsch incorporated Merleau-Ponty's insights into the embodied character of perception into his own account of consciousness, and Merleau-Ponty imported some of the key insights of Gestalt psychology into his writings, though without acknowledging Gurwitsch's contribution (Gurwitsch, 1964, 305, 418; see Toadvine, 2001, 198–199).

In the remainder of this chapter I will draw, in turn, upon Gurwitsch, Merleau-Ponty, and Bernhard Waldenfels to follow a particular thread of critical elaboration upon Husserl's basic insights. Gurwitsch is most useful for his investigation of the structuring of thematic fields, for which he draws insights from Gestalt psychology. His writings also involve the most detailed discussion of attentional issues, so I will dwell on them at some length. Merleau-Ponty furthers the process of de-centering by insisting on the fundamental role of embodiment in founding our relation to the world. In this he corrects the lingering cognitivism Gurwitsch had inherited from Husserl. Finally, Waldenfels builds upon the insights of Gurwitsch and Merleau-Ponty while arguing that both of their approaches continue to remain too focused upon the active constitution of worlds by individuals. Waldenfels's "pathic" approach to attention emphasizes its process-character, as a movement of "answering", and puts this pathic aspect in explicit connection to the politics of media and culture. This more differentiated account of attention developed through these approaches to attention then suggest ways of supplementing Schatzki's theory of practice in Chapter 3. Heidegger will be marginal to the discussion. A number of aspects of his analysis of *Dasein* in *Being and Time* (Heidegger, 1962) seem implicitly to raise issues of attention, for example his discussion of everydayness [*Alltäglichkeit*] and the anonymous *Man* (Blumenberg, 2007, 191).

Attention plays a supporting role in his elucidation of directionality [*Ausrichtung*] (Schatzki, 2017, 44–45). Yet on the whole Heidegger gave attention only a very tightly circumscribed place in the context of his writings on readiness-to-hand and presence-at-hand, and was not interested in it as a phenomenon to be analysed in detail (Waldenfels, 2004, 29). Nevertheless, it will be useful to return at more length to Heidegger's concepts of directionality and de-severance [*Ent-fernung*] in the introduction to Part II, as a way of sharpening the contours of the notion of directed practice developed in the present book.

Structures of the field of consciousness

As is clear from the passage cited earlier, a central metaphor in Husserl's writings on attention is the visualistic image of a spotlight, "ray" or "beam" of regard (Husserl, 2012, 52). Gurwitsch objected to the way this image seemed to imply an unstructured field in which consciousness relates to contents:

> Consciousness is, in general, not the presence of a content surrounded by a chaotic manifold of any other contents whatever; and thematic consciousness does not consist, as one usually asserts of attention, in a beam of light being cast upon a certain content while a chaotic confusion of other contents fills the region of shadow and darkness. [...] In general, the distinction between "noticed" = "illuminated," and "unnoticed" = "unilluminated" parts of consciousness misses essential phenomenological structures. [...] [T]he phenomenological structure, to which all studies concerning attention and the like must refer, is the following: there is a partial domain of what has a special connection with the theme, materially belongs to it, or however we wish to express it. We shall call this partial domain, which determines the attitude in which we are dealing with the theme, the thematic field.
>
> Gurwitsch, 1966, 202

The significance of Gestalt psychology for Gurwitsch was that it had insisted on seeing sense data, the "raw materials" of perception, not as a collection of independent, unconnected stimuli but as inherently *organized*: "That which presents itself in direct and immediate experience, is structured and organized to a greater or lesser extent" (Gurwitsch, 1964, 115). As Wolfgang Köhler, one of the foremost Gestalt psychologists, put it:

> [I]nstead of reacting to local stimuli by local and mutually independent events, the organism responds to *patterns* of stimuli to which it is exposed; and [...] this [...] is a unitary process, [...] which gives, in experience, a sensory scene rather than a mosaic of local sensations.
>
> Köhler, 1947, 102

For Gurwitsch, Gestalt psychology offered an analogy for how to approach phenomenological description (Gurwitsch, 1966, 194). If we take the task of describing conscious experience *as it presents itself* with the utmost seriousness, in other words, we must set aside all assumptions about the presence or absence of "real" connections among objects as such (i.e., we must perform the transcendental reduction). Insofar as we do this, we must acknowledge that "[w]hat is immediately given, the primal phenomenological material, is given only as articulated and structured" (Gurwitsch, 1966, 256). It is this structuring, and the way it renders every perception specific as a whole, that Husserl's spotlight image obscures. As Gurwitsch puts it in a later passage of the same essay, Husserl seems to overlook the fact that "by being actually singled out, the content in question undergoes a qualitative change and is, phenomenally speaking, no longer 'the same'"(Gurwitsch, 1966, 262, 265; cf. Merleau-Ponty, 1962, 35).

Gurwitsch illustrates this by returning to Husserl's tableau of the inkwell among other objects related to writing found on his desk:

> The inkwell belongs to the surrounding field; it is bound up with this field as with its "natural" environment. Even though it is singled out and made the theme of a "special attention", the singling out requires and presupposes the surroundings from which the theme cannot be totally severed. It always remains attached to a surrounding "fringe".
>
> Gurwitsch, 1966, 199

The notion of the "fringe" taken up by Gurwitsch is one of James's important legacies. Gurwitch wants to make clear that this "fringe" or "halo" is not essentially a matter of spatial proximity but of thematic relatedness, which can vary in complex ways: "Phenomenal 'distances' always exhibit qualitative features; they are thus not distances in the genuine sense of the term" (Gurwitsch, 1966, 199). The different things related to writing on the desk, along with some items unrelated to writing, constitute for Gurwitsch a Gestalt, a specific configuration, a thematic field. There is a larger horizon of other co-given matters and things both spatially and thematically unrelated to the inkwell. That is, attention is embedded in a structured field with a number of components. Most centrally, the Gestalt structure of "figure" and "ground" is always at work in some way, and in a sense, attention can be seen as another term for any particular actualization of this figure-ground structure. Further, Gurwitsch distinguishes between formative or organizing features of the thematic field and those that are organized or formed in relation to the formative features, and to different degrees of clarity or distinctness among the elements of the thematic field (Gurwitsch, 1966, 205ff, 225). Importantly, this structuring of the thematic field *is not the sole and spontaneous accomplishment of a pure ego that remains the same throughout.* The effectivity of Gestalt connections, figure-ground relations and other forms of organization within the theme-thematic field structure, and the alterations and modifications these can undergo, necessarily relativize the independence of the perceiving subject in relation to the phenomena of intentional experience.

> Hence, the pure ego can no longer be said to confront the stream [of consciousness], to stand in any sense outside or beyond it, any more than the stream of consciousness can be considered as a field for free activities of the pure ego.
>
> Gurwitsch, 1966, 285

On the basis of Gurwitsch's critical adaptation of Husserl's ideas, it is possible now to offer a provisional summary of how attentional fields are structured. As we shall see, temporal questions will lead to important further elaborations. But for the time being, Gurwitsch's main claim in *The Field of Consciousness* can serve as an initial stock-taking:

> [e]very field of consciousness comprises three domains, or, so to speak, extends in three dimensions. First, the *theme*: that with which the subject is dealing, which at the given moment occupies the "focus" of his [*sic*] attention, engrosses his mind, and upon which his mental activity concentrates. Secondly, the *thematic field*, which we define as the totality of facts, co-present with the theme, which are experienced as having material relevancy or pertinence to the theme. In the third place, the *margin* comprises facts which are merely co-present with the theme, but have no material relevancy to it.
>
> Gurwitsch, 1964, 55–56

In the conclusion of *Fields of Consciousness*, Gurwitsch further differentiates the "margin":

> Marginal consciousness [...] is of interest and importance because, whatever our theme, our mental activity is always accompanied by an awareness of facts and data belonging to the following three orders of existence: 1. *The stream of our conscious life*; 2. *our embodied existence*; 3. *the perceptual world*.
>
> Gurwitsch, 1964, 415

In the next section, the embodied character of attention will be examined more closely.

Embodied attention

Maurice Merleau-Ponty, while agreeing with Gurwitsch on the importance of Gestalt psychology and on many other points as well, would challenge his continued allegiance to the cognitive perspective taken by Husserl. Instead Merleau-Ponty would unfold a phenomenology organized around an account of bodily capabilities initially inaccessible to reflective consciousness, in effect, moving the body from the margin to the thematic center. In the process, he would open the door to acknowledgment of a much more important role for non-cognitive, non-focused, passive and routine forms of attention. Merleau-Ponty has for this reason been an important touchstone for humanistic (Seamon, 2015) and later, non-representational (Anderson and Harrison, 2010) and neohumanistic (Simonsen, 2013) geographies. His emphasis on embodiment is important for the present argument because it helps equip the account of attention here to be articulated with the ineluctably embodied dimensions of practice. For Merleau-Ponty,

> the perception of our own body and the perception of external things provide an example of *non-positing* consciousness, that is, of consciousness not in possession of fully determinate objects, that of a *logic lived through* which cannot account for itself.
>
> Merleau-Ponty, 1962, 57

This logic is an incipient logic of practice, of actions and interactions within the body's environment:

> I can therefore take my place, through the medium of my body as the potential source of a certain number of actions, in my environment conceived as a set of *manipulanda* and without, moreover, envisaging my body or my surroundings as objects in the Kantian sense.
>
> Merleau-Ponty, 1962, 120

In his major text *Phenomenology of Perception*, Merleau-Ponty lays the groundwork for his own approach in part through an extended critique of what he calls "empiricist" and "intellectualist" analyses of attention in psychology (Merleau-Ponty, 1962, 30–36). These two approaches are invalid because each loads one side or the other of the perceiver-perceived couplet with all responsibility for explaining the movement of attention. A valid account of attention, according to Merleau-Ponty, must take as its starting point the generative role of the body as a "third term" through which perceiver and perceived are dynamically connected. Attention is then fundamentally framed by bodily space:

> Bodily space can be distinguished from external space and envelop its parts instead of spreading them out, because it is the darkness needed in the theatre to show up the performance, the background of somnolence or reserve of vague power against which the gesture and its aim stand out, the zone of not[-]being *in front of which* precise beings, figures and points can come to light. In the last analysis, if my body can be a "form" and if there can be, in front of it, important figures against indifferent backgrounds, this occurs in virtue of its being polarized by its tasks, of its

> *existence towards* them, of its collecting together of itself in pursuit of its aims [...]. [O]ne's own body is the third term, always tacitly understood, in the figure-background structure, and every figure stands out against the double horizon of external and bodily space.
>
> Merleau-Ponty, 1962, 115

The introduction of this third term effectively corporealizes the figure-ground structure Gurwitsch had adapted from Gestalt psychology, so that, in place of Husserl's Ego we can now discern a "surging" bodily salience at work.

> [T]he subject, when put in front of his scissors, needle and familiar tasks, does not need to look for his hands or his fingers, because they are not objects to be discovered in objective space: bones, muscles and nerves, but potentialities already mobilized by the perception of scissors or needle, the central end of those "intentional threads" which link him to the objects given. It is never our objective body that we move, but our phenomenal body, [which] [...] as the potentiality of this or that part of the world, surges toward objects to be grasped and perceives them.
>
> Merleau-Ponty, 1962, 121

This "surging" takes place along the "intentional threads":

> My flat is, for me, not a set of closely associated images. It remains a familiar domain round about me only as long as I still have "in my hands" or "in my legs" the main distances and directions involved, and as long as from my body intentional threads run out towards it.
>
> Merleau-Ponty, 1962, 150

This sensibility to these various bodily connections motivates Merleau-Ponty's substitution of the term "intentional arc" for Husserl's spotlight or searchlight metaphor. "It is this intentional arc which brings about the unity of the senses, of intelligence, of sensibility and motility" (Merleau-Ponty, 1962, 157).

Merleau-Ponty thinks of attention as having two dimensions or levels, an actual, creative dimension and an habitual dimension rooted in cultural, historical, biographical contexts. The actual dimension he describes as follows: "To pay attention is not merely further to elucidate pre-existing data, it is to bring about a new articulation of them by taking them as *figures*" (Merleau-Ponty, 1962, 35). The image of intentional threads connecting Merleau-Ponty to his apartment nicely illustrates the second, habitual dimension by which the body incorporates practical relations to its surroundings. This incorporation may presuppose repetition and practice but is not reducible to them.

> To get used to a hat, a car or a stick is to be transplanted into them, or conversely, to incorporate them into the bulk of our own body. Habit

expresses our power of dilating our being-in-the-world, or changing our existence by appropriating fresh instruments.

Merleau-Ponty, 1962, 166

This habitual dimension is important also because it points to the entire range of *non-focused, non-deliberate, non-cognitive* qualities our attention can have. Insofar as our bodily engagements are in part automatic or unreflected (tying shoes, turning door knobs, etc., but also using language), our attention to them is of a passive, routine or "monitoring" nature: we are capable of noticing them, but usually do so only when something prompts a break in the normal flow of practice. Byung-Chul Han refers to these unreflected capabilities as "actomes" (Han, 2014, 88). Although Heidegger does not present it in attentional terms, his famous workshop scenario in which the previously "ready-to-hand" hammer goes missing or ceases to function and provokes a more distanced and objectifying attention to its "presence-at-hand" can be seen to illustrate this point (Heidegger, 1962, 102–103). Non-cognitive, often unfocused attention plays an enormous role in our everyday lives, and thus deserves more scrutiny (Harrison, 2008; Dewsbury, 2015). As suggested earlier, it is the interplay between focused or active attention and passive, distracted or routine modes of attention that lies at the center of political questions about the directedness of practice. As J.D. Dewsbury puts it:

> We could say that habits offer a background of *preoccupation* in the face of life's incessant becoming, our sense of who we are is anchored by dispositions that, literally pre-occupy us, both pre-existing us and occupying at least part of our attention. [...] This anchoring, however, frees up another part of our attention – namely, that which is attentive to the new – and thus is able to provide space to reevaluate the efficacy of our ongoing habit dispositions.
>
> Dewsbury, 2015, 32

In line with a Deleuzian sensibility that programmatically privileges "active living", Dewsbury portrays habitual attention's complexity-reducing effects primarily as a condition of possibility for "more active orientations to what befalls us" (Dewsbury, 2015, 37). I share some of Paul Harrison's reservations about this particular ethico-political line (Harrison, 2015). However, Dewsbury's characterization of attention in terms of (pre-)occupation is suggestive. Dewsbury helpfully highlights the dynamics of interplay between focused, oriented and less-focused forms of attention. In our embodied experience, these different attentional modes are constantly animating, soliciting and referring to each other, such that a truly moment-by-moment description of attentional states would be an extremely complex matter. Habitual movement, thoughts, emotions and affects can all evoke each other in an ongoing tangle.

David Seamon already offers an interesting typology of attention in his classic 1979 *A Geography of the Lifeworld* (Seamon, 2015). There he distinguishes between, on the one hand, a spectrum of different forms of relatively focused attentive modes ranging from inward-directed "obliviousness" regarding the external world to outward-directed "heightened contact", and on the other hand, an underlying "basic contact" or "pre-conscious attention" roughly equivalent to Merleau-Ponty's or Dewsbury's habitual attention (Seamon, 2015, 103–120). Using the example of driving, he notes that:

> [b]asic contact is the essential foundation for more conscious modes of encounter. Because basic contact automatically synthesizes our driving movements with the road ahead, we can turn our attention to the autumn foliage or notice skaters in the park as we pass. Or we can ignore the trip and think about the morning ahead or worry about a friend in the hospital. Basic contact, in harmony with the powers of habit, integrates the routine portions of our daily living. We can thus turn our attention to new and unfamiliar things.
>
> Seamon, 2015, 117

Attention as pathic and mediated

If Husserl's ideal-typical model of attention was that of a focused consciousness relentlessly captivated "by a single object and its inexhaustibility", recent work has dwelt instead upon the other end of the spectrum, that of attention as "impressionistic opening to a universe of diffuse affection" (Blumenberg, 2007, 182; Böhme, 2013). Bernard Waldenfels takes up such non-autonomous, unreflective aspects of attention in his *Phenomenology of Attention* (Waldenfels, 2004). He builds on the work of Gurwitsch, Merleau-Ponty and Husserl, but his subtle phenomenological analysis poses a number of challenges to the picture of attention that has emerged thus far. First, he radicalizes Gurwitsch's and Merleau-Ponty's de-centering of the autonomous, cognitively conceived subject by identifying an originary "pathic" moment of attentional movement. Second, he calls into question some of the dualisms, heuristic or otherwise, that structure foregoing discussions of attention, especially the distinctions between noetic subject or Ego and noematic objects of perception, and between active, free or autonomous and passive or heteronomous movements of attention. The aspect of his account of most interest here is the insight that the process of becoming alert or attending to something [*Aufmerken*] or merely noticing it *as* something [*Bemerken*] is inaugurated by a previous becoming obtrusive or noticeable [*Auffallen*] on the part of the matter we begin to attend to. Corresponding to this noticeability is a primordial turning-toward or initial answering, a "primary attention", that may or may not ripen into full, "secondary" attention, depending on what answer is given to the initial solicitation posed by some newly obtrusive matter (Waldenfels, 2004, 86, 117). This more complex process characterizes our attention not just to what we conventionally think of as "external" objects or events but also to internal thoughts and feelings. In a certain sense, even that which appears to express our spontaneous freedom always comes to us, not from us (see Chapter 4).

For Waldenfels, the paying of attention is first and foremost an answering. The first stage of attentional movement is thus the awakening of activation [*Weckung der Erregung*]:

> If we ask ourselves under what conditions something activates our attention and rises above the threshold of attention, we encounter minimal preconditions such as the raising of a shape [*Gestalt*] from a neutral background and a sufficient intensity [*Prägnanz*] of shape formation to prevent the shape from becoming indistinct from the background.
>
> Waldenfels, 2004, 96

The processes of turning and noticing already introduced by Husserl then come into play in subsequent stages, but the initial "subliminal attention" is not yet "conscious" (Waldenfels, 2004, 96). The obtrusiveness of things that awaken our attentiveness can vary dramatically, and our corresponding "room for attentional maneuver" can narrow the more insistent they become (Waldenfels, 2004, 97; see also Strohmayer, 1993). In this connection, Waldenfels's analysis of shock as an extreme form of obtrusiveness is interesting:

> The awakening of attention moves [...] between the extremes of a sleepy monotony in which nothing is noticeable any longer and the over-awakeness of a shock, where something falls entirely outside the frame and stuns us. [...] A shock doesn't raise itself as a figure from a background but rather intensifies itself to an absolute impression that fills the moment to its brim.
>
> Waldenfels, 2004, 130

Once our attention has been awakened and we are aware of something obtrusive, the next question is that of the initial valence of our response, whether positive or negative: the obtrusive matter may exercise attraction and encourage turning toward, or may exercise repulsion, provoking a turning away (Waldenfels, 2004, 97, 136). This of course has to do with the specifics of how we are socialized into particular "habitual attentional styles" (Wehrle, 2013, 271), or what Ludwik Fleck defined as community-specific "styles of thought" (Fleck, 1981). Attentional styles are themselves arenas for important power relations. Additionally, these elementary reactions are already so saturated with what Waldenfels calls "in-between events", articulations of internal and external, autonomous and heteronomous moments, that it makes no sense to distinguish clearly between the effects of the attending subject and those of the object (Waldenfels, 2004, 100). Certainly there are instances of relatively helpless fascination, or alternatively, of sovereign and arbitrary control over one's attentional answers, but usually we are somewhere between these two poles.

The third moment Waldenfels identifies is the transition from attending to thematically apprehending something in a "formation of relief". This function of attention:

> brings it about that, in the constitution of an "attentional relief" [*Beach-tungsreliefs*] some things *step forward*, others *step backward*. [...] On the side of the attentive person this corresponds to a "pulling forward" and a "setting back". In this way something becomes a *theme*. That which steps forward not only steps out of a flat surface, it constitutes the middle-point of a *thematic field*, graduated according to proximity and distance to the thematic core. What doesn't belong to the theme goes to the *margin*. More exactly: it is pushed to the margin. Center and margin are in no sense static magnitudes but rather products of an ever-self-renewing centering and marginalization.
>
> Waldenfels, 2004, 102

Here Waldenfels infuses Gurwitsch's tripartite schema with a dynamism that brings us closer to a political phenomenology of attention. This dynamism is not a simple binary matter, Waldenfels insists, of the difference between actuality and potentiality, "it is far more a question of the possibility of a *reorganization* of the field of experience in the course of which weightings are redistributed" (Waldenfels, 2004, 102–103).

Even these preliminary points, which do not exhaust the subtlety of Waldenfels's analysis of attention, already enrich our sense of what goes on in our turning toward and turning away from matters of concern. Waldenfels goes beyond Gurwitsch and Merleau-Ponty in linking the pathic foundation of attentional processes explicitly to cultural media, which are responsible for generating "forms of obtrusiveness" (Waldenfels, 2004, 129). Media have become ever more adept at producing and manipulating the "seductive power" of the sensory materials and narratives they place in our perceptual fields: "the seductive power of things opens a gateway for all kinds of influence, also for the media-transported influence of economic advertising and of political propaganda" (Waldenfels, 2004, 136–137). A related degradation is discerned by Hans Blumenberg, who worries about an age in which "the competition for the allocation of disposable perception is carried out through the escalation of stimuli instead of through the refinement of attention" (Blumenberg, 2007, 184). This concern is in turn closely related to Stiegler's analysis of the erosion of deep attention (see Chapter 1). A direction that Waldenfels does not take, and that I will not pursue very far in the present book, would be to explore wider cultural variations in the construction of attentional styles and of obtrusiveness that have more to do with cultural and social categories such as race, ethnicity, gender or sexuality than with consumer fascination. For example, some of the basic insights of whiteness studies (Roediger, 2007; Gilroy 2002; Garner, 2007) or of feminist research on cultures of masculinity (Adams and Savran, 2002; Kimmel, 2012), have to do precisely with the unobtrusiveness of "unmarked categories". The particular arrangements of obtrusiveness and unobtrusiveness that allow the privileged not to notice their privilege as specific and power-laden, are culturally constructed and potentially contestable (Fanon, 2008). Following this line of critical inquiry would be one very important elaboration upon the argument presented in this book.

Waldenfels's anatomy of processes of attention develop the points made by Husserl, Gurwitsch and Merleau-Ponty in a way that offers a number of analytical tools. Specifically, he points the analysis explicitly in the direction of power relations. As he puts it, "the occurrence of power stands in close relation to the occurrence of attention, where something *and not something else* becomes noticeable to me" (Waldenfels, 2004, 235). His conviction that "being concerned with the special phenomenon of the solicitation of attention [*des Aufmerkenlassens*] seems an appropriate way to think of power relations in general differently than certain traditions have allowed" (Waldenfels, 2004, 235). Two supplemental points need to be made however. First, it is important to avoid a one-sided understanding of solicitation of attention only as a matter of threats to our political and ethical autonomy. The pathic or "receptive" character of our attention is also what opens us to the ethical appeals of others in relations of care or solidarity (Noddings, 2013, 30). More will be said on this point in Chapters 4 and 7 . For the moment it is enough to note that questions of which way we turn, what we turn to doing, who this turning turns us into, and who or what determines our turning bring us back to James's conviction that the course of our attention is a core dimension of who we are. These questions return us as well to Stiegler's concerns about the larger impacts of the increasingly sophisticated methods by which we are hailed and solicited upon our ability to sustain focused attention at all.

The second supplemental point to make is that the politics of attention is always a matter of unobtrusiveness and non-solicitation as well as the obtrusiveness resulting from solicitation. This point will be picked up again in Chapters 4 and 7. The pathic-responsive features of attention, in short, form an important battleground for the ethical and political issues political economies of attention have primarily interpreted with reference to active-selective attention. Maren Wehrle's sweeping attempt to trace the convergence of psychological and phenomenological research on attention ends on exactly this point. Like Waldenfels, whom she cites, she zeroes in on the key question of "[w]hich things become noticeable to us at all and whether we remain with them", and links this issue with Foucault's questions about the conditions under which we are able to think and perceive otherwise than we normally do (Wehrle, 2013, 353–354).

References

Adams, R. and Savran, D., eds. (2002). *The Masculinity Studies Reader*. Oxford: Wiley.

Anderson, B. and Harrison, P., eds. (2010). *Taking Place: Non-Representational Theories and Geography*. Farnham: Ashgate.

Blumenberg, H. (2007). *Zu den Sachen und zurück*. Frankfurt am Main: Suhrkamp.

Böhme, G. (2013). *Atmosphäre: Essays zur neuen Aesthetik*. Frankfurt am Main: Suhrkamp.

Crary, J. (1999). *Suspensions of Perception: Attention, Spectacle, and Modern Culture*. Cambridge, MA: MIT Press.

Depraz, N. (2004). Where is the phenomenology of attention that Husserl intended to perform? A transcendental pragmatic-oriented description of attention. *Continental Philosophy Review*, 37, pp. 5–20.

Dewsbury, J.D. (2015). Non-representation landscapes and the performative affective forces of habit: from "Live" to "Blank". *Cultural Geographies*, 22(1), pp. 29–47.

Fanon, F. (2008). *Black Skin, White Masks*. Trans. R. Philcox. New York: Grove Press.

Fleck, L. (1981). *Genesis and Development of a Scientific Fact*. Trans. F. Bradley. Chicago, IL: University of Chicago Press.

Garner, S. (2007). *Whiteness: An Introduction*. London: Routledge.

Gilroy, P. (2002). *There Ain't No Black in the Union Jack: The Cultural Politics of Race and Nation*. London: Routledge.

Gurwitsch, A. (1964). *The Field of Consciousness*. Pittsburgh, PA: Duquesne University Press.

Gurwitsch, A. (1966). Phenomenology of thematics and of the pure ego: studies of the relation between Gestalt Theory and phenomenology. In: A. Gurwitsch, *Studies in Phenomenology and Psychology*. Evanston, IL: Northwestern University Press, pp. 175–286.

Han, B.-C. (2014): *Psychopolitik: Neoliberalismus und die neuen Machttechniken*. Frankfurt am Main: Fischer Verlag.

Harrison, P. (2008). Corporeal remains: vulnerability, proximity, and living on after the end of the world. *Environment and Planning A*, 40(2), pp. 423–445.

Harrison, P. (2015). After affirmation, or, being a loser: on vitalism, sacrifice and cinders. *GeoHumanities*, 1(2), pp. 285–306.

Heidegger, M. (1962). *Being and Time*. Trans. J. Macquarrie and E. Robinson. Oxford: Blackwell.

Husserl, E. (1991). *On the Phenomenology of the Consciousness of Internal Time (1893–1917)*. Trans. J. Brough. Dordrecht: Springer.

Husserl, E. (2001). *Logical Investigations, Volume 1*. Trans. J. Findlay. London: Routledge.

Husserl, E. (2012). *Ideas*. Trans. W.R.B. Gibson. London: Routledge.

James, W. (1950). *The Principles of Psychology*. 2 Volumes. New York: Dover.

Kimmel, M. (2012). *Manhood in America*, 3rd ed. New York: Oxford University Press.

Köhler, W. (1947). *Gestalt Psychology: The Definitive Statement of the Gestalt Theory*. New York: Liveright.

Malpas, J. (2006). *Heidegger's Topology: Being, Place, World*. Cambridge, MA: MIT Press.

Merleau-Ponty, M. (1962). *Phenomenology of Perception*. Trans. C. Smith. London: Routledge and Kegan Paul.

Moran, D. (2005). *Husserl: Founder of Phenomenology*. Cambridge: Polity Press.

Noddings, N. (2013). *Caring: A Feminine Approach to Ethics and Moral Education*. 2nd ed. Berkeley: University of California Press.

Posner, M. (ed.) (2004). *Cognitive Neuroscience of Attention*. New York: Guilford Press.

Roediger, D. (2007). *The Wages of Whiteness: Race and the Making of the American Working Class*, 2nd ed. London: Verso.

Schatzki, T. (2017). *Martin Heidegger: Theorist of Space*. 2nd unrevised ed. Stuttgart: Franz Steiner Verlag.

Seamon, D. (2015). *A Geography of the Lifeworld*. London: Routledge.

Simonsen, K. (2013). In quest of a new humanism: embodiment, experience and phenomenology as critical geography. *Progress in Human Geography*, 37(1), pp. 10–26.

Steinbock, A. (2004). Introduction to this special issue. *Continental Philosophy Review*, 37, pp. 1–3.

Strohmayer, U. (1993). Beyond theory: the cumbersome materiality of shock. *Environment and Planning D: Society and Space*, 11(3), pp. 323–347.

Strohmayer, U. (1998). The event of space: geographical allusions in the phenomenological tradition. *Environment and Planning D: Society and Space*, 16, pp. 105–121.

Styles, E. (2006). *The Psychology of Attention*. 2nd ed. New York: Psychology Press.

Toadvine, T. (2001). Phenomenological method in Merleau-Ponty's critique of Gurwitsch. *Husserl Studies*, 17, pp. 195–205.

Waldenfels, B. (2004). *Phänomenologie der Aufmerksamkeit*. Frankfurt am Main: Suhrkamp.

Wehrle, M. (2013). *Horizonte der Aufmerksamkeit: Entwurf einer dynamischen Konzeption der Aufmerksamkeit aus phänomenologischer und kognitionspsychologischer Sicht*. Munich: Wilhelm Fink Verlag.

3   The directedness of practice

This chapter builds upon some of the insights from the previous chapters about the directedness of attention to suggest ways of understanding the directedness of practice more generally. The political economy of attention sketched earlier, along with the survey of phenomenological insights, already point up some urgent issues that have led some commentators to talk of a "crisis of attention" (Jackson, 2009). And yet this crisis is not merely one of what we pay attention to, or how and by whom our selective attention is steered. Attention is ultimately only one dimension of embodied practice, and our embodied practices more generally are also structured by our directional asymmetry. What we are thinking, feeling or experiencing are subsets or dimensions of *what we are doing*, and what we are doing, our practices, involve structures and processes of directedness that are related but not necessarily identical to those discussed above for attention. In this chapter, the sensibility for attentional direction is carried over to highlight directional aspects of practice hitherto not so central to practice theory. Along the way, I will argue that the movement of attention helps explain the movement of practical engagements.

"Practice theory" is a broad category encompassing approaches from a range of disciplines. According to Hilmar Schäfer:

> Basically it is possible to understand as practice theory those approaches in which "practices" form the fundamental theoretical category and which attempt thereby to overcome a series of established philosophical and sociological dichotomies, for example the difference between structure and action, a rule and its application, the macro- and micro-perspective as well as between society and individual.
>
> Schäfer, 2016, 11

The emergence of practice theories can be understood as a critical response to earlier functionalist approaches in sociology and anthropology (Everts, Lahr-Kurten and Watson, 2011, 323–324; Schäfer, 2016, 10). Practice theories developed since the 1970s usually blend a continued cognizance of structuring contexts with interpretive and action centered perspectives in which actors are neither fully determined nor completely autonomous. According to Schatzki, Knorr Cetina and von Savigny (2001), practice theories have more recently enjoyed a higher profile across a number of disciplines, amounting to a "practical turn", in part as a way of responding to the challenges thrown up to theorization of the social by poststructuralist cultural theories (see Hui, Schatzki and Shove, 2017).

Because of the breadth and diversity of the field of practice theories, it is no easy matter to decide which approach or combination of approaches is most suitable to be brought into the present project. Geographers have drawn prominently upon the writings of so-called "first generation" practice theorists such as Giddens and Bourdieu (Everts, Lahr-Kurten and Watson, 2011, 323–324; Hui, Schatzki and Shove, 2017, 1). Bourdieu has been mobilized for example in the work of Joe Painter and his students (Painter, 2000). Thus, Alex Jeffrey's study of the "improvised state" in Bosnia-Herzegovina since the Dayton Accords (Jeffrey, 2013), and Craig Jeffrey's ethnography of educated but unemployed young men in rural India (Jeffrey, 2010) both infuse Bourdieu's notions of social, cultural and symbolic capital with relevance for situated spatial processes. Interesting as these studies are, though, they do not address the directedness of practice as such. Bourdieu's portrayal of *habitus* in terms of the "learned ignorance" (Bourdieu, 1990, 19), "censorship" or "genesis amnesia" (Bourdieu, 1977, 18, 79) inherent in unreflected and involved practice, and his related critique of the "objectifying" perspective of science (Bourdieu, 1990, 86ff) can be seen to raise the issue of selectivity of attention and practice in potentially fruitful ways. The work of Anthony Giddens (1984) has been interesting to geographers because it displays a more developed spatial sensitivity than most of his contemporary social theorists. This spatial sensitivity is expressed in a critical engagement with time geography, and in interesting theorizations of the spatial structuring of "locales" through "regionalization", a process explored most systematically by his one-time collaborator Benno Werlen (Werlen, 1992, 1997, 1999). These lines of thought are broadly relevant to the present project. But other lines of practice theory provide more suitable vocabularies.

For my purposes the most promising version of practice theory is the "second generation" approach developed by the philosopher Theodore Schatzki. There are a number of reasons Schatzki's work is particularly helpful. First of all, as Everts, Lahr-Kurten and Watson point out in their piece recommending it to geographers, his approach is "the most elaborate and explicitly fleshed out practice theory" available at this juncture (Everts, Lahr-Kurten and Watson, 2011, 325). Second, it is developed in a detailed, ongoing and commendably even-handed conversation with a wide range of other approaches, including poststructuralist approaches from which many practice theorists have until recently tended to shy away. This contributes to the overall convincingness of his practice theory. A third feature that strengthens its general plausibility is the way Schatzki portrays practice as a finely textured web or weave through which human activities "hang together", but avoids placing substantive limits on what kinds of activities qualify as practices. In other words, his theory hugs the level of empirical detail quite closely while remaining widely applicable across a range of areas of life. Fourth, and more specifically, his sensitivity to the spatial organization of practices, manifested most strongly in his theorization of the "site of the social" (Schatzki, 2002; Everts, Lahr-Kurten and Watson, 2011) but also the "timespace of human activity" (Schatzki, 2010), forms a detailed context in which to bring forward the issues surrounding the directedness of practice. Finally, in his notions of "teleoaffective structures" and "activity-place-spaces", Schatzki already addresses the directedness of practice more explicitly than do most practice theorists, and in ways that I believe can be linked to the phenomena of attention outlined above. For all these reasons, the conversation carried out in this chapter is largely with Schatzki, though, again, there is nothing standing in the way of widening it to include other interlocutors.

Schatzki's theory of practice is presented in its most developed form in a three-volume series (Schatzki, 1996, 2002, 2010). In the first volume, *Social Practices: A Wittgensteinian Approach to Human Activity and the Social*, Schatzki surveys the theoretical landscape in which any practice theory today must make claims for plausibility, lays out the basic features of his practice theory, and distinguishes it carefully from some other important recent approaches to practice, notably those of Bourdieu, Giddens, Taylor and Lyotard (Schatzki, 1996). In the second volume, *The Site of the Social: A Philosophical Account of the Constitution of Social Life and Change*, Schatzki elaborates his notion of social practice by arguing that:

> [t]o theorize sociality through the concept of a social site is to hold that the character and transformation of social life are both intrinsically and decisively rooted in the site where it takes place. In turn, this site-context [...] is composed of a mesh of orders and practices.
>
> Schatzki, 2002, xi

In *The Site of the Social*, Schatzki develops his account through extended engagement with two empirical examples: Shaker practices in the context of the medicinal herb business in mid-19th century New Lebanon, New York, and late 20th century trading practices on the NASDAQ exchange. The third volume, *The Timespace of Human Activity: On Performance, Society, and History as Indeterminate Teleological Events*, in Schatzki's words:

> turns the accounts of its predecessors inside-out. It moves inside practice-arrangement nexuses to theorize the indeterminate temporalspatial activity events, as simultaneously effect-features and determining contexts of which practices, social phenomena, and the course of history at large occur. Building on the accounts of the preceding books, the book ties practices and social affairs back to activity as the happening through which practices, society, and history exist.
>
> Schatzki, 2010, xii

In this third volume, the work of Heidegger on human spatiality, which had provided a relatively unobtrusive background tone in the first two volumes, is brought more explicitly to the fore as a basis for understanding the performative happening or evental character of practice and the social (Schatzki, 2017). Schatzki's highly detailed and spatially sensitive anatomy of practices and sites can, I am convinced, help to extend the notion of directedness beyond the purview of attention to include practices more generally. In the process of attempting to sketch such an extension, I will also suggest ways in which specifically directional questions can in turn sharpen certain aspects of Schatzski's account.

In what follows, I will first summarize Schatzki's conception of social practice, laying special emphasis upon his notions of the "teleoaffective structure" of practices and the associated "activity-place-spaces". Next, I gloss his discussion of "the site of the social". With these basics in place, the third section suggests how these conceptions can be articulated with some of the insights gleaned from the foregoing chapters to characterize what Schatzki calls "integrative practices" as involving a triple directionality composed of attention and two levels of practical *telos*. Seeing practice through these enhanced lenses, I submit, also improves the explanatory power of Schatzki's practice theory, and in fact adds a missing element to his culminating account of "the timespace of human activity". As is true of practice theory more generally, Schatzki has much less to say about how and why practitioners sometimes switch from one practice to another than about the character of involvement in each practice. Bringing in a heightened awareness of attentional dynamics can, I want to suggest, address this gap. The fourth section will discuss Schatzki's "residual humanism" and thus set up the more extended account of directionally asymmetrical subjectivity laid out in Chapter 4.

Social practice and teleoaffective structure

Schatzki defends a position according to which it is neither individuals, their "minds" and "actions", nor social orders that lie at the root of social reality but social practice; indeed social orders and individuals are the results of practices (Schatzki, 1996, 13). This approach is initially shaped by a creative but careful reading of Wittgenstein. Wittgenstein's texts suggest, according to Schatzki, that we abandon talk of "the mind" and distinctions between internal and external worlds in favor of analyzing "how things stand and are going for people", that is, "conditions of life" that are expressed in "bodily doings and sayings" (Schatzki, 1996, 22). The idea of "expression" is important here: it already transports the idea of the intelligibility of practices to others, and this is a key point for Schatzki.

> [T]he performance of behavior that expresses such and such a condition presupposes practices on the background of which others are able, on the basis of that behavior, to understand and say that this is the actor's

> condition; and people are able to understand and say this by virtue of
> participating in these presupposed practices [themselves].
>
> Schatzki, 1996, 24

In a sense, then, the mutual intelligibility of conditions of life among social
actors shows that these conditions always transcend the individual bodies that
express them. The "hanging together" that defines sociality in the most basic
sense, are rooted in connections wrought by practices (Schatzki, 1996, 14).

What, then, does Schatzki understand "practice" to be? Practice is:

> a temporally unfolding and spatially distributed nexus of doings and
> sayings. Examples are cooking practices, voting practices, industrial
> practices, recreational practices, and correctional practices. To say that
> the doings and sayings forming a practice constitute a nexus is to say that
> they are linked in certain ways. Three major avenues of linkage are
> involved: (1) through understandings, for example, of what to say and do;
> (2) through explicit rules, principles, precepts, and instructions; and (3)
> through what I will call "teleoaffective" structures embracing ends, pro-
> jects, tasks, purposes, beliefs, emotions, and moods.
>
> Schatzki, 1996, 89

In the second volume of the trilogy he adds to these three principles of the
composition of practices a fourth element, "general understandings" or more
broadly shared interpretations not directly determinative of practices but
acting as a backdrop to them (Schatzki, 2002, 86ff.).

Within this compound umbrella definition of practices, Schatzki makes a
series of further distinctions and specifications. First of all, he distinguishes
between "dispersed" and "integrative" practices. The former kind is composed of generally applicable, modular practices "widely dispersed among
different sectors of social life". Examples include "describing" or "following
rules". (Schatzki, 1996, 91). A signal difference between dispersed and integrated practices is that dispersed practices lack teleoaffective structure
(Schatzki 1996, 92). Integrative practices are more complex and constitutive
of specific domains of social life. They are composed of all four linkages
between doings and sayings mentioned above (practical understandings, rules,
teleoaffective structures and general understandings) (Schatzki, 1996, 98–99;
2002, 86ff.). Crucially, for Schatzki, much of social life is "held together",
conducted or performed through integrative practices. Integrative practices
are not just collections of contingently related dispersed practices: some dispersed practices are transformed by their incorporation into integrative practices, as, for example, when practices of keeping one's things in order are
transformed by the specific form they take in military life (Schatzki, 1996,
100). Other dispersed practices, such as imagining, may remain relatively
stable in how they are carried out regardless of whether they play a part
within larger integrative practices. Additionally, Schatzki emphasizes that

specific actions may be part of more than one practice, and many practices, both dispersed and integrated, vary significantly both historically and geographically (Schatzki, 1996, 104). Even these few additional considerations already clearly suggest how complex Schatzki's view is of the weave of practices through which the social "hangs together".

Especially because it will be so central to my own adaptation of Schatzki's ideas, it is worth dwelling in some depth upon the "teleoaffective structures" characteristic of integrative practices. Teleoaffective structures can be thought of as variably flexible logics or orderings inherent in the pursuit of the ends, projects, tasks, and the doings and sayings that make them up, specific to an integrative practice. These logics and orders are usually not stringent and linear.

> Western cooking practices, for instance, embrace a range of ends, projects, purposes, and tasks such as making snacks, lightly browning, whipping up appetizers, chopping, pickling, readying the grill, and preparing healthy meals. These ends and projects form myriad possible hierarchical orders in the sense that certain actions and projects can be carried out for the sake of certain other projects and ends. [...] Notice that the greater part, sometimes the entirety of a practice's teleoaffective structure concerns teleology alone instead of also or exclusively affectivity. No particular emotions and moods, for instance, are appropriate for cooking. By contrast, certain emotions are appropriate for, and nearly inherent to, rearing practices.
>
> Schatzki, 1996, 100–101

Within a given integrative practice, the components of the teleoaffective structure may be organized in a straightforwardly hierarchical way, and Schatzki usually discusses the relation between ends, projects, tasks, and doings and sayings as if these comprise a nested hierarchy. Teleoaffective structures are inherently, though not always explicitly, normative, in the general sense that more or less acceptable ways of doing the practice are understood, may invest the emotional and affective experience of carrying out practices, and may in some circumstances be enforced. Schatzki, following Charles Taylor, asserts that teleoaffective structures, like the other components of integrative practices (understandings and rules) are not located within the individual but are "out there" in social space, and only derivatively appropriated within individuals (Schatzki, 1996, 105–106). Put differently, teleoaffective structure is "not a set of properties of actors" but rather of practices; it "is (1) expressed in the open-ended set of doings and sayings that compose the practice and (2) unevenly incorporated into different participants' minds and actions" (Schatzki, 2002, 80). This "out-thereness" holds as well for intelligibility, both in the sense of "how the world makes sense" and of "which actions make sense". Both of these forms of intelligibility "are articulated through the organization of practices" (Schatzki, 1996, 111). Since their intelligibility is external to actors, practical situations and their structures can be thought of as "signifying" actions to participants. So, for example, in a fictional scenario involving "Michael" and "Teresa":

> the idea is that an end, say, winning Teresa, signifies (to Michael) a particular project, say, buying her flowers, which in turn signifies a particular task, say, driving to the nearest florist, which itself signifies to him the action of getting the keys, which in turn signifies looking for them – so he stands up and begins to look about the room, these being doings in his bodily repertoire.
>
> Schatzki 1996, 122

Teleoaffectivity, in other words, "governs action by shaping what is signified to an actor to do" (Schatzki, 1996, 123). Further below I will argue that the concept of teleoaffective structure provides an excellent basis on which to understand the sense in which practices are inherently directed.

The site of the social

In the first volume of his trilogy, Schatzki is chiefly occupied with the task of spelling out an account of practice. In the second volume, he embeds practice within material "sites" and social "orders". Based upon a review of different conceptions of order within sociological theory, and drawing explicitly upon Foucault, Laclau and Mouffe, Law and others, Schatzki develops an idea of order that accents the relative openness and contingency of the "hanging together" of phenomena: "social orders are thus the arrangements of people, artifacts, organisms and things through and amid which social life transpires, in which those entities relate, occupy positions, and possess meanings" (Schatzki, 2002, 22). "Arrangements" as he intends the term here:

> are not inherently regular. Entities can be, and often are, arranged irregularly, as in an English garden. Arrangements are also not inherently stable. Relations, positions and meanings, like the arrangements of which they are aspects, are labile phenomena, only transitory fixations of which can be assured.
>
> Schatzki, 2002, 24

Schatzki further specifies a set of dimensions of arrangements or ways in which they are held together and given an at least provisionally stable anatomy through practices. The first of these dimensions he designates with the umbrella category "social relations", the second with "being". The key social relations are: (1) causal relations; (2) spatial relations; (3) intentionality; and (4) "prefiguration" (Schatzki, 2002, 40–47). The first of these four relations is broken down further into "making things happen" vs. "leading to" things happening. This is an important distinction because it underpins Schatzki's argument for continuing to see human agency (which can "make things happen") as qualitatively different from non-human agency (which can "lead to" things happening) and more central to social relations (Schatzki, 2002, 42).

By spatial relations, Schatzki means both physically anchored "activity space" and "activity-place-space". "Activity space is not a physical matrix because its constituents are actions. Its objectivity nonetheless derives from the locations in physical space where activities take place" (Schatzki, 2002, 43). Subtly different but ultimately important for my own adaptation of Schatzki's ideas is the concept of "activity-place-space", which he describes as a "matrix of places and paths where activities are performed. These places and paths are stationed, furthermore, at particular entities" (Schatzki, 2002, 43). Crucially for my purposes, "to the extent that the activities that are to occur in a given locale are interdependent, sequenced, and nested, the places where these activities are to take place are similarly interdependent, sequenced, and nested. Indeed, rooms, building, and housing complexes, even whole communities and urban expanses, are laid out with an eye to such activity-place relations" (Schatzki, 2002, 43). As a way to illustrate the interplay between practices and arrangements Schatzki introduces the extended example of nineteenth century Shaker manufacturing of herbal products in New Lebanon, New York (Schatzki 2002, 25–38). Thus he can exemplify activity-place-space within the context of Shaker manufacturing activities:

> The laboratory's kettles, stills, and chests were laid out with an eye to what would be done with them, how these activities interconnected, and thus what places these entities would anchor in the activity-place space of the laboratory. For instance, the place to draw liquors from the fluid extract barrels needed to be convenient, sufficiently expansive, and so anchored as to permit the smooth transition from extraction to reduction of the liquors via boiling.
>
> Schatzki, 2002, 43–44

We can already begin to see in this description how the directionality of practice in the context of a site might be thematized. Directionality lurks as well behind the third form of social relation Schatzki finds in arrangements, namely "intentionality":

> [t]wo entities can be related by way of one of them performing actions or having thoughts, beliefs, intentions and emotions about the other. [...] When an entity is directed toward an object in this way, it can be said to stand in an "intentional" relation to this object.
>
> Schatzki, 2002, 44

In Chapter 2 we saw that intentionality in the phenomenological sense can be understood as the general directional matrix for the more detailed movements of attention. There is clearly no practice without some form of intentionality in this sense, either.

The fourth and final form of social relation within an arrangement is what Schatzki calls "prefiguration", or, as he felicitously puts it, "how the world channels forthcoming activity" (Schatzki, 2002, 44). Prefiguration is Schatzki's term for the operation of blends of enablement and constrain upon practices, and he approvingly cites Foucault's insight that prefiguration consists not just in grand structures but in the capillaries of everyday social relations and institutions. Yet he extends the underlying focus on actions. "What enables and constrains actions [...] is not actions alone. Artifacts, organisms, and things, typically in combination and as arranged, also constrain one another's activities" (Schatzki, 2002, 45). The imagery of directionality is salient in prefiguration:

> The future is made in the ceaseless advance of human and nonhuman agency. This advance is not, however, a leap into an empty, unfurrowed, isotropic space that receives motion in any direction. Agency does not invent the future wholesale from its own resources. Instead, it arcs through a variegated and folded landscape of variously qualified paths: Agency makes the future through an extant mesh of practices and orders that prefigures what it does – and thereby what it makes – by qualifying paths before it.
>
> Schatzki, 2002, 210

Thus, prefiguration as Schatzki defines it, cannot be grasped:

> through either Bourdieu's structuring structures (habitus), Giddens's rule-resource structures, or Foucault's "capillaries" of power. The prefiguring effect of all these phenomena is the delimitation of possible actions. [...] [A]ttention [should] be instead directed to the multitudinous ways that the mesh of practices and orders makes courses of action easier, harder, simpler, more complicated, shorter, longer, ill-advised, promising of ruin, promising of gain, disruptive, facilitating, obligatory or proscribed, acceptable or unacceptable, more or less relevant, riskier or safer, more or less feasible, more or less likely to induce ridicule or approbation. [...] [The mesh of practices and orders] figures them as more distinct or fuzzy, more threatening or welcoming, more unsurveyable or straightforward, more cognitively dissonant or soothing, smoother or more jagged, more disagreeable or appealing, and so on.
>
> Schatzki, 2002, 225–226

Through the interplay of causal relations, spatial relations, intentionality and prefiguration, practice-arrangements not only exhibit social relations but also produce dimensions of "being". The bottom line here is that "what something is understood to be in a given practice is expressed by those of the practice's doings and sayings that are directed toward it. Meaning, consequently, is carried by and established in social practices" (Schatzki, 2002, 58). One adjustment to Schatzki's approach that I will propose in Part II of this book can be anticipated by supplementing this passage. "What something is understood to be", I will argue, is expressed not only by "those of the practice's doings and saying that are directed toward it" but also, crucially, by those that are *not directed toward it*. The meaning of a thing, person or process in the context of practices is expressed not just in how it is actively addressed, engaged, mobilized or intended but also in *how it is not addressed, how it is taken for granted, treated as irrelevant to a specific practice, left in the background*. Put differently, I would like to claim that Schatzki's concept of prefiguration can be seen as the practice-theoretic analogue of the Gestalt-character of thematic fields as explained by Gurwitsch.

After the extended discussion of arrangements and orders, and then a condensed account of his conception of social practice, Schatzki offers a definition of the social site. The social site can be defined as a "mesh of practices and orders" (Schatzki, 2002, 123) or "the site specific to human coexistence: the context, or wider expanse of phenomena, in and as part of which humans coexist" (Schatzki, 2002, 147). Social sites for Schatzki are textured and performatively intertwined with the practices they host. Everts, Lahr-Kurten and Watson nicely evoke this in suggesting how a site ontology would conceive of "place": "places only exist within and through activities that arrange surrounding entities and meanings. On the other hand, activities occur amidst these arrangements" (Everts, Lahr-Kurten and Watson, 2011, 327).

Practices, attention and direction

There is a great deal more to be said of Schatzki's conception of practices and the site of the social, and I will continue to bring in additional facets of these concepts in the chapters to follow. The summary presented above is not even close to exhaustive. In this section, though, I leave aside further summary and turn to the question of how Schatzki's account of integrated practices could be combined with the analyses of attention from the previous chapters to yield the outlines of an approach to directed practice. Schatzki is not completely silent on the directedness of practice. For example, he does acknowledge that one of the four kinds of social relation lending arrangements their cohesion is intentionality (see above). In *The Timespace of Human Activity*, the third volume in his trilogy, he will briefly treat Heidegger's notion of orientation [*Ausrichtung*] and dis-tance [*Ent-fernung*] in ways that touch upon directed attention (Schatzki 2010, 53–54). More generally, Schatzki notes, the Heideggerian conception of being-in-the-world that anchors his analysis fundamentally understands human life as a directed "being on the move", a "doing-from-toward" (Schatzki, 2010, 195). There he also discusses visual encounters with landscapes in directional terms (Schatzki 2010, 99–100). But these passages are not developed in a way that focuses upon direction as such. This may in part be traceable to Heidegger's neglect of directionality (see the Introduction to Part II). One contention of mine is that our understanding of "the timespace of human activity" is deepened by a more systematic focus upon direction. However, the materials with which to make this point are mostly to be found in the conception of practices in Schatzki's second book, especially in the notion of teleoaffective structures, and the account of sites as practice-arrangement meshes, or "practice-order bundles" (Schatzki 2002, 173). The raw materials for a better account of the directedness of practice are to be found, on the one hand, in the explanation of teleoaffectivity as involving an organized hierarchy of ends, projects, tasks and doings and sayings, and on the other, in the account of activity-place-spaces, in which material arrangements of things, people and processes express and support specific paths and sequences of activity. Each of these features of practice-order bundles implies direction in a slightly different sense. Teleoaffectivity evokes direction in the sense of orientation toward a goal, which may not necessarily be spatial at all, whereas activity-place-spaces more explicitly involve spatially expressed sequences. Identifiable spatio-temporal sequences of activities manifest different possible ways of realizing the basic teleoaffective structures that organize integrated practices. As Schatzki makes clear, there are often many different specific ways to carry out such practices. But it is usually possible to point to a set of baseline things that have to happen, and often also some unavoidable sequences, if a practice is to be successfully carried out.

I would like to argue that the directedness of practice can be made more intelligible, and its importance become more obvious, if Schatzki's conception of practice-order bundles is leavened with an additional focus upon the direction of attention. There is nothing in Schatzki's account of practice that bars consideration of attentional dynamics. Attention is already implicitly at work in his assertion that "intentionality" is among the social relations causing arrangements to hang together (Schatzki 2002, 44). In one sense, my proposal is merely to emphasize this aspect of practice-order bundles more strongly and to focus on the effects of both passive, ambient attentional phenomena and the selectivity of active attention in the context of practices. If we do so, it becomes easier to recognize that practices usually involve a *triple directionality*:

- the purposive, if flexible directionality toward specific ends inherent in teleoaffective structures;
- the closely related spatial directionality laying down paths through activity-places-spaces compatible with teleoaffective structure; and
- the "thematic" directionality of attention on the part of human participants.

My claim will be that the connections between these three kinds of directionality form the context in which political economies of attention acquire their significance for social practice. More specifically, the structures of thematic fields and the ongoing selectivity of responses to solicitation from the different horizons of attention have an impact on whether, how, and how effectively we carry out practices, as well as how much control we are able to exercise over these matters, and what kinds of effects our selectively directed practices have upon the world. Attention, in short, is a key factor in explaining what we do and how we do it. The politics of attention and the politics of directed practice are inseparable. This is an important message of Matthew Crawford's account of skilled craft practices in *The World Beyond Your Head: How to Flourish in an Age of Distraction* (Crawford, 2015).

How can we characterize the ways in which human attention is at work in the carrying out of practices? As we saw in previous chapters, there are different qualities and intensities of attention: deep, sustained focused attention; momentary or episodic attention; routine, passive, monitoring attention; hyper attention; and drifting attention (Harrison, 2008). These interact with each other in a dynamic fashion. An important feature of human attentionality is our fundamental openness or answerability to address from all directions (Waldenfels, 2004). We can further supplement Schatzki's somewhat underdeveloped explanation of the affective dimension of teleoaffective structures by recognizing that affects are important motivators for the play of attention in practices (Reckwitz 2017, 119–121). These points taken together also raise the crucial issue of how different kinds of practical engagement are vulnerable to distraction, interference and appeals.

It is possible to clarify the interplay between modes of attention and practices by asking which of these kinds of attention are necessary for which aspects of integrative practices. Importantly, attentional states accompany practice at its most basic level of "doings and sayings". It is always from within the stream of awareness that moves along with doings and sayings that we inhabit or change attentional relations to practices. As Schatzki emphasizes throughout his work, much of the flow of practice does not require explicit thematization of intelligibility and understandings. In attentional terms, we could say that the sequence of doings and sayings flows within a sheath of largely routine, passive or "monitoring" attention that is the result of learning and is closely related to Bourdieu's "habitus" (Bourdieu, 1990, 52–53). Bourdieu's suggestive reference to the "censorship inherent in [...] habitus", which "cannot give what it does give to be thought and perceived without *ipso facto* producing an unthinkable and an unnameable" (Bourdieu, 1977, 18) and his closely related description of the practical relation to the world as one of "learned ignorance" (Bourdieu, 1990, 19) can be understood in attentional terms. Both formulations point to the routine, tacit flow of passive attention within practice that can be successful only because episodes of more executive, focused attention are at most occasional interruptions. Heidegger's famous scenario of the damaged tool would be an example of such an episode (Heidegger, 1962, 102ff). The carrying out of practices *is only possible* because the vast majority of the doings and sayings involved in integrative practices have become routine or automatic and unreflective. It is precisely because we don't need to pay explicit attention to most things, processes and arrangements that we are able to use them effectively.

Teleoaffective structures lend a larger set of orderings to the flow of doings and sayings in an integrated practice. As Andreas Reckwitz points out, teleoaffective structures are affective in the sense that in participating in practices, people usually assume some constellation of positive and/or negative affective states typical for those practices, and these states in turn shape the layout of prominence and unobtrusiveness, aversion and anticipation attaching to the people, objects and ideas involved in the practice (Reckwitz, 2017, 120). Margaret Archer observes, further, that affective and emotional experiences of rightness or competence often suffuse practices (Archer, 2000, 210–213). Layered over these unreflective substrata, many integrated practices involve planning and preparatory stages, forms of anticipation that go beyond the unremarked protentions and "intentional threads" (Merleau-Ponty, 1962, 150) accompanying all activity. The setting of what Schatzki calls "ends" or goals and initial decisions about the ordering of tasks and projects through which those ends are pursued often require more focused and deliberate attention. In the flow of practice, it is also not unusual that decisions to switch between tasks or between projects can be made more or less spontaneously, because the flexible nature of teleoaffective structures does not typically lay down stringent orderings but rather allows a wide range of acceptable sequences of activities. At these decision points, more reflective and focused attention may briefly be called for. Finally, as Crawford (2015) shows so vividly, integrated practices often require ongoing evaluations and comparisons in which the progress of a task being carried out is compared with an intermediate goal or with expectations of how things are supposed to be going. This kind of reflective evaluation generally also requires focused attention, though it can be as much bodily as cognitive in character. In sum, it is generally the relation between doings and sayings, on the one hand, and the larger orderings that integrate them into a structure, on the other, that requires more focused and deliberate states of attention. It needs to be emphasized, again, though, that even these focused states are always accompanied by the non-reflective embodied know-how involved in manipulating objects, communicating, etc., and thus by an underlying stratum of routine-monitoring attention.

There is always the possibility of distraction and interruption within integrative practices, as in all phases of human life, because of our directional asymmetry, which involves openness and answerability to the world. This openness and answerability, discussed at greater length in Chapter 4, is a crucial feature of individual embodied existence, inseparable from the relational character of human beings. Thus it would be mistaken to think of distraction or interruption as necessarily deleterious in the wider frame of a person's life. For example, all parents would want to be interrupted in whatever they were doing by the news that a child was ill. Distraction can also have a positive role within the logic of a practice: participants need to be capable of interruption, whether by other participants engaged in related tasks who must communicate something relevant, by things unexpectedly going wrong or requiring adjustment in some particular activity, or by the emergence of the feeling or the conviction that it is appropriate to switch to doing something else. Even where interruptions are unrelated to the practice, a task that is highly routinized, or in which the person doing it has done it many times, often leaves ample room for cognitive or affective wanderings of attention. In a discussion of the mechanization and rationalization of manufacturing processes, Antonio Gramsci saw this very possibility as in fact an opening for subversive consciousness:

> Once the process of adaptation [to mechanized work] has been completed, what really happens is that the brain of the worker, far from being mummified, reaches a state of complete freedom. The only thing that is completely mechanized is the physical gesture; the memory of the trade, reduced to simple gestures repeated at an intense rhythm, "nestles" in the muscular and nervous centers and leaves the brain free and unencumbered for other occupations. [...] American industrialists have understood all too well this dialectic inherent in the new industrial methods. [...] [N]ot only does the worker think, but the fact that he gets no immediate satisfaction from his work and realizes that they are trying to reduce him to a trained gorilla, can lead him into a train of thought that is far from conformist.
>
> Gramsci, 1971, 309–310

A similar idea is put forward by J.D. Dewsbury in his remark, noted in Chapter 2, that routine or habitual attention emancipates our more critical and creative directedness (Dewsbury, 2015). The notion that attention could be directed inside or outside a practice allows us to mobilize the concept of thematic fields developed by Gurwitsch. Still operating with a broadly cognitive concept of attention, Gurwitsch characterized thematic fields in terms of matters relating to the current theme or focus of attention (Gurwitsch, 1964). It makes sense to adapt this notion to the context of an integrated practice and to identify what I will call "pragmatic fields" as the range of attentional states relating to the practice in question. These states, as noted above, are not all species of focused attention: they always include routine or monitoring attention. Pragmatic fields would also include forms of potential interruption or distraction occurring *within* the overall practice. And finally, pragmatic fields would include the spatial contexts within which practices take place, the spatial arrangements and paths Schatzki calls activity-place-spaces, which are core structuring elements of sites (Schatzki, 2002, 43).

To anticipate the argument in Chapter 7, it is possible to distinguish broadly between interruptions to practical involvement to which one would want to be exposed and those to which one would not want to be exposed. The first category would include appeals and other forms of contact from friends, family, co-workers or distant others to whose needs and wishes we want to be responsive. As Schatzki notes, people as well as many objects, spaces, or doings and sayings are involved in more than one practical constellation (*Zusammenhang*) at the same time (Schatzki, 2002). It would also include many bodily sensations that indicate one's own needs, memories of hitherto forgotten important events, etc. Finally, it might include knowledge in the form of newspaper headlines or other media venues that keep us informed about the world. When these kinds of matters break into the flow of practice, we are in some sense glad they did, even if they interfere with the practice. Probably the quintessential example of the second, unwanted kind of interruption faced by privileged denizens of the 21st century Global North is that of a notification from an advertiser popping up on the screen of one's work computer, tablet or smartphone. But of course a whole range of more serious interruptions up to and including war or natural disasters would also have to be included in this second category.

The relevance of bringing attentional processes into contact with Schatzki's account of practices is that doing so helps clarify how the interplay between the directedness of practice and the directedness of attention forms a site for a political economy. My basic hypothesis is that distraction and interruption of attention is often the reason for changes in the direction of practice. This perspective could enhance the explanatory power of accounts of practice because, as yet, changes between practices are generally undertheorized in a good deal of practice theory. The dynamics of attention are a key source of the indeterminacy Schatzki highlights in his critique of the traditional dualism of constraint and enablement:

> That [...] arrays of possibility constrain and enable little is suggested by the fact that a person can suddenly shift from acting for one end to acting for another, or from carrying out one project for a given end to carrying out another, and so on. Until action occurs, it is never determinate which end a person will have acted for, what project he will have carried out for that end, what emotions will have affected this, and even whether he will have acted for any end at all.
>
> Schatzki, 1996, 166

The formulations in this passage already offer some purchase for my claims. People "suddenly shift[ing]" from one action to another is undeniably often caused by a shift in attention. In the third book of the trilogy, Schatzki will cast this aleatory and contingent character of action in terms of performance and events (Schatzki, 2010). But I want to suggest that the performative, evental character of what we actually do is much more closely related to the pathic character of attention, its inherent distractability, than hitherto recognized. The constitutionally unstable movements of attention are an important reason that it is difficult to say in any concrete situation exactly which sequence of doings and sayings someone will follow, as well as whether this sequence will remain within the current pragmatic field of tasks, projects and ends or instead will turn in a different direction.

A focus on attention can clarify not only the micro-level movements of attention as a factor in directing practices, but also more generally issues of the "style" individuals develop through learning how to undertake the range of practices structuring their lives. The acquisition of attentional skills is as crucial for learning practices outside formal education settings as it is for learning in the classroom. Through these educational processes in a broad sense, furthermore, different individuals do not all develop identical ways of carrying out practices. As Schatzki acknowledges:

> [a]lthough the expressive significance of bodily activity is socially insti-
> tuted, each person, in his bodily activity, exhibits a unique style. [...] A
> person's unique style of bodily expression evidences an active being who
> learns social forms but then expresses itself. [...] The expressive body
> cannot be locked into the traditional dichotomy of free will versus
> determinism.
>
> Schatzki 1996, 53

A not insignificant part of what constitutes a person's style of carrying out practices is, I would suggest, "attentional style" (Wehrle, 2013, 341). Practical style and attentional style are features of individual activity that transcend specific practical engagements. What is more, or so I claim, attentional style can go some way toward helping us explain why individuals actually do what they do in the way they do it when the teleoaffective structures and physical contexts of practices would allow things to be done differently. If as Schatzki asserts, people do the things they do because practice-order bundles or sites "signify" particular courses of action, the process of signification is a form of address. The experience of being addressed unavoidably involves the media-tion of various forms of attention, whether explicit and focused or more pas-sive and unreflected, and these are composed in each individual in a somewhat unique way, a style. It is not difficult to see echoes of Gestalt theory in this notion of signification: in both cases an organization of the field of involvement is experienced as external. The link between signifying and attention is rendered all the more plausible by the fact that Schatzki explains "signifying" as a matter of "singling out" an action to be done (Schatzki, 1996, 122). We comprehend what is singled out for us to do in part through responding to this singling out "proposed" by the practice with the "singling out of what is singled out" characteristic of our own attentional styles, which weave together our past experiences, acquired interests and affective tenden-cies into a series of horizons that are irreducibly both social and individual.

Chapter 1, on recent discussions of political economies of attention, cul-minated in an extended encounter with the ideas of Bernard Stiegler. It will be recalled that his critique of the degradation of attention under technology-intensive neoliberal capitalism was focused on threats to the ability of young people to acquire the attentional skills – particularly "deep attention" – needed to access the external "tertiary memories" through which processes of culturally specific individuation (what Stiegler calls "transindividuation") must take place (Stiegler, 2010). Concretely, these threats endanger our control over how we use focused attention, where we direct it, and how long we are able to sustain it (Gazzaley and Rosen, 2016, 33). Although practice involves complex combinations of different kinds of attention, not merely focused attention, most practices cannot do entirely without focused attention. And, as I have suggested above, deleterious interruptions of practice are often traceable to shifts in attention. If attention is in fact a constant dimension of practice, and if, as I have suggested here, attentional dynamics play an important (if complex) steering role in practices, then the recent intensification of technological, social and economic pressures on attention can be expected tendentially to degrade practices. Less judgmentally, "degradation" could be understood as a shift in the attentional styles we acquire. Either way, the openness and answerability to the world that render us vulnerable to the possibility of unwanted distraction are simultaneously the portals for forms of contact and appeal that we would not want to close off (Noddings, 2013). Thus the politics of direction cannot simply be a matter of increasing control over our surroundings. In Chapters 5 and 6, I will extend these suggestions by arguing that problems in the intensity and rhythm of turnings of attention, and the shifts between practical involvements they may prompt, can lead to forms of alienation and reification of potentially wider social significance. In Chapter 7 I will draw together the foregoing arguments to place Stiegler's concerns within a richer political-economic context. In all of these subsequent stages of the argument, I will repeatedly refer to "attention and practice". This should be understood as a shorthand for the potentially very complex interactions inherent in the "triple directionality" of practice outlined above. The details will not be rolled out again further on, although they should be evoked to some extent by the phrase itself. At bottom, and despite the complexity folded into the term, "attention and practice" should be taken to signify the links between the two and the potentially leading or steering function of attention in relation to practice.

Residual humanism

To close the present chapter in a way that sets up the argument in Chapter 4, I will briefly discuss the evolution of Schatzki's perspective on the centrality of human agency in practice. My argument involves the claim that human beings, while relational, are not featureless, formless relata but have specific suites of physically, cognitively and affectively determined traits that inevitably shape the way our being-in-the-world-with-others goes. Not all of these traits are purely social, the result of having learned or acquired competence in a wide array of practices; some are even more basic biological, physiological or existential traits. These traits will be the focus of Chapter 4. However, focusing upon the properties and capabilities of embodied individuals may seem to run afoul of Schatzki's practice theory. In *Social Practice*, Schatzki is at pains to stress the socially constructed, derivative nature of embodied individuals:

> A person is not a substance or inner kernel. [...] [I]ndividuality is a socially constructed and achieved status. Personhood is an *effect* of social practices, in that expressive bodies, life conditions, and ascriptions/com-prehensions of these conditions exist (for the most part) only within practices.
>
> Schatzki, 1996, 35

Schatzki has developed his practice theory in part to do justice to the fact that "in many prominent twentieth-century schools of thought, [...] the individual human subject is neither given, foundational, nor in charge of human action and the processes of meaning and significance" (Schatzki, 1996, 8–9). Enough different thinkers have challenged notions of autonomous human subjectivity "as to render problematic any attempt to conceive social life as fundamentally nothing but interrelations among acting and experiencing subjects" (Schatzki, 1996, 9). In line with many features of this general trend, Schatzki under-stands his theory of practice as one that "furthers refutation of the foun-dational utility of the individual in general social ontology" (Schatzki 1996, 210).

This position seems fairly clear. On the other hand, with the progression of his argument through the three volumes, his emphasis shifts toward a more robust acknowledgment of the indispensability to social practices of indivi-dual embodied human beings. In *The Site of the Social*, Schatzki declares his allegiance to what he terms "residual" or "cautious humanism" (Schatzki 2002, 111, 116, 210). He reconciles these two positions in the following way. In the first place, it is clear that:

> [i]ndividual human beings and their interactions are an overwhelmingly significant feature of experience. When, consequently, "social" is intui-tively understood to mean pertaining to the coexistence of human beings, approaching the nature of the social through properties associated with individual persons enjoys a certain experiential obviousness and palpable convincingness.
>
> Schatzki 1996, 179

Schatzki does not reject this everyday understanding as completely mis-guided. Indeed, reference to the coexistence of human beings as a baseline for social theory is indispensable (Schatzki 1996, 170). Furthermore, *contra* some versions of "posthumanism", Schatzki defends the aforementioned "residual humanism" by affirming "the special constitutional, causal and prefigura-tional significance of human activity in both human life in general and social existence in particular" (Schatzki 2002, 116). By the third volume, the focus of Schatzki's theorizing has shifted to the temporality and spatiality of *Dasein*'s being-in-the-world, and he aligns his approach with others built upon "the background conviction that society and history are largely human affairs and [...] what people do is central to these affairs" (Schatzki, 2010, ix). This is roughly my own position. Some sort of residual humanism is necessary.

In discussing the Heideggerian account of human spatiality upon which he draws in the final book, Schatzki makes a crucial point upon which I would like to elaborate. He argues that there are two overall gaps in Heidegger's thoughts on spatiality. First, there is "a general lack of clarity about how the human body and the phenomenon of embodiment are tied up with questions of space" (Schatzki, 2010, 54). Second:

> it is fair to say that Heidegger did not sufficiently think through the relations between existential spatiality and objective space. Instead of prioritizing the former over the latter, human activity is better thought of as inherently and crucially related to both.
>
> Schatzki, 2010, 56

Schatzki's project in *The Timespace of Human Activity* is primarily to address the first gap, relating to the body. He approaches this problem by means of Heidegger's concepts of "the clearing" and "the event". My own project here is, in a sense, to address both the first and the second gap together. I argue that focusing upon embodiment without simultaneously recognizing the body itself as *part of objective space*, yields an incomplete picture. Put provocatively, I will claim in the next chapter that the partly "objective" or "corporeal" spatial shape of the human body actually lies at the core of directed practice and thus of "the timespace of human activity". At the very beginning of his third volume, Schatzki asserts that the "activity timespace" of human practice he will describe is opposed to a view in which things "have spatial and temporal properties by virtue of 'occupying' or occurring "in" time and space conceived of as abstract realms or containers of some sort" (Schatzki, 2010, ix). This may be the case, but if instead of conceiving of time and space as containers, we think of them as *the directed time of embodied human beings*, then "occupation" does very much become a central feature of human social life. "Occupation" will be the subject of Chapter 7. To lay the groundwork for explaining it, Part II elaborates upon Schatzki's claim that human activity is "better thought of as crucially related to both" existential spatiality and objective space (Schatzki, 2010, 56).

References

Alkemeyer, T. and Buschmann, N. (2017). Learning in and across practices: enablement as subjectivation. In: A. Hui, T. Schatzki, and E. Shove, eds, *The Nexus of Practices: Connections, Constellations and Practitioners*. London: Routledge, pp. 8–23.

Archer, M. (2000). *Being Human: The Problem of Agency.* Cambridge: Cambridge University Press.

Bourdieu, P. (1977). *Outline of a Theory of Practice.* Trans. R. Nice. Cambridge: Cambridge University Press.

Bourdieu, P. (1990). *The Logic of Practice.* Trans. R. Nice. Stanford, CA: Stanford University Press.

Crawford, M. (2015). *The World Beyond Your Head: How to Flourish in an Age of Distraction.* New York: Viking.

Dewsbury, J.D. (2015). Non-representation landscapes and the performative affective forces of habit: from "Live" to "Blank". *Cultural Geographies,* 22(1), pp. 29–47.

Everts, J., Lahr-Kurten, M., and Watson, M. (2011). Practice matters! Geographical inquiry and theories of practice. *Erdkunde,* 65(4), pp. 323–334.

Gazzaley, A. and Rosen, L. (2016). *The Distracted Mind: Ancient Brains in a High-Tech World.* Cambridge, MA: MIT Press.

Giddens, A. (1984). *The Constitution of Society.* London: Polity Press.

Gramsci, A. (1971). *Selections from the Prison Notebooks.* Trans. Q. Hoare and G. N. Smith. New York: International Publishers.

Gurwitsch, A. (1964). *The Field of Consciousness.* Pittsburgh, PA: Duquesne University Press.

Harrison, P. (2008). Corporeal remains: vulnerability, proximity, and living on after the end of the world. *Environment and Planning A,* 40(2), pp. 423–445.

Heidegger, M. (1962). *Being and Time.* Trans. J. Macquarrie and E. Robinson. Oxford: Blackwell.

Hui, A., Schatzki, T., and Shove, E. (2017). Introduction. In: A. Hui, T. Schatzki, and E. Shove, eds, *The Nexus of Practices: Connections, Constellations and Practitioners.* London: Routledge, pp. 1–7.

Jackson, M. (2009). *Distracted: The Erosion of Attention and the Coming Dark Age.* New York: Prometheus Books.

Jeffrey, A. (2013). *The Improvised State: Sovereignty, Performance and Agency in Dayton Bosnia.* Oxford: Wiley-Blackwell.

Jeffrey, C. (2010). *Timepass: Youth, Class and the Politics of Waiting in India.* Stanford, CA: Stanford University Press.

Merleau-Ponty, M. (1962). *Phenomenology of Perception.* Trans. C. Smith. London: Routledge and Kegan Paul.

Noddings, N. (2013). *Caring: A Feminine Approach to Ethics and Moral Education.* 2nd ed. Berkeley, CA: University of California Press.

Painter, J. (2000). Pierre Bourdieu. In: M. Crang and N. Thrift, eds, *Thinking Space.* London: Routledge, pp. 239–259.

Reckwitz, A. (2017). Practices and their affects. In: A. Hui, T. Schatzki, and E. Shove, eds, *The Nexus of Practices: Connections, Constellations and Practitioners.* London: Routledge, pp. 114–125.

Schäfer, H. (2016). Einleitung. In: H. Schäfer, ed., *Praxistheorie: Ein soziologische Forschungsprogramm.* Bielefeld: Transcript, pp. 9–25.

Schatzki, T. (1996). *Social Practices: A Wittgensteinian Approach to Human Activity and the Social.* Cambridge: Cambridge University Press.

Schatzki, T. (2002). *The Site of the Social: A Philosophical Account of the Constitution of Social Life and Change.* University Park, PA: Penn State Press.

Schatzki, T. (2010). *The Timespace of Human Activity: On Performance, Society, and History as Indeterminate Teleological Events.* Lanham, MD: Lexington Books.

Schatzki, T. (2017). *Martin Heidegger: Theorist of Space.* 2nd unrevised ed. Stuttgart: Franz Steiner Verlag.

Schatzki, T., Knorr Cetina, K., and von Savigny, E., eds. (2001). *The Practice Turn in Contemporary Theory.* London: Routledge.

Stiegler, B. (2010). *Taking Care of Youth and the Generations.* Trans. S. Barker. Stanford, CA: Stanford University Press.

Waldenfels, B. (2004). *Phänomenologie der Aufmerksamkeit.* Frankfurt am Main: Suhrkamp.

Watson, M. (2017). Placing power in practice theory. In: A. Hui, T. Schatzki, and E. Shove, eds, *The Nexus of Practices: Connections, Constellations and Practitioners.* London: Routledge, pp. 169–182.

Wehrle, M. (2013). *Horizonte der Aufmerksamkeit: Entwurf einer dynamischen Konzeption der Aufmerksamkeit aus phänomenologischer und kognitionspsychologischer Sicht.* Munich: Wilhelm Fink Verlag.

Werlen, B. (1992). *Society, Action and Space: An Alternative Human Geography.* New York: Routledge.

Werlen, B. (1997). *Sozialgeographie alltäglicher Regionalisierungen, Band 2: Globalisierung, Region und Regionalisierung.* Stuttgart: Franz Steiner Verlag.

Werlen, B. (1999). *Sozialgeographie alltäglicher Regionalisierungen, Band 1: Zur Ontologie von Gesellschaft und Raum.* Stuttgart: Franz Steiner Verlag.

Part II

Turning-in-the-world

Part I of this book advanced the following arguments:

- that recent writings on the political economy of attention point toward a new way of understanding the importance of directed engagement as an arena of social power relations;
- that understanding these power relations requires grasping in more phenomenological depth what "attention" is; and
- that bringing together this more detailed concept of attention with recent theorizations of practice yields a concept of directed practice that can form the basis for a broader appreciation of the role played by direction in power relations and social processes more generally.

The argument presented thus far has taken for granted that embodied human subjects are embedded non-dualistically in relations with the world, other people and the objects encountered within the world. The directional features of these relations have been highlighted but not systematically grounded. Part II is intended to accomplish – or at least begin – this grounding. As such it can be considered the heart of the entire argument.

The three chapters to follow all highlight a characteristic lacuna of much socio-spatial theory and philosophy. This lacuna expresses itself in the common interpretation of dynamics and potential problems of subject-world relations in terms of distance or separation, remoteness or proximity, but not in terms of direction or orientation. There are many subtly different specific versions of this oversight. One important and influential version is to be found in Martin Heidegger's analysis of human being-in-the-world. Heidegger is particularly important to the present argument because Schatzki has organized the final volume of his practice theory, *The Timespace of Human Activity* (Schatzki, 2010), around Heideggerian conceptions of human spatiality. One goal of the present book is to supplement Schatzki's account of the timespace of human activity by exploring the features and significance of the *directedness* of practice. Thus it is necessary to see how Heidegger occludes directedness. A critical look at Heidegger's treatment of distance and direction as spatial features of human being-in-the-world is intended to set the stage for the three chapters to follow, which turn up other versions of the "distance bias" exemplified by Heidegger.

Distance and direction in Heidegger's *Being and Time*

The claim here will be that Heidegger's description of the spatiality of *Dasein*'s being-in-the-world obscures the importance of direction in the sense of *turning*. Heidegger describes the fundamental spatiality of being-in-the-world, as immersed in dealing with "entities encountered within the world [...] concernfully and with familiarity" (Heidegger, 1962, 138). As already noted in Chapter 2, the spatiality of this concernful dealing involves both "de-severance" or "de-distancing" [*Ent-fernung*] and "directionality" [*Ausrichtung*] (Heidegger, 1962, 139, 143). Only a brief review of these terms is necessary here. De-severance is a matter of the "closeness" or "bringing-near" we experience in relation to the matters with which we are dealing. "Dasein is essentially de-severant: it lets any entity be encountered close by as the entity which it is". It is only on the basis of this existential closeness that the more mundane characteristics of nearness or remoteness in terms of "distances" can be accessible to us (Heidegger, 1962, 139). This aspect of our spatiality is fundamental and existential: "*In Dasein there lies an essential tendency towards closeness*" (Heidegger, 1962, 140). De-severance is "always a kind of concernful Being towards what is brought close and de-severed" (Heidegger, 1962, 140). In his book on Heidegger as a "theorist of space", Schatzki identifies four different senses in which de-severance (or as he translates it, "dis-tance") can be understood, only the first three of which are explicitly treated in *Being and Time*: (1) the de-severance of "what is attended to"; (2) the "nearness of being used in current activity"; (3) the maintenance of "an average field of reaching, grasping, and seeing (SZ 106–7 [...])" in which entities are available; and (4) nearness as relevance (Schatzki, 2017, 44–45).

"Directionality" [*Ausrichtung*] is intimately linked to de-severance. "Every bringing-close [...] has already taken in advance a direction towards a region out of which what is de-severed brings itself close, so that one can come across it with regard to its place" (Heidegger, 1962, 143). Much in the way that mundane distances can only be accessed on the basis of our underlying de-severant relation to the world, Heidegger claims that directions in the normal sense of left or right can only emerge on the basis of existential directionality (Heidegger, 1962, 143). Jeff Malpas defines directionality (which he translates alternatively as "orientation") as:

> the way in which, in being involved in a certain task, I find myself already situated in certain ways with respect to the things and places around me – in working at my desk I have the computer in front of me, bookshelf to one side, a pad of paper to the right, a desk lamp to the left, and so on.
>
> Malpas, 2006, 91

There are three related problems with the way Heidegger conceives of spatiality in terms of de-severance and directionality. The first problem, Heidegger's neglect or insufficient development of inherently spatial aspects of human embodiment, has been remarked upon by a number of commentators. Drawing upon Hubert Dreyfus, Malpas argues that "orientation in space [...] itself depends on the way spatiality is articulated in and through one's own body", a point Kant had recognized (Malpas, 2006, 130). Neglecting this, Heidegger subordinates spatiality and embodiment to temporality. Stuart Elden remarks that for Heidegger, "the spatiality of Dasein is not a *primary* characteristic. Even its spatiality in a secondary way is not what would normally be termed spatial" (Elden, 2001, 16). For example, the "towards which" of our involved engagements with the world is characterized temporally as a teleology of activity, not originally in spatial terms.

> Yet what this hides, or at least leads us to overlook, is the way in which our activity, and our orientation to things and places within that activity, is not merely determined by the end *to which* we are directed, but also by the structure of the spatiality *in which* that activity is situated.
>
> Malpas, 2006, 127

This amounts to distinguishing between two of the three forms of the directedness of practice identified in Chapter 3. Similarly, Graham Harman argues that "nothing in the analysis of directionality enlightens us as to how spatial direction is different from any *other* kind of placement in the tool-system" (Harman, 2002, 52). Schatzki concludes that Heidegger's account "suffers from a lack of clarity about how embodiment and the human body are bound up with spatiality" (Schatzki, 2017, 46).

The second problem with Heidegger's account concerns the privileging of the aroundness of the world and its equipmental contexts as realms of possibility over the actual, performative directedness of any particular engagement. Here we come closer to the core of the problem for the present argument. Heidegger writes that "[b]oth directionality and de-severance, as modes of Being-in-the-world, are guided beforehand *by the circumspection* of concern" (Heidegger, 1962, 143). "Circumspection" [*Umsicht*] is defined by Heidegger as a kind of non-objectifying "sight" appropriate to the familiar readiness-to-hand of equipment we use in our immediate environment (Heidegger, 1962, 98). We are not "blind" to the things around us with which we deal, but we are also not normally looking at them "theoretically" as isolated objects. It is through circumspection that "a totality of equipment has already been discovered" before any particular piece of equipment "shows itself" (Heidegger, 1962, 98). The German "*Umsicht*", like the English "circumspection", involves a prefix that evokes "aroundness", though *Um-* in German can also signal "in order to" (Heidegger, 1962, 98, trans. note 2). The connotation of aroundness is the important issue here. Heidegger calls the spatial involvement associated with circumspection a "region": "By reason of such an involvement, the ready-to-hand becomes something which we can come across and ascertain as having form and direction" (Heidegger, 1962, 145). Heidegger describes this process as a "making room": "As a way of discovering and presenting a possible totality of spaces determined by involvements, this making-room is what makes possible one's factical orientation at the time" (Heidegger, 1962, 146). Heidegger's discussions of *aletheia* shows similar features (Strohmayer, 1998).

Within this awareness of surrounding equipmental involvements, any particular orientation that could be described as, say "left" or "right", have the character of "permanent possibilities" (Schatzki, 2017, 46). Our "factical orientation at the time" is an incidental matter; what counts is the totality of possibilities embedding our being-in-the-world. I would like to suggest that this foregrounding of possibilities as against actual directed involvement constitutes a "petri-dish" model of human worldly existence, a model implying that humans exist or stand out as potentiality in all literal and figurative directions at once. This petri-dish model is to be found in a wide array of otherwise quite divergent accounts of the human world, for example in Giddens (1984) and Schütz and Luckmann (2003), or in Bergson's notion of living beings as "centers of real action" (Bergson, 1991, 33, 44–45). It is closely associated with an emphasis upon possibility and becoming. The petri-dish model is implicit as well in the alternative, "organic" philosophical anthropology laid out by Heidegger's contemporary Helmuth Plessner (Plessner, 1981). Plessner's characterization of human being as "eccentric positionality", that is, as capable of taking reflective distance from the self and comprehending the self simultaneously from within and without as being physically and actively related to its environment, is suffused with the language of centrality, distance and centrifugal or centripetal relations (Plessner, 1981, 364–365). As in Heidegger, there are some indications in Plessner of an interest in the directedness of relations to the world. His characterization of the "frontality" in relation to the environment that living beings establish at and through their boundaries (Plessner, 1981, 308, 311, 353), his description of the human being as eccentrically "behind itself" (Plessner, 1981, 363, 368), or his more Husserlian discussion of the "ray" of intentional relations (Plessner, 1981, 404–406, 411–412) all suggest a latent directional sensibility. Plessner does not develop these suggestive ideas very far, but I will pick up some of his insights in framing Chapter 4. In any event, what is lost or discounted in the petri-dish model is the importance in *limiting possibilities* of actual directedness *at any given moment*. Directionality is performative, that is, it is instantiated in a particular way at every living moment. This means that a constellation of possibility *and impossibility* always structures our engagements, and thus that the ontological omnidirectionality of our circumspection is of little practical importance. The notion of embodied directionality presented in Chapter 4 will be deliberately opposed to this petri-dish model of human being-in-the-world.

The third problem in Heidegger's spatial thinking is that this subordination of actual directedness to circumspection is coupled with a collapsing of directedness into relations of distance. This becomes clearer when we look more closely at Heidegger's account of how the realization of fundamental directional possibilities through our "factical orientation at the time" occurs. As already noted, "every bringing-close [...] has already taken in advance a direction towards a region out of which what is de-severed brings itself close" (Heidegger, 1962, 143). De-severance thus at least strongly implies a selective directedness. Schatzki's paraphrase renders the daylight between the two terms even smaller:

> [T]he equipment that compose a world are always differentially near and far vis-à-vis the activities carried on there; these nears and fars are thus relative to what people are doing. [...] As a person carries on in a region, his or her activity so changes that equipment that was far is brought near. If the person cutting boards suddenly notices a leaky pipe, a wrench that earlier was far might suddenly be brought near.
>
> Schatzki, 2017, 44

What this passage suggests is that the meaning of directionality is nothing other than de-severance.

> What does "direction" mean? Only that a thing is harbored in a specific place in our concern. And what does "distance" mean? Again, only that a thing is harbored in a specific place in our concern. But this means that de-distancing [de-severance] and directionality are *one and the same*.
>
> Harman, 2002, 53

Being directed toward something *is simply* bringing it close. The occlusion or absorption of any independent sense of directionality by de-severance is reproduced in a range of works interpreting or drawing upon Heidegger (see, for example, Pickles, 1985, 165).

The last sentence of the quote from Schatzki, about noticing a leaky pipe, bears closer scrutiny. For what does this sentence, and indeed the entire Heideggerian account of the relation between directionality and de-severance that Schatzki paraphrases, airbrush out? *The process of turning.* Even if it is the case that the state of *being directed toward* something is equivalent to bringing it close, the entire suite of concepts of distance, de-severance, nearness and farness *cannot account for turning as a process.* It is telling that Heidegger introduces directionality by saying that every bringing-close "has already taken in advance a direction" (Heidegger, 1962, 143). But of course we are not always bringing the same matters close, so this having "already taken in advance a direction" must be a dynamic process, namely that of turning. Put differently, what is distinctive about directionality, what cannot be reduced to an equivalent of distance or nearness, is turning itself. In turning, a certain analogue to distance and nearness is at work, but it is a qualitatively different, directional analogue. Turning toward something involves moving our engagement "toward" it, while turning away from it moves us "away from" it. But this is a "rotational" toward and away from, and thus qualitatively different from distancing. The three chapters to follow seek to flesh out a conception of the rotational movement of our directed engagements with the world, and thus can be seen to comprise an initial account of "turning-in-the-world".

References

Bergson, H. (1991). *Matter and Memory*. Brooklyn, NY: Zone Books.

Elden, S. (2001). *Mapping the Present: Heidegger, Foucault and the Project of a Spatial History*. London: Continuum.

Giddens, A. (1984). *The Constitution of Society*. Cambridge: Polity Press.

Harman, G. (2002). *Tool Being: Heidegger and the Metaphysics of Objects*. Chicago, IL: Open Court Press.

Heidegger, M. (1962). *Being and Time*. Trans. J. Macquarrie and E. Robinson. Oxford: Blackwell.

Malpas, J. (2006). *Heidegger's Topology: Being, Place, World*. Cambridge, MA: MIT Press.

Pickles, J. (1985). *Phenomenology, Science and Geography: Spatiality and the Human Sciences*. Cambridge: Cambridge University Press.

Plessner, H. (1981). *Die Stufen des Organischen und der Mensch: Einleitung in die philosophische Anthropologie*. Frankfurt am Main: Suhrkamp.

Schatzki, T. (2017). *Martin Heidegger: Theorist of Space*. 2nd unrevised ed. Stuttgart: Franz Steiner Verlag.

Schütz, A. and Luckmann, T. (2003). *Strukturen der Lebenswelt*. Konstanz: UVK Verlagsgesellschaft.

Strohmayer, U. (1998). The event of space: geographic allusions in the phenomenological tradition. *Environment and Planning D: Society and Space*, 16(1), pp. 105–121.

4 Turning subject

The line of thinking developed in the first three chapters raises a series of fundamental questions about the nature of embodied being-in-the-world. This middle section of the book offers some preliminary answers to these questions by reconceiving subject-world relations. As noted at the end of Chapter 3, this project can be thought of as a complement to Schatzki's account of "the timespace of human activity". All three moments of the phrase "subject-world-relations", that is, "subject", "world", and "relations" can be better understood if we cease to think of them only in terms of separation or distance but think of them as well them in directional terms. This weave of moments is of course lived as an inextricable tangle, but pulling them out in succession for heuristic purposes can improve our understanding of what is at stake here. It is precisely in the directional aspects of our relations with the world, so I will argue, that systematic disablement threatens even some relatively privileged groups in the 21st century Global North.

This chapter begins at the "subject" end of subject-world relations. I would like to propose a heuristic model of the "turning subject" based upon the directional asymmetry of human embodiment. This model is heuristic because it brackets the relational origins and character of human subjects for the purposes of seeing what it is about our individual embodiment that equips us to be relational. As discussed in the last chapter, Schatzki advances his "cautious humanism" despite a detailed knowledge *and acceptance* of the many de-centerings and denaturalizations undergone by the category of the human subject. The directedness of embodied human existence, so this chapter argues, offers one explanation of how some kind of humanism can in fact be reconciled with the critiques leveled by many anti- and post-humanist approaches (Simonsen, 2013). What kind of subjectivity can be recuperated without automatically reconstituting the "masterful subject" of modern Western thought? And more specifically, which features of subjectivity are necessarily complicit in the project of mastery? Lise Nelson asks, "Why are notions of intentionality/reflexivity/purposeful action immediately suspect and otherized as capitulating to the transparent, masterful subject?" (Nelson, 1999, 336). I agree with Nelson and Simonsen that these issues need more careful consideration than they have sometimes received in recent years. My approach to them will be through certain little-discussed aspects of the embodied character of human life. In pursuing this issue I will focus upon natural features of human bodies. There are clearly risks involved in doing this, but I follow Reecia Orzeck's reasoning on this point:

> The temptation to avoid the possibility of inadvertently shoring up dubious and harmful claims by steering perfectly clear of all talk of the natural is understandable. Still, arguments are not wrong just because they are susceptible to manipulation and abuse, and we would be remiss to avoid holding ideas up to scrutiny, which means taking them seriously, out of fear of endorsing the uses to which they can be put.
>
> Orzeck, 2007, 504–505

In the introduction to Part II some of the difficulties with Heidegger's treatment of bodily aspects of directionality were noted. But the account of directionality assembled in the present book may well seem riven by an internal tension between broadly physical-material dimensions of embodiment, on the one hand, and more immaterial, cognitive or affective dimensions associated with attentional processes on the other. Throughout the sections to follow, the argument deliberately articulates two senses of embodiment distinguished in the German language but not in English: the physical body [*Körper*] and the non-objective "lived body" [*Leib*] (Elden, 2001, 55; Dörfler and Rothfuß, 2018). The latter concept denotes the body as experienced, not merely as a physical object. The lived body is important, for example, in Merleau-Ponty's phenomenology of embodied perception (Merleau-Ponty, 1962). The lived body connects the argument as well with the so-called "new materialism". This discourse engages material and affective dimensions of human existence (e.g. Thrift, 2007; Anderson and Harrison, 2010) and the mode of being of "objects" (e.g. Latour, 1987; Harman, 2002). In effect, I argue that the complex phenomena of attention and practice introduced in previous chapters must be understood as involving *both* the physical body of objective space and the lived body, and further, that the organization of the physical body – often ignored in phenomenology – is a crucial determining framework for the experiences of the lived body (see Malpas, 2006, 130, 132). The argument of the present chapter lends the *leibliche* dimension more "backbone" by deliberately introducing a more literally physical and geometrical imagery. In this specific sense it accords relatively well not only with Schatzki's acknowledgement of embodiment but with Plessner's organically grounded account of the human (Plessner, 1981). The eccentric positionality, the capability of being outside the self, characteristic of humans, does not for Plessner in any way "free" humans of our existence as physically embodied living beings. We are always embodied for Plessner as "*Leibkörper*" in a "here and now" (Plessner, 1981, 304–305).

Corresponding to the two senses of corporeal and lived embodiment are two sense of human temporality. On the one hand, I will treat time in the conventional modern sense as "a finite resource for which practices compete" (Shove, Pantzar and Watson, 2012, 127). On the other hand, I will argue that recent historical changes in how time as a finite resource is organized threaten a certain kind of qualitative, lived time that Bernard Stiegler evokes with the notion of "deep attention" (see Chapter 1). This latter experience of focused absorption in a matter of concern, applying not just to attention but to practices more generally, can be thought of as a kind of "timelessness" (Berg and Seeber, 2016, 25). Critiques of conventional notions of time have proceeded from one or more of three basic angles:

- a phenomenological perspective, in which temporality is understood not to be external to us but rather rooted in human consciousness, experience or being-in-the-world (Moran, 2005, 139–140);
- a poststructuralist perspective arguing strenuously against the idea that lived time should be understood in terms of "arborescent" structures of mutually exclusive possibilities, and reframing temporality as far richer, more multi-dimensional, heterogeneous, embodied, affective, and interwoven with space than can be adequately captured in the stale, abstract, divisible schema of clock time (Bergson, 2001, 101, 1991; Deleuze, 1988, 97–98; Grosz, 2005; Massey, 2005); and
- an historical-genealogical perspective focusing upon the historical and geographical specificity and variety of notions and practices of time (e.g. Glennie and Thrift, 1996; May and Thrift, 2001).

In none of these cases is the practical usefulness of linear, continuous notions of time flatly denied; but their sufficiency as an ontological account of temporality as such is rejected. I have no quarrel with these critiques as enrichments of our understanding of ontologies of time. In fact, another way to put my critical argument is to say that, still finding ourselves within the modern, capitalist geo-historical context described by critiques in the third vein, we may be facing developments that pose a threat to certain experiences of lived time as laid out in phenomenological critiques of the first category. Category 2 is ontologically interesting but has little purchase on the more banal aspects of the temporality of everyday practice discussed in this book.

The two doublings of embodiment and time are intimately related, in the sense that corporeal organization (including neurological and physiological dimensions) is what makes conventional, linearizable time relevant, while the lived body is the setting for different forms of lived time. This linked doubling of human embodiment and temporality locates the present argument, as noted in the Introduction, firmly within what Foucault called the analytic of finitude, which I do not believe we have managed to escape (yet?) despite strenuous efforts. This focus on physical dimensions of embodiment and time as a scarce resource is also necessitated by the project of sketching the "political economy of oriented practice" mentioned in the book's subtitle. What I eventually present in Chapter 7 is not a full-fledged political economy but rather a collection of concepts and ideas that could deepen and enhance existing critical analyses of capitalism. Nevertheless, these concepts must be relatable to the fundamental starting points of historical-geographical materialism. In the tradition of work drawing upon or inspired by Marx, any political economy rests upon particular conceptions of human social life as rooted in material processes. This in turn implies some particular understanding of physical or corporeal features of human beings such that they need to be – and can be – involved in material processes in the ways described (Orzeck, 2007, 508; Fracchia, 2005). As should already be clear, "directionality" is at least in part an embodied feature of human life, and thus, I will argue, the directional selectivity of human attention and practice is an important basis for political economy.

This chapter seeks to reframe "the embodied subject" as a *directionally asymmetrical* being characterized by an omnidirectional openness, receptivity or vulnerability, on the one hand, and the limited directional scope of our active "outward" engagements, on the other. The term "omnidirectional" here should be understood in a broad sense to include internal experiences – thoughts, affects, emotions, etc. – as well as physically localizable external orientations. Put schematically, our susceptibility or passive porosity with respect to the world is not directionally selective but our active engagement is. Accordingly, the process of turning results from the interplay of these two basic bodily conditions: when an impulse or appeal reaches us from our bodies, our thoughts, our affects, or from any external source, we may or may not respond by turning our active orientation toward it. The discussion of vulnerability in the first section takes its cues from the work of Judith Butler, the geographer Paul Harrison, and from aspects of Schatzki's practice theory. In the next section, Joseph Fracchia's Marxist account of corporeal organization is used to frame the argument for the other side of directional asymmetry, namely, the directional finitude of our active engagements. The embodied context for active engagement is then spelled out in more detail with reference to the anthropological ideas of André Leroi-Gourhan. This context is contrasted with the petri dish model of human embodiment common to much social and cultural theory. The final section builds upon David Wills's interpretations of Leroi-Gourhan to propose a tripartite zonal structure to our embodied engagement with the world, and to concretize further what Schatzki calls the "timespace of human activity".

Vulnerability and direction

Human subjects *as physical bodies* will be conceived here as "obligatory points of passage" for social processes, and at the same time, as *lived bodies*, as the only "points of live awareness" of these processes to which social scientists have access. The sociologist Hartmut Rosa explains this starting point well in justifying his own retention of a working concept of "subjects":

Subjects are marked by two essential characteristics invariant with respect to the variations in relations to the world: they are, first, those entities that *have experiences,* or, if one takes into account the fact that experiences are always intersubjectively constituted, [those entities] in which experiences are manifested; and they mark, secondly, the place at which psychic energy materializes itself in motivations, at which, in other words, drives to action become effective (Rosa, 2015, 65).

Neither claim should be understood to deny that animals can have experiences, or that animals, naturally occurring things or human artifacts play a role in making, remaking or experiencing the world. Indeed, one way to understand my argument is as a Plessnerian plea to recognize the ongoing importance of certain features of our biological animality (Plessner, 1981). But the vast question of what kinds of beings have agency and accessible awareness is not the chief concern here and will be left aside.

My starting point here is similar to Kirsten Simonsen's starting point in her pursuit of a form of humanism "after" posthumanism (Simonsen, 2013, 15). In keeping with the general approach here of asking about the conditions of possibility of relational existence, it makes sense to ask what features of embodied human being make it possible for us to be involved in relations. Certainly "agency" as a general ability to act willfully is one such condition. Our fundamental vulnerability and passivity with respect to processes both within and outside our bodies has been addressed to some extent already in Chapter 2, in the discussion of Waldenfels's writings on the pathic character of attention (Waldenfels, 2004). It is also a major theme running through some strands of non-representational theory (Anderson and Harrison, 2010; Dewsbury, 2015; Ash and Simpson, 2016). Here I want to generalize the insights of Waldenfels by engaging with Judith Butler in her work on "precarious life", with Schatzki, and with Paul Harrison. The intent is to bring out more strongly the first of the two components of our directional asymmetry as human beings, that is, our openness to solicitations, appeals or address from our bodily, social and material worlds *from any direction.* The central, ineliminable ambiguity of this openness or receptivity is that it represents the possibility of receiving appeals for care or solidarity (Noddings, 2013), and of responsiveness to our own desires, but is at the same time the gateway for solicitations and appeals of a manipulative kind that tend to erode rather than support healthy social relations.

Some of Judith Butler's writings after September 11th, 2001, have addressed the issue of bodily vulnerability (Butler, 2004, 2006). Here some basic points of orientation for understanding the sense in which I mean vulnerability are helpful. In an essay originally given as a talk in 2002, Butler draws upon the then still very raw experiences of the attacks of September 11th, 2001 to reflect upon the centrality of bodily vulnerability to human life.

The body implies mortality, vulnerability, agency: the skin and the flesh expose us to the gaze of others but also to touch and to violence [...]. Given over from the start to the world of others, bearing their imprint, formed within the crucible of social life, the body is only later, and with some uncertainty, that to which I lay claim as my own.

Butler, 2004, 21

This vulnerability, however, is ambivalent, always both the condition that allows us to be threatened and the very possibility of meaningful connection with others. Thus, Butler, notes, the formation of political communities such as that of sexual minorities must face a problem that is perhaps insoluble:

We ask that the state, for instance, keep its laws off our bodies, and we call for principles of bodily self-defense and bodily integrity to be accepted as political goods. Yet, it is through the body that gender and sexuality become exposed to others, inscribed by cultural norms, and apprehended in their social meanings. In a sense, to be a body is to be given over to others even as a body is, emphatically, "one's own," that over which we must claim rights of autonomy.

Butler, 2004, 20

Butler is reflecting on this dilemma in the context of extraordinarily violent events and of theories of gender and sexuality. But her point, I submit, is generally valid for other aspects of everyday life as well. We are vulnerable not just to violence, however conceived, but also to much more mundane negative or positive forms of touch and contact with others. The argument I seek to develop here must include an acknowledgement both of the fundamental fact of bodily vulnerability and of the futility of trying to counteract this vulnerability through comprehensive protection, as protecting ourselves too thoroughly, even where it is possible, can easily cut off more necessary and nourishing forms of connection with others. In Chapter 7 this latter point will be discussed at greater length in dialogue with feminist care ethics (Held, 2006).

I would like to specify and elaborate Butler's basic insight by turning to the work of Harrison. The wider frame for Harrison's focus on vulnerability, susceptibility and passivity is what he rightly perceives to be a consistently selective tendency in human geography and social and cultural sciences more generally to attribute to the human "a positive *capacity* or *power*, in terms of a 'being-able-to'" (Harrison, 2008, 427). As noted earlier, Sara Ahmed calls this "the phenomenology of the 'I can'" (Ahmed, 2006, 138). Harrison suggests that "theories of life, of vitality, and of affirmation are in the ascendant", but that this affirmative mode of theorizing is in danger of "forgetting finitude" (Harrison, 2015, 1, 2). Briefly reviewing Marxist approaches, Nietzschean vitalism, certain strands of identity politics and some phenomenological work, Harrison identifies a common suite of organizing principles and desires animating conceptions of subjectivity: autonomy, sovereignty, affirmation of creativity, purposeful activity, and intentional teleology of action. These priorities conspire to render invisible, derivative, incidental or undesirable what Harrison calls the "heterological determination of sensibility".

> The idea that sensibility may take place as a relation with an exterior, may be composed from the outside, through and as a passive exposure which inspires, holds and binds the subject in relations which it does not and did not choose and which lie before and beyond any of its abilities to comprehend, conceptualize or represent.
>
> Harrison, 2008, 430

This view has implications for how we think of embodied relationality (as lived): we need to "think interiority as somehow already involved with and turned towards it exterior" (Harrison, 2008, 436). In developing this critique of affirmative-autonomous conceptions of human agency, Harrison draws strongly upon the work of Emmanuel Levinas, whose original ethical philosophy places vulnerability to the appeal of the other at the root not only of ethics but of human existence (Levinas, 1969; see also Caputo, 1993; Rose, 2014). In a broad sense, this perspective chimes with that of Nel Noddings, whose feminist phenomenological account of care is centered upon attentiveness to the needs of others (Noddings, 2013, 24).

This sense of openness, of passivity, exposure and vulnerability, not as defective states to be overcome or remedied but as fundamental conditions of possibility for the embodied experience of events, is in broad agreement with Waldenfels's phenomenology of attention as pathic and with Butler's thoughts on precarious life. It is fundamental to our attentional makeup as human beings that we are "answerable" to solicitations and appeals from our own bodies, thoughts, and feelings, and from our external surroundings. This is an "omnidirectional" answerability, receptivity and vulnerability. It does not imply that we always or necessarily respond or answer to signals and appeals, but that we receive them. This vulnerability is at work even where it appears not to be, in the very midst of what we experience as deliberate or willed actions. This important insight brings us back to Schatzki's analyses of practices in the third volume of his trilogy, *The Timespace of Human Activity* (Schatzki, 2010). There Schatzki radicalizes his portrayal of the contingency of practice by reframing practices as events and performances. Crucially, though, performances are not to be understood here as originating in and moving outward from some center of action:

> Performances, as events, befall people, that is, they happen to people. A person, to be sure, performs, or carries out, an action. She does not, however, perform, or carry out, the performance: the performance befalls her. Its befalling her is, at once, her carrying out the action.
>
> Schatzki 2010, 170

Thus, "befalling" is, in Schatzki's account, not radically opposed to freedom (Schatzki, 2010, 170). Their coexistence in performances is a sign of the "indeterminacy of action" (Schatzki, 2010, 175). Seen in this way, Harrison's emphasis on passivity, vulnerability and exposure need not be understood simply as opposing the more typical emphasis on activity. Schatzki's argument in effect asserts that even what we normally think of and experience as self-initiated activity involves a moment of passivity or heteronomy. This may seem a strange way to understand practices. As Schatzki notes, however, it seems to be supported by recent neurological research, which "has discovered that the brain processes that lead to voluntary movement (say, the voluntary movement of a finger) precede conscious awareness of wanting to perform such movement" (Schatzki, 2010, 182). The reality of wanting to perform it is then a sign of the freedom involved, but we can think of the preceding brain and nervous-system processes as the trace of "befalling". Significantly for the present argument, psychological research on attention has long struggled with a similar strangeness, known to psychologists as the "homunculus problem" (Styles, 2006, 5, 10, 239). Neuropsychological experiments have suggested that the subjective experience of conscious control of attention and actions may happen *after* the primary brain and nervous-system processes that in fact exercise this control (Styles, 2006, 280–281). And yet something or some suite of processes in us *can and does* control attention in ways we are able to experience as "our own" accomplishments. To the extent that this "something" is not identical with what we experience as our "will", however, it can be thought of as a "homunculus". As Elizabeth Styles puts it, if you are watching a leaf, are distracted by a falling apple, and then "voluntarily" return your attention to the leaf, in what sense is it really "you" who returns to the leaf (Styles, 2006, 5)? Certainly people can "behave in goal-directed ways, initiating and changing behaviours, apparently 'at will'" (Styles, 2006, 239). But it appears that "willing", like the performances of which Schatzki writes, "befalls" us. This perspective dovetails with Deleuze's claim, in *Difference and Repetition*, that:

> the spontaneity of which I am conscious in the I think cannot be understood as the attribute of a substantial and spontaneous being, but only as the condition of a passive ego feeling that its own thought, its own intelligence, by which it says I, takes place in it and on it, not by it.
>
> Deleuze, 1994, 86

Our thoughts, desires and feelings are not "our own" in any simple sense, though we may constantly "appropriate" them (see Chapter 5). We are responsible for our actions in the sense that they are initiated by us as embodied individual agents, even though both our motivations and the kinaesthetic processes through which we act may "befall" us. This is one important sense in which the physical body and the lived body must be understood as articulated with each other. It also integral to our directional asymmetry. The difficulty Butler sees in reconciling notions of vulnerability with claims for autonomy, like the difficulties Schatzki raises in grasping the sense in which actions that "befall" us can be thought of as "free", may fruitfully be reframed as questions of direction. In both cases, the difficulty can be relieved to some extent by recognizing that our exposure, receptiveness and answerability can be addressed from anywhere, from all directions both internal and external, while what we experience as relatively autonomous, self-determined action generally "points forward". This latter suggestion will be supported at more length below.

To summarize this first argument, embodied human beings are characterized fundamentally by vulnerability, passivity and exposure at a number of levels, from the existential level of our being-in-the-world to more mundane levels of our relations to external solicitations and events occurring in the flow of our everyday practices, even to the level of our own thoughts, feelings and actions. On the one hand, it is important to recognize that this vulnerability is not something we can or should wish simply to minimize. It is at the root of our aliveness to ourselves as loving, desiring, fearful, hopeful beings, and of other relational capabilities as discussed in non-representational affect theory in human geography, for example (Thrift, 2007; Anderson and Harrison, 2010; Dewsbury, 2015). More importantly for the present argument, our openness or answerability to the world is a crucial precondition for our responsiveness to the appeals and needs of others so central to the ethics of care (Held, 2006). At the same time, though, this openness, coupled with the inherent directional finitude of our active engagements – to which I turn momentarily – forms the subjective basis for the political economy of directed practice. If we are fundamentally exposed and susceptible, and if our responsiveness to address always has us dealing with the possibility of turning away from some things in order to turn toward what addresses us, we are perforce involved in an economy, and one that is inherently political. Despite all the subtlety and ambiguity the concept of embodied attention has acquired in the course of the literatures reviewed in Chapter 2, the chief claim of Goldhaber and Franck, discussed in Chapter 1, namely, that focused attention is also always a scarce resource, remains valid. The practical focus that is often led or steered by movements in our attention, is likewise a scarce resource.

Corporeal organization and direction

One underlying difficulty with perspectives that appeal to embodied needs or constraints is that any attempt to specify these features and processes runs the risk of universalizing and essentializing them (Orzeck, 2007, 497). The risk is heightened here by my distinction between *leibliche* or lived dimensions of embodiment and corporeal or physical dimensions. The latter almost necessarily become the locus of universalist claims (although of course the former can as well). Similar difficulties have stoked ongoing disputes in critical disability studies around the extent to which "impairments" can be seen as inherent features of individual bodies, as performatively constituted or as both (Hall and Wilton, 2017, 728). Here I will follow those strands of critical disability studies that work with stable notions of bodily constraints, because in my view the benefits of seeing how the directedness of practice is anchored in general features of embodiment outweigh the dangers or reification, essentialization, universalization, etc.

Taking a similar approach, Lena Gunnarsson argues with respect to feminist theory that questions raised by approaches within the discourse of so-called "new materialism" make it more difficult than before to ignore concrete and relatively stable features of human embodiment (Gunnarsson, 2013). Gunnarsson pinpoints a key assumption in some recent feminist theory, derived at least indirectly from Deleuze, which she believes needs to be challenged. This is the assumption that natural, bodily dynamics are fundamentally unpredictable and transgressive rather than structured. Against what she terms the "glorification of indeterminacy" and the attendant "celebration of transgression as such" (Gunnarsson, 2013, 8–9), Gunnarsson urges a refocusing of attention upon the ways in which embodiment not only enables but constrains human possibilities. Put differently, it is necessary to recognize that the experiences of the lived body are impacted in a range of ways by the characteristics of the physical body. An argument along related lines within the Marxist tradition by Fracchia will serve to elaborate on Gunnarsson's points and to deepen the background to the second component of directional asymmetry (Fracchia, 2005). Fracchia, like Gunnarsson and Orzeck, is well aware of the monumental difficulties facing attempts to settle on any suite of stable corporeal features of "human nature". Such attempts:

> must negotiate a variety of dilemmas, not least of which are the following: they must determine the relation between the natural/biological and the social; they must speak of universals, yet avoid universalizing a particularist notion, and still be able to account for how one species can produce a seemingly endless variety of cultural forms; they must be able to account for historical change without falling into a transhistorical Whiggishness and to discern the directions of historical changes without falling into teleologies.
>
> Fracchia, 2005, 34

Fracchia acknowledges that there has been no shortage of attempts to define human nature within recent historical materialism, but he argues that all of them have been insufficiently literal in their materialism, and too afraid of running afoul of recent critiques of essentialism and naturalism.

His own argument begins with a passing comment from Marx in the *German Ideology*, a comment Marx himself did not develop further. According to Marx, the "first fact" of any plausible historical theory must be "the corporeal organization of human beings" (quoted in Fracchia, 2005, 39). Fracchia's development of the significance of this "first fact" takes place within an historical materialist framework, which he stakes out with the familiar principle that "people make their own histories, but not as they please" (Fracchia, 2005, 43). The way he links the two facets of this familiar idea with embodiment is helpful:

> [B]ehind changing social capacities such as the specific character of technology, it is the set of corporeal capabilities that establishes the possibilities for humans to make their own histories; and beyond the changing limits of inherited socio-cultural conditions, it is the set of corporeal constraints, the needs and limits embedded in human corporeal organization, that prevents humans from making their histories as they please, that imposes limits on the variability of human cultures and on human malleability.
>
> Fracchia, 2005, 43

Fracchia goes on to discuss a range of capabilities, including the body's perceptual systems, the dexterous hand, and the "uniquely flexible human supralaryngeal tract" allowing subtle vocalizations (Fracchia, 2005, 46–47). Taking a cue from Engels (1962, 444), he highlights the importance of bipedality and the upright gait in freeing up the hands for manual work. Under the heading of corporeal limits, Fracchia discusses bodily needs for warmth, nourishment, oxygen, sleep, terrestriality (restricting our activities largely to the landmasses of the earth) and at least a minimal amount of physical activity (Fracchia, 2005, 49–51). Significantly, one form of corporeal constraint he mentions is that imposed by human sense organs. The perceptual systems through which we are enabled to engage in material processes of making our own histories are characterized at the same time by limitations. This is one important context in which I claim we need to place the inherent directionality of human attention and practice. This directionality is, again, corporeal, in a sense that includes and frames the cognitive and affective features of the lived body.

The limitations imposed by corporeal organization in the very broad sense of Fracchia's argument are not narrowly relative to historically, geographically or culturally specific contexts of human life (Fracchia, 2005, 55). It is also not necessary to oppose an acknowledgment of corporeal organization to culturally specific semiotics of bodily inscription: "these inscriptions themselves pertain to the textured materiality of corporeality as the site of needs, wants, desires, limits, constraints and capacities" (Fracchia, 2005, 58). It is this incredibly flexible but still specific and partly limiting suite of corporeal characteristics of the thinking, feeling, affected and active body that forms the framework for processes of ablement and disablement, and for shifting relations to the need for care, addressed in the critical disability studies and feminist care ethics literatures. These features of corporeal organization are particularly helpful in specifying the ways in which disablement and incapability are present also in the lives of the generally "abled": sensory capacities, forms of mobility, motility and dexterity, etc. are all simultaneously forms of inability. Embodied directionality is a feature of corporeal organization anchored in, though not reducible to, our bipedality and our upright gait. While it enables a great range of accomplishments, it also renders many things impossible for us. As with many other forms of corporeal organization, our directedness can be compensated and its limiting effects overcome to some extent by technological prostheses. However, and this is crucial, no amount of automation and prosthesis can allow us to be actively engaged in a "live" and focused way with more than one or at most a couple of matters at a time. Especially the psychological research on attention makes this clear (Styles, 2006; Gazzaley and Rosen, 2016). As already suggested, focused attention is a central and indispensable part of many forms of practice more generally.

The ideas of André Leroi-Gourhan (1911–1986), a French archaeologist, paleontologist and anthropologist, can help specify more clearly the fundamental shaping role of the directionality of our active engagements. Leroi-Gourhan is an interesting background figure who appears in the work of French poststructuralists such as Derrida (2016, 90–93) and Deleuze and Guattari (2004, 281), and in that of their inheritors (Wills, 2008, 8). Stiegler, who studied with Derrida, is certainly in this lineage. But Leroi-Gourhan appears, too, in Fracchia's Marxist argument for acknowledging the role of corporeal organization in explaining social and historical processes (Fracchia, 2005, 52–53). This interest in his work derives from Leroi-Gourhan's specific hypotheses about how humans evolved, and how our physical evolution led to the emergence of art, writing and other cultural forms. Leroi-Gourhan conceives of the place of humans in evolution in terms of "functional dispositions" (Leroi-Gourhan, 1993, 36). According to him, the long processes of animal evolution eventually resulting in the distinctive features of humans can be seen as:

> a series of "emancipations" following one upon another [...] that of the entire body from the fluid element, that of the head from the ground, the freeing of the hand from [the task of] locomotion and, finally, of the brain from the front of the face.
>
> Leroi-Gourhan, 1993, 25

These evolutionary emancipations can be understood as gradually divesting hand and face of functions that limited their availability for manipulation, communication, and cooperation. At the same time, the emergence of upright posture freed the skull from earlier structural responsibilities, allowing it to accommodate a larger brain. Leroi-Gourhan convincingly argues that the enlargement of the brain cavity in the evolutionary path he traces was not driven by growth of the brain; rather, it was a gradual result of decreasing mechanical burdens associated with the arrangement of the lower jaw and the suspension of the head from the end of the backbone (Leroi-Gourhan, 1993, 45–46). The evolution of the brain and the nervous system, in other words, follows rather than leads the evolution of the bodily apparatus (Leroi-Gourhan,

1993, 50). And when this process has gone far enough to free the hands and the face, tool use and communication accelerate it. Humans' upright posture leads to qualitative changes in the human brain. "In the development of the brain the relation between face and hand remained as close as ever: the tool assigned to the hand and speech assigned to the face are only different poles of the same unity" (Leroi-Gourhan 1993, 19–20). Leroi-Gourhan interprets evidence of the closely coupled evolutionary growth of areas in the brain's frontal lobe associated with manual dexterity and speech as a trace of the technical in human evolution. Freedom of the hand calls forth tool use different from that of other primates. In sum, an upright posture, a relatively short face, and hands freed from tasks of locomotion, allowing them to work with and on tools, are fundamental characteristics of the human (Leroi-Gourhan, 1993, 19).

Crucial for Leroi-Gourhan, as well for my argument here, is the fact that the hands and the face, as organs of tool use and speech, combine to give humans a uniquely flexible "anterior field" (Leroi-Gourhan 1993, 31ff; Stiegler 1998, 149). Many species are characterized by a division of the anterior or frontal relational field into two complementary regions: one for the activities of the frontal limbs and the other for the activities of the facial organs. But humans are the only species in which there is "a far-reaching connection between the facial and manual poles" without the hands being involved in travel (Leroi-Gourhan, 1993, 34–35). This field fundamentally orients our technicity, creating a space within arm's reach where our powers of vision, touch, vocalization, smell and taste are brought together with our manual dexterity, allowing fine operations on and with other subjects or objects. The anterior relational field of course does not fully determine or exhaust the structuring even of our sensory attention (think of hearing and touch), much less of cognitive or affective dimensions of attentional phenomena. Again, attentional openness or exposure is part of our omnidirectional answerability. Nevertheless, the space where our vision and manual activities converge plays a strong role in the selective direction of our attention and our practices in a wide range of situations.

The anterior relational field is implicated in modern social theory in the notions of the "front region" in the work of Goffman (1990) or Giddens (1984). More directly relevant conceptualizations of the anterior relational field as the condition of possibility of human action are found in George Mead's conception of the "manipulative zone" (Mead, 1938) and in Schütz and Luckmann's adaptation of this concept, which they term the "zone of operation" [*Wirkzone*] (Schütz and Luckmann, 1973, 41–42). Schütz and Luckmann define the zone of operation as the most intimate region of actual or potential action, and like Mead, consider it "the kernel of the lifeworld" (Schütz and Luckmann, 1973, 42). The zone of operation is nested within a broader set of spatial "reaches" [*Reichweiten*] of experience, namely "actual", or "potential" reaches, structuring the everyday lifeworld. The world within actual reach is characterized as the spatial extent of what is currently experienceable through perception; potential reach includes "recoverable reach", places and things one was engaged with in the past that are still accessible, and "attainable" reach, the extent of potential future reach (Schütz and Luckmann, 1973, 36–40). Within this set of spatial structures, the zone of operation is defined as "a zone which I can influence through *direct* action", in which things can be both seen and touched (Schütz and Luckmann, 1973, 41). Schütz and Luckmann acknowledge the prosthetic extension of effectivity enabled by tools and technology more broadly, further distinguishing between a "primary" and a "secondary" zone of operation, the latter being that reachable with the aid of technology (Schütz and Luckmann, 1973, 44–45; see also Adams, 1995). The notion of the zone of effectivity is a potentially useful way of approaching the directedness of practice because it spatializes activity as fundamentally conditioned by frontality.

But Schütz and Luckmann elide in a characteristic way the implications of the selectivity of our bodily directedness. The zones of *non-engagement* they discuss ("recoverable" and "attainable reach") are always couched in terms of *possible engagement*, of the possibility of engaging with them demonstrated by our having engaged with them in the past and potentially (again) in the future. They show little interest in the constitutive role of intimate or more distant zones of non-engagement *as current zones of non-operation* for social orders: however possible it may be that some nearby objects, persons or activities might be actively engaged later, the effects of our activity at any moment are shaped by that fact that we are *not* currently engaging them. The tendency to sideline this issue also runs through the work of Anthony Giddens and Benno Werlen, whose theories of everyday regionalization have both extended Giddens's arguments and brought Schütz and Luckmann's work to the attention of human geographers (Werlen, 1992, 1997, 1999; cf. Hannah, 2015).

As noted in the introduction to Part II above, this inattention to real non-engagement in favor of possible engagement suggests a "petri-dish" model of the transformative effect of acting individuals, that is, a model in which we are able in principle to activate potentials for change in all directions at once. This assumption occludes the directional insight contained in the idea of a frontal zone of operation, or Leroi-Gourhan's anterior relational field. Against the petri-dish model, it must be emphasized that every zone of operation simultaneously defines a (much more extensive) zone of non-operation significant *as such* for social processes, not merely as a zone of past or potential future effectivity. A second, equally crucial point to make is that the petri-dish model occludes our omnidirectional vulnerability or passivity. If we are "centers of action" pointing outward, it is harder to recognize that we are also the destination of solicitations and address from within and outside ourselves. It is only by virtue of this fundamental fact that we are able to recognize and respond to ethical appeals from others or to recognize the emergence of needs or desires in ourselves. The petri-dish model thus obscures the first part of our directional asymmetry as embodied human beings. The finite directedness of focused thoughts, feelings, affects and actions are of course not physically limited by the anterior relational field. However, as phenomena of the lived body, they still involve an experience of figurative "frontality": they are "before" us as long as we are actively engaged with them, and are thus temporarily exclusive of other possible matters of concern. Neurologically, having something "before us" in the sense of attending to it seems to be correlated with modulation of neural activity by the pre-frontal cortex (Gazzaley and Rosen, 2016, 54; Styles, 2006, 233–234).

The notion of directional asymmetry to a significant extent reverses the petri-dish model, in the sense that it is not our *potential activity* but our *actual vulnerability* that points in all directions. However, the model of directional asymmetry does not fully reverse the petri-dish model by denying our active capabilities entirely. Instead it recognizes that they are directionally limited. This is the significance of Leroi-Gourhan's notion of the anterior relational field. It forms the anchor for the second part of our directional asymmetry, namely, the directionally limited scope of our outward activity. Many of the key aspects of attention and practice upon which previous chapters have focused are mediated in important ways by the lived bodily experience anchored in the physical structure of the anterior relational field. The lived structuring of our attentional fields into theme, thematic field, and margin, explored by Gurwitsch, is strongly inflected – though again, not completely determined – by the space framed by our hands and face. Likewise, the lived activity place-spaces Schatzki describes as the settings within which practices follow their teleoaffective structures are encountered primarily through this anterior relational field. Competing claims on our attention and alternative paths for the sequencing of our practices can, by contrast, emerge and prove irresistible as easily from the margins outside our anterior fields – from the zones of non-effectivity encompassing our narrow zones of effectivity – as from within them. Again, this is due to the fundamentally pathic, omnidirectionally vulnerable character of the lived human body.

Frontal, dorsal and lateral space

This general, asymmetrical zonation of different relations of activity and passivity anchoring the lived body in the physical body can be specified further through a reading of the work of queer theorist David Wills, who likewise dwells at length upon the significance of Leroi-Gourhan's account of the human (Wills, 2008). Wills is interesting for the present argument because his main focus is upon the meaning for the human of "the dorsal" or back-side constituted with and by upright posture and the anterior relational field, and upon "turning" as a constitutive process. Wills "rotationalizes" Stiegler's claim that the human is inherently technical, arguing that technicity is inextricably related to our structuring into front and back regions (Wills, 2008, 3). Unlike Stiegler, Wills frames the technological not as something that originally emerges in concert with the anterior relational field through the work of hands, eyes and mouth emancipated by an upright posture, but as something *that comes from behind* to constitute the human, something already inherent in the upright posture itself. Technology is thus something neither visible nor foreseeable that both enables and "surprises". Wills suggests that "[a] technology of the human itself, a technology that defines and so produces the human, cannot be part of the human self-image; it comes at the human from behind, is already at its back. Or indeed, *in* its back" (Wills, 2008, 7). It may be that "discovery and invention are henceforth consistently understood as being ahead, around the corner, or on the horizon of forward progression", but this view of technology forgets "the primary or primal vertebral articulation that frees the hands to pick up stones and fashion tools, that redistributes the weight of the head and jaw to allow the brain to develop and the tongue to speak" (Wills, 2008, 9).

With some qualification, Wills's focus upon the dynamics of turning and "dorsality" thus sharpens the sensibility I seek to cultivate here. It is consistent with my contention that there is a directional asymmetry between our answerability to the world and the scope of our active interventions in it. The technical and other human processes we typically think of as taking place *in front of us* presuppose a *behind*, a region invisible and less accessible out of which matters of concern, the ethical appeal of others, or unlooked-for technological possibilities may emerge. This specifies further Merleau-Ponty's claim that the body is always in some sense the "background" of action (see Chapter 2). Wills's analysis suggests a way of further specifying how the movements of attention and practice are structured by embodied spatialities. In Chapter 2 we saw in connection with Gurwitsch that the structures of attention include the tripartite division between active "theme", associated "thematic field" and "margin" or background, and that this basic division is embedded in a range of "horizons" (biographical, cultural, bodily and external/physical) from which new appeals or solicitations may emerge at any time (Gurwitsch, 1964). Merleau-Ponty's focus upon bodily aspects of attention additionally highlighted the range of unreflective, incorporated, routine and automatic forms of attention accompanying our activities. This range of more habitual relations to our concerns and their surroundings is, so I argued in Chapter 3, likewise a central structuring element in understanding practices in Schatzki's sense as inherently directed and to some extent led by attentional stasis or movement.

Wills's dorsal supplementation of Leroi-Gourhan's notion of the anterior relational field allows a consolidation of these heuristic suggestions in the idea that we can broadly map attention and practice onto a differentiated picture of lived bodily space. The difference between more focused and deliberate and more routine, unreflected and automatic dimensions of attention and practice can be anchored to the distinction between the frontal and the dorsal. However, here Wills's notion of the relation between front and back is too binary. His conception knows only front or back, not sides.

> Even if in turning, one (the human) deviates from itself in the simplest or most minimal fashion, turns just a little to the left or to the right […] it

turns, for all intents and purpose, *toward the back*. For my purposes and according to my interpretation, every deviation is a form of retroversion [...]. Any departure, however slight, from a pure and strict [...] forward linearity makes reference to what it behind.

Wills, 2008, 5

I want to argue that this collapsing of all deviation into dorsality is too undifferentiated, and renders the process of turning itself inconsequential. Each of these criticisms is important. First, matters of focused, active practice generally – though of course not always – take place in front of us, and especially within the complex and shifting anterior relational field where our manual, vocal and visual spaces converge and overlap. Explicit, concentrated attention is focused either in this same field or "in front of us" in a more figurative, *leibliche* register encompassing the cognitive and the affective. In either case it makes a good deal of sense, in my view, to ensconce this physically framed frontal experiential field within a *lateral* space of embodiment which is not immediately dorsal. To this lateral space we can heuristically assign many of the habitual, routine and unreflectively monitored aspects of what we are doing, saying, thinking or feeling, as well as the currently dormant elements of our thematic fields. "Tools", in the broadest sense – familiar objects, language, tacit knowledge – belong here as well. This lateral space is not simply a dorsal space, an invisible space behind us out of which matters emerge. It is characterized by the fact that some aspects of attention and practice, whether utterances, visual focus or the dexterous workings of our hands, are *involved* in practices in the anterior field, and perceived as such, without themselves usually being brought into explicit focus. Perhaps most easily envisioned in manual terms, these tools, embodied capabilities, habits and routines *extend from the side into the front*. Thus, they can be thought of as inhabiting an in-between space, neither explicitly remarked nor purely unremarked.

The tripartite division proposed here between anterior field, lateral space and dorsal space can be thought of as a refinement of one half of our directional asymmetry. This asymmetry can now be thought of as composed, on the one hand, by our vulnerability or answerability to solicitations or significations from anywhere, including from within the body, the less tangible world of thoughts, feelings or affects, and on the other hand, by the tripartite zonation of our possibilities for active engagement with the world. Our active practices are very often directed, and are surrounded by lateral and dorsal spaces of embodiment to which our relation is fundamentally unreflected, passive or completely uninvolved. What transpires within our anterior relational fields, or more accurately, in the interplay between our anterior and lateral fields, may be described, for example, in the agency-foregrounding terms of Giddens's structuration theory. But this is not the whole picture. Whatever it is we are actively *doing*, we are also *in so doing*, not actively engaged with the vast realm of what is behind us. More importantly, this non-engagement always swinging around behind us as we engage with what is in our anterior relational fields can be understood as an *active form of social reproduction*, a claim I will elaborate more fully in Chapter 7.

In her *Queer Phenomenology*, Sara Ahmed writes that "[o]rientations shape not only how we inhabit space, but how we apprehend this world of shared inhabitance, as well as 'who' or 'what' we direct our energy and attention toward" (Ahmed, 2006, 3). Inhabiting space, according to Ahmed, "'decides' what comes into view. The point of such decisions may be precisely that we have lost sight of them; that we take what is given as simply a matter of what happens to be 'in front' of us" (Ahmed, 2006, 14). More broadly, "[t]he body becomes present as a body, with surfaces and boundaries, in showing the 'limits' of what it can do" (Ahmed, 2006, 55). Ahmed elegantly summarizes the point I am making here:

> The field of positive action, of what this or that body does do, also defines a field of inaction, of actions that are possible but not taken up, or even actions that are not possible because of what has been taken up.
>
> Ahmed, 2006, 58

This is one way to express our directional asymmetry: the ongoing, shifting definition of fields of non-actualized possibilities, of zones of non-effectivity, is a fundamental accompaniment inherently bound to our more narrowly focused positive and active capabilities. And all of these zones are permeable to solicitations.

The argument of this chapter has highlighted the role of the anterior relational field, a lateral region "adjacent" to it, and a dorsal space in structuring the possibilities and impossibilities of active practice. Again, these are features of the *lived body* [*Leib*] that are framed by and can be at least loosely tied to features of the physical body. It may be helpful to depict this tripartite structure in the form of Figure 4.1.

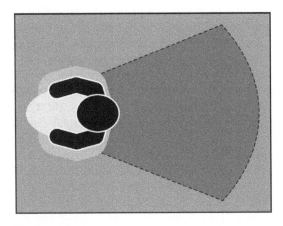

Figure 4.1 The directional body

Here we see the spaces encompassing the body differentiated into a dark dorsal space, a lateral space of lighter grey, encompassing the arms, and a bright space in front of the face and between the arms. The lateral space is the realm, roughly speaking, of tools and capabilities we can draw upon unreflectively and without paying focused attention, things and skills we can "bring in from the side" in whatever we are doing. The white space is the anterior relational field itself, the frontal zone of operation, in Schütz and Luckmann's terms, in which matters are accessible to vision, voice and hand all at once. The dark dorsal space is truncated into a wedge shape for graphical convenience, and in order to enable the graphical argument in Chapter 8. But dorsal space should be understood as indefinitely extended, as suggested by the dashed line around it. The direction taken by the figure should be understood as lived, experienced or felt direction anchored in but not reducible to the physical body. The physical body's framing relevance is represented as the generically anthropomorphic shape of the figure itself. This helps highlight the fact that in being oriented toward one matter of concern, we generally must be turned away from others. This directional exclusivity is as much a neurological, perceptual and kinaesthetic as it is a straightforwardly anatomical issue, but the anatomical demarcation of "front", "back", and "sides" in the diagrams should be understood to include these non-visible dimensions as well. To retain a minimum degree of recognizably human form, the head is separated from the body, but this should not be understood to imply a mind-body dualism.

The omnidirectional vulnerability or answerability through which we are open to the world is graphically represented by the fact that new matters of concern can appear to or address us from any internal or external source, as pictured in Figure 4.2. The different stars are different possible sources of appeal (sounds or movements, thoughts or ideas, pains, itches or hunger, emotions or shifts in atmosphere, for example).

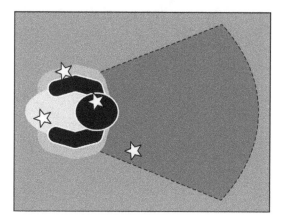

Figure 4.2 Omnidirectional vulnerability

Figure 4.3 places the directionally asymmetrical subject within the "activity-place-space" of integrated practices as defined by Schatzki (2002). In this schematic space, a sequence of tasks must be performed at a sequence of stations (represented by squares), and moving between these stations involves both covering distance and turning. The roughly path-like structure of the space is intended to indicate the association between a sequence of tasks and a corresponding sequence of places at which they are performed.

Figure 4.3 could also be seen metaphorically to depict the movement of cognitive attention or a thinking process within a figurative space defined by elements of what Gurwitsch called the "thematic field", that is, matters relevant to the currently engaged theme. By placing the image of the practitioner within the external spatial structure of the practical task-space, we have the complete context within which the spatially structured flow of practice, as well as possible changes of direction through attentional shifts, runs its course. The dorsal zone of the body emphasizes the fact that turning toward one task within a practice-space usually means turning away from others.

These diagrams will serve as a basis for depicting the dynamic process of turning itself in the next chapter. Turning is initiated by an impulse, solicitation or appeal coming to us from the realm of external occurrences, or from

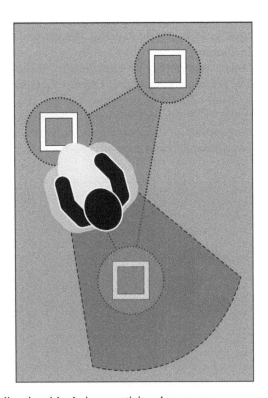

Figure 4.3 The directional body in an activity-place-space

thoughts, feelings, memories, affective states and other sensations. It can originate in front of us, behind us, to the side, within us, etc. The impulse may immediately trigger a reflex, as in the case of sharp pain. But often there is a period of "hesitation" (Ricœur, 2007) during which it is not yet clear whether we will turn to address the appeal. If we do, this involves a shift of the "front" of the lived body, that is, the focus of attention and possibly also practice, toward the source of the appeal. To the extent that attention and practice involve sensorimotor or communicative capabilities, we often also turn our anterior relational fields toward the new matter of concern. This allows not only direct engagement of attentive focus but the bringing to bear of our unreflected capabilities and skills or tools of all sorts from our lateral spaces upon the new concern. In contrast to Wills's rather binary vision, turning thus is not always destined to "go all the way" around to the back but involves partial turnings or responses to solicitations. The present but unreflected tools, resources and elements of the thematic field associated with whatever theme we have in front of us may form the infrastructure for infinitesimal shifts and incomplete rotations through which we remain "on course" with what we are doing, take a "detour" or "turn off" completely. As we shall see in the next chapter, how all of this happens for embodied, directed subjects is important.

Again, the sensibility presented here is located in a deliberately double way between embodiment as experienced *Leib* and embodiment as more physical, corporeal organization, and between time as scarce resource and time as lived quality. Only this doubleness allows the full range of forms of attention and practice their place. What Schatzki calls the "timespace of human activity" necessarily involves a physical component of corporeal organization, which shapes and anchors, while not fully determining the *leibliche* dimension. If the directionally asymmetrical turning subject is at the core of the timespace of human activity, this implies that the turning subject is temporal as well as spatial. The interplay between what we are turned toward and what we are turned away from take place in and on our *embodied, directed time.* The concept of directed time deliberately fuses temporal and spatial movement. As we shall see in Chapter 7, the directed time through which we live our directional asymmetry is at the center of a politics of occupation.

This political perspective necessarily implies that I hold onto a desire to defend or expand some appropriately chastened and amended notion of human "autonomy". This is a tension Butler takes seriously, and a similar ethical tension pervades Simonsen's insistence on retaining some altered form of humanism (Simonsen, 2013). But what kind of autonomy is appropriate here? As will be discussed further in Chapter 7, ideas about "relational" or "mutual autonomy" developed in feminist care ethics are helpful, because they detach the notion of autonomy from the goal of achieving a splendid, sovereign isolation from external influence (Held, 2006, 48–49, 55). These considerations bring us to the issue of alienation. The larger frame for the argument here has been that of subject-world relations. If, as I claim, embodied human subjects are fundamentally characterized by directional asymmetry, how does this affect the way we experience our relations with the world in which we are embedded? The concept of alienation as a problem of subject-world relations is well suited to begin to construct a deeper sense of the problems touched upon by the literature on the political economy of attention. Like other concepts treated here, alienated relations with the world have largely been grasped in terms of distance and separation. On the basis of the notion of directional asymmetry, I will propose another way of understanding alienation.

References

Adams, P.C. (1995). A reconsideration of personal boundaries in space-time. *Annals of the Association of American Geographers*, 85(2), pp. 267–285.

Ahmed, S. (2006). *Queer Phenomenology: Orientations, Objects, Others*. Durham, NC: Duke University Press.

Anderson, B. and Harrison, P., eds. (2010). *Taking Place: Non-Representational Theories and Geography*. Farnham: Ashgate.

Ash, J. and Simpson, P. (2016). Geography and post-phenomenology. *Progress in Human Geography*, 40(1), pp. 48–66.

Berg, M. and Seeber, B. (2016). *The Slow Professor: Challenging the Culture of Speed in the Academy*. Toronto: University of Toronto Press.

Bergson, H. (1991). *Matter and Memory*. Brooklyn, NY: Zone Books.

Bergson, H. (2001). *Time and free will: an essay on the immediate data of consciousness*. Trans. F. Pogson. Mineola, NY: Dover.

Butler, J. (2004). *Undoing Gender*. London: Routledge.

Butler, J. (2006). *Precarious Life: The Powers of Mourning and Violence*. London: Verso.

Caputo, J. (1993). *Against Ethics*. Bloomington, IN: Indiana University Press.

Deleuze, G. (1988). *Bergsonism*. Trans. H. Tomlinson and B. Habberjam. Brooklyn, NY: Zone Books.

Deleuze, G. (1994). *Difference and Repetition*. Trans. P. Patton. New York: Columbia University Press.

Deleuze, G. and Guattari, F. (2004). *A Thousand Plateaus*. Trans. B. Massumi. London: Continuum.

Derrida, J. (2016). *Of Grammatology*. 40th Anniversary Edition. Trans. G. Spivak. Baltimore, MD: Johns Hopkins University Press.

Dewsbury, J.D. (2015). Non-representation landscapes and the performative affective forces of habit: from "Live" to "Blank". *Cultural Geographies*, 22(1), pp. 29–47.

Dörfler, T. and Rothfuß, E. (2018). Lebenswelt, Leiblichkeit und Resonanz: Eine raumphänomenologisch-rekonstruktive Perspektive auf Geographien der Alltäglichkeit. *Geographica Helvetica*, 73, pp. 95–107.

Elden, S. (2001). *Mapping the Present: Heidegger, Foucault and the Project of a Spatial History*. London: Continuum.

Engels, F. (1962). Anteil der Arbeit an der Menschenwerdung des Affen. In: *Karl Marx/Friedrich Engels – Werke*, vol. 20. Berlin: Karl Dietz Verlag, pp. 444–455.

Fracchia, J. (2005). Beyond the human-nature debate: human corporeal organization as the "first fact" of historical materialism. *Historical Materialism*, 13, pp. 33–61.

Gazzaley, A. and Rosen, L. (2016). *The Distracted Mind: Ancient Brains in a High-Tech World.* Cambridge, MA: MIT Press.

Giddens, A. (1984). *The Constitution of Society.* London: Polity Press.

Glennie, P. and Thrift, N. (1996). Reworking E.P. Thompson's 'Time, work discipline and industrial capitalism'. *Time and Society,* 5(3), pp. 275–299.

Goffman, E. (1990). *The Presentation of Self in Everyday Life.* New York: Penguin.

Grosz, E. (2005). *Time Travels: Feminism, Nature, Power.* Durham, NC, and London: Duke University Press.

Gunnarsson, L. (2013). The naturalistic turn in feminist theory: a Marxist-realist contribution. *Feminist Theory,* 14(1), pp. 3–19.

Gurwitsch, A. (1964). *The Field of Consciousness.* Pittsburgh, PA: Duquesne University Press.

Hall, E. and Wilton, R. (2017). Towards a relational geography of disability. *Progress in Human Geography,* 41(6), pp. 727–744.

Hannah, M. (2015). Aufmerksamkeit und geographische Praxis. *Geographische Zeitschrift,* 103(3), pp. 131–150.

Harman, G. (2002). *Tool Being: Heidegger and the Metaphysics of Objects.* Chicago, IL: Open Court Press.

Harrison, P. (2008). Corporeal remains: vulnerability, proximity, and living on after the end of the world. *Environment and Planning A,* 40(2), pp. 423–445.

Harrison, P. (2015). After affirmation, or, being a loser: on vitalism, sacrifice and cinders. *GeoHumanities,* 1(2), pp. 285–306.

Held, V. (2006). *The Ethics of Care: Personal, Political and Global.* Oxford: Oxford University Press.

Latour, B. (1987). *Science in Action.* Cambridge, MA: Harvard University Press.

Leroi-Gourhan, A. (1993). *Gesture and Speech.* Trans. A. Bostock Berger. Cambridge, MA: MIT Press.

Levinas, E. (1969). *Totality and Infinity.* Trans. A. Lingis. Pittsburgh, PA: Duquesne University Press.

Malpas, J. (2006). *Heidegger's Topology: Being, Place, World.* Cambridge, MA: MIT Press.

Massey, D. (2005). *For Space.* London: Sage.

May, J. and Thrift, N., eds, (2001). *TimeSpace: Geographies of Temporality.* London: Routledge.

Mead, G.H. (1938). *Philosophy of the Act.* Chicago, IL: University of Chicago Press.

Merleau-Ponty, M. (1962). *Phenomenology of Perception.* Trans. C. Smith. London: Routledge and Kegan Paul.

Moran, D. (2005). *Husserl: Founder of Phenomenology.* Cambridge: Polity Press.

Nelson, L. (1999). Bodies (and spaces) do matter: the limits of performativity. *Gender, Place and Culture,* 6, pp. 331–353.

Noddings, N. (2013). *Caring: A Feminine Approach to Ethics and Moral Education.* 2nd ed. Berkeley, CA: University of California Press.

Orzeck, R. (2007). What does not kill you: historical materialism and the body. *Environment and Planning D: Society and Space,* 25, pp. 496–514.

Plessner, H. (1981). *Die Stufen des Organischen und der Mensch: Einleitung in die philosophische Anthropologie.* Frankfurt am Main: Suhrkamp.

Ricœur, P. (2007). *Freedom and Nature: The Voluntary and the Involuntary.* Trans E. Kohak. Evanston, IL: Northwestern University Press.

Rosa, H. (2015). *Social Acceleration: A New Theory of Modernity.* Trans. J. Trejo-Mathys. New York: Columbia University Press.

Rose, M. (2014). Negative governance: vulnerability, biopolitics and the origins of government. *Transactions of the Institute of British Geographers*, 39(2), pp. 209–233.

Schatzki, T. (2002). *The Site of the Social: A Philosophical Account of the Constitution of Social Life and Change*. University Park, PA: Penn State Press.

Schatzki, T. (2010). *The Timespace of Human Activity: On Performance, Society, and History as Indeterminate Teleological Events*. Lanham, MD: Lexington Books.

Schütz, A. and Luckmann, T. (1973). *Structures of the Lifeworld*, Vol. 1. Trans. R.N. Zaner and H.T. Engelhardt, Jr. Evanston, IL: Northwestern University Press.

Shove, E., Pantzar, M., and Watson, M. (2012). *The Dynamics of Social Practice: Everyday Life and How It Changes*. London: Sage.

Simonsen, K. (2013). In quest of a new humanism: embodiment, experience and phenomenology as critical geography. *Progress in Human Geography*, 37(1), pp. 10–26.

Stiegler, B. (1998). *Technics and Time, 1: The Fault of Epimetheus*. Trans. R. Beardsworth and G. Collins. Stanford, CA: Stanford University Press.

Styles, E. (2006). *The Psychology of Attention*. 2nd ed. New York: Psychology Press.

Thrift, N. (2007). *Non-Representational Theory: Space | Politics | Affect*. London: Routledge.

Waldenfels, B. (2004). *Phänomenologie der Aufmerksamkeit*. Frankfurt am Main: Suhrkamp.

Werlen, B. (1992). *Society, Action and Space: An Alternative Human Geography*. New York: Routledge.

Werlen, B. (1997). *Sozialgeographie alltäglicher Regionalisierungen, Band 2: Globalisierung, Region und Regionalisierung*. Stuttgart: Franz Steiner Verlag.

Werlen, B. (1999). *Sozialgeographie alltäglicher Regionalisierungen, Band 1: Zur Ontologie von Gesellschaft und Raum*. Stuttgart: Franz Steiner Verlag.

Wills, D. (2008). *Dorsality: Thinking Back through Technology and Politics*. Minneapolis, MN: University of Minnesota Press.

5 Turning and alienation

Near the beginning of Chapter 2, I approvingly cited William James on the centrality of directed attention to the possibility of subjective self-determination. The passage bears quoting again:

> When we reflect that the turnings of our attention form the nucleus of our inner self; when we see [...] that volition is nothing but attention; [...] we must admit that the question whether attention involve such a principle of spiritual activity or not is metaphysical as well as psychological, and is well worthy of all the pains we can bestow on its solution. It is in fact the pivotal question of metaphysics, the very hinge on which our picture of the world shall swing from materialism, fatalism, monism, towards spiritualism, freedom, pluralism,—or else the other way.
>
> James, 1950, 447–448

How can we interpret this exhortation in view of the picture painted of attention in Chapter 2, of practice in Chapter 3 and of directional asymmetry in Chapter 4? I have argued:

- that the direction of attention involves a complex interplay of internal and external solicitations, social and personal horizons and styles of attending, as well as differentially structured culturally specific arrangements and processes of obtrusiveness and unobtrusiveness;
- that the ways in which our hours, days and lives are composed through sequences of practices are in part determined by the "leading" influence of attention, which holds steady or turns within and outside the teleoaffective structures of practices according to whether and how it answers various solicitations; and
- that the embodied human beings who serve as the obligatory points of passage for these processes are both fundamentally affected, vulnerable and open, and at the same time directionally limited in our active engagements. This directional asymmetry ties together our corporeal organization and our *leibliche* embodied experiences.

This chapter concerns the kinds of relations to the world that human beings, embodied in the ways described in the previous chapter, can have. In theories of alienation, reification and fetishism (but also more broadly in discussions of essentialism and hypostatization), the relation between subject and world is traditionally posed in terms of distance or separation and objectification. The goal here will be to reframe subject-world relationality in terms of direction, in terms of turning toward and turning away. This "rotational" dimension, I want to claim, subtends and frames that of distancing or separation. The chapter proceeds through three steps. The first section lays out the ideas of Rahel Jaeggi and Hartmut Rosa on alienated and non-alienated relations to the world. Both thinkers provide useful concepts that outfit the traditional critical category of alienation for use in a context in which sovereign subjectivity is no longer assumed either as a description or as a norm for theory. The second section "spatializes" Rosa's notion of "resonance" in terms of the dimensions of directionally asymmetrical subjectivity sketched in the previous chapter, and supplements this concept with the notion of "critical-creative engagement". The third section takes this directional framing of our relations to the world as the background for returning to the concept of montage proposed by Jonathan Beller and Bernard Stiegler as a way to understand "cinematic consciousness". Here Jaeggi's insights on alienation can render more precise what is at stake. The fourth and final section relates the issues of montage and rupture to alienation via a discussion of Henri Lefebvre's "rhythmanalysis" (Lefebvre, 2004). This then prepares the ground for the issue of reification and "objecthood" that is the focus of Chapter 6.

Alienation, appropriation and resonance

Much has been written about how the artificial split between "subjects" and "objects" is constituted in practice and in theory. Numerous accounts of subjectivation are mirrored by equally numerous critical accounts of "objectification" in all its varieties. The same is true of critiques of other familiar dualisms that have structured modern Western thought, often in combination: nature/culture, human/animal, self/other, masculine/feminine, reason/madness, normal/abnormal, civilized/savage, Western/Oriental, etc. The basic motif of most such accounts is that of a simplifying separation or distancing, a breaking, obscuring, denial or circumscription of underlying continuities, connections, interdependencies or flows. Such breaks are seen to produce a misleading picture of two separate, independent poles. Bertell Ollman, for example, defines alienation very broadly as "the separation of what does not allow separation without distortion" (Ollman, 1976, 47). For the purposes of the present argument, however, it makes some sense to establish a basic distinction between ways in which such distancing and separation is experienced from the "subject"-side, which we can call *alienation*, and the effects distancing and separation have upon our understanding of the "object"-side, that is, *reification.* It should be kept in mind in this and the subsequent chapter, however, that both alienation and reification are names for problems with the connective relation itself (Bewes, 2002, 3–4).

Rahel Jaeggi identifies Marx and Heidegger as two highly influential anchor-points for many critiques of modern relations to the world. For Marx, "[w]hat is alienated or reified is something that has been *made* but appears as *given* (by nature, as it were, and in such a way that it appears not subject to our will)" (Jaeggi, 2014, 15). Closely related is Marx's distinction between "living" and "dead" labor, the point of the latter expression being to highlight the fact that inanimate as well as animate factors of production have their origins in creative human labor (Kirsch and Mitchell, 2004). For Heidegger, by contrast, the key distinction in the relation to objects is between the practical entanglement of things in our involved dealings and a detached view of them as inert objects (Jaeggi, 2014, 17). Heidegger's corresponding analysis of the relation of self to itself centers on inauthenticity and the "fallenness" of *Dasein* in considering itself to exist in the same way as a thing (Jaeggi, 2014, 18–19). Here again we see the difficulty of cleanly distinguishing between alienation and reification.

With this caveat in mind, alienation can be defined initially as follows: "Being alienated from something means having become distanced from something in which one is in fact involved or to which one is in fact related – or in any case ought to be" (Jaeggi, 2014, 25). In the Marxist tradition, where the concept of alienation has been most thoroughly developed, the problem of alienation is seen as relevant to a number of different kinds of involvement, all deriving from Marx's original treatment in his 1844 manuscripts: human relations to nature, to ourselves as individuals and our individual activity, to our "species being", and to other individual humans (Mészáros, 2006, 14). Jaeggi's recent theorization of alienation is relevant to the argument here because she, too, seeks to give the concept substantive ethical and political content, but without resorting to the regulative ideal of the individual subject in immediate communion with the world. Jaeggi's core assertion is that alienation should more specifically be understood as:

> a *relation of relationlessness.* […] According to this formulation, alienation does not indicate the absence of a relation but is itself a relation, if a deficient one. Conversely, overcoming alienation does not mean returning to an undifferentiated state of oneness with oneself and the world; it too is a relation: a *relation of appropriation.*
>
> Jaeggi, 2014, 1

Defining alienation in this formal way avoids the pitfalls of a substantive account of what one is alienated from and focuses instead on the nature of the relation. One consequence is the possibility that an unalienated life could in principle be unhappy or in some other way not "good" (Jaeggi, 2014, 33). This formal approach has the advantage of being able to acknowledge the fundamental "lateness" of human beings with respect to the world we find ourselves in, the pre-existence of that world and our state of "thrownness" into it (Jaeggi, 2014, 115–117). Our fundamental lateness explains why an unalienated relation with the world can only be developed through processes of appropriation. "Appropriation" means "a way of *establishing relations* to oneself and to the relationships in which one lives (relationships that condition or shape who one is)" such that these relations can be experienced as one's "own" (Jaeggi, 2014, 33). Jaeggi acknowledges the links between the concept of appropriation and property relations, but argues that the concept as she uses it is not merely reducible to capitalist ideologies. There is, she claims, "an interesting tension in the idea of appropriation between what is previously given and what is formable, between taking over and creating, between the subject's sovereignty and its dependence" (Jaeggi, 2014, 39).

The notion of appropriation frees the question of alienation from the often deadening clutches of an unattainable opposite term. The issue, according to Jaeggi, is not some phantasm of pure or complete self-creation or self-determination, it is not whether we ourselves are the causes of or responsible for our situations. We need not strive for complete *control over* the events that determine our lives, nor find it troubling that we are not always their authors, or that the actions of ourselves or others develop dynamics independent of us. "Not everything that is not in our command makes our life alien to us" (Jaeggi, 2014, 62). Although I will not pursue this line of thought here, Jaeggi's focus on the often heteronomous sources of the materials we must appropriate could form the basis for more systematic analysis of the experience of oppressed, exploited or marginalized groups. For although it may be the case that even the most privileged members of any social formation must engage in appropriation, it is surely also the case that there are important and systematic differences in how easy or difficult this is, in the degree to which the materials "provided" by society support or hinder positive experiences of the identity one is able to build out of them, the degree of individual control over the ways in which such appropriation takes place, etc. Clearly, if the everyday cultural resources provided by a particular social formation include deeply embedded racist, sexist or homophobic elements, it will, generally speaking, be more difficult for racial and sexual minorities as well as women to feel at home in the identities it is easiest to build out of these materials.

According to Jaeggi, we also need to take into account the fact that "a certain fixity of relations is always necessary in order to frame the setting within which we live and that therefore we cannot make transparent *all* the conditions under which we live and regard them as always fluid and at our command" (Jaeggi, 2014, 61). Rather we need to be able to a significant extent to *integrate* events and circumstances, many initially beyond our ken and control, into our sense of ourselves (Jaeggi, 2014, 63). As she makes plain throughout her book, this integration is not merely the unchanged adoption of external roles or imperatives but is often transformative. An important aspect of integration is that we should be able to maintain a relatively coherent self-conception. It is not "a question of whether what I want and do really *fits me* but whether the various things I want and do – the things I identify with and that matter to me – *fit together with one another*" (Jaeggi, 2014, 122). And this fitting together must take place at the level of my interpretation. "It is not traits and desires themselves that must fit together but a person's interpretation of them. What is important is whether I can integrate what I want into the conception I have of myself as a person" (Jaeggi, 2014, 122). Jaeggi's many-layered and sensitive account of the inability to appropriate and integrate experiences and materials explains the "distance" at the heart of alienation.

The same general approach shapes Jaeggi's conception of the will and the role of volition in the question of whether one's relations with the world or with people or events is alienated. Drawing on the work of Ernst Tugendhat and Harry Frankfurt, she develops a concept of will that neither relies upon an essentially sovereign notion of subjective self-command nor denies to subjects the competence to interpret their will. Again, appropriation is key. Following Tugendhat, she argues that we demonstrate a will to be able to will things by our very acts of willing. Immanent in these acts, in other words, is an ideal of the "functional capacity of willing" (Jaeggi, 2014, 33). But our will is not simply "what we want". A further question needs to be asked, namely "whether we have ourselves at our command in what we will" (Jaeggi, 2014, 34). As is common for individuals addicted to substances, gaming, or what have you, it is possible that we can will something at one level but not want to will it at another level. This would be an example of an alienated relation with our acts of willing: we cannot "make them our own". In this connection, Frankfurt distinguishes between "first order desires" and "second order volitions", the latter being "a desire to have or not to have a first-order desire" (Jaeggi, 2014, 104). Here it is clear that affective, emotional and psychological dynamics beyond our control may or may not be integrated into a coherent, that is, non-alienated self-interpretation. The point isn't so much where our decisions, desires, goals, etc. *come from* but whether we can *take them on* successfully. This way of approaching the matter makes room for the insights of phenomenology and psychology as to the pathic, often passive and vulnerable dimensions of our relations to the world.

A second recent attempt to retheorize relations to the world, one that likewise gives an important role to the concept of alienation, is that of Hartmut Rosa (Rosa, 2015; 2016). Rosa, like Jaeggi, provides a set of helpful concepts with which to approach the problematic of world-relations as faced by directionally asymmetrical subjects. In his work *Social Acceleration*, Rosa offers a comprehensive and multifaceted explanation of how and why the overall pace of life in the Global North has increased in the last few decades (Rosa, 2015). Rosa weaves together strands of explanation from the Marxist tradition centered on neoliberal capitalism, from the social systems theory of Luhmann and others, which highlights processes of functional differentiation and decoupling of ever more spheres of social life, as well as from a range of other research on technology, social psychology and related topics. In his massive 2016 tome *Resonanz: eine Soziologie der Weltbeziehung* [*Resonance: A Sociology of Relation to the World*], Rosa seeks to deepen his account of what it is that is threatened by acceleration, above all by focusing upon the *qualitative* aspects of relations to the world more than he had in the earlier book. The name he gives to healthy or successful relations to the world is *resonance*; the contrasting term – though not simply representing "unsuccessful" relations – is alienation. Further developing his earlier diagnosis of acceleration, Rosa suggests that alienation is related to the constant pressures brought to bear upon individuals, groups and institutions by the logic of escalation in 21st century capitalism to pursue "extension of reach" [*Reichweitenvergrößerung*]. This concept concerns the extent of our ability to experience and affect the world outside of us, and is thus broadly in line with Schütz and Luckmann's discussion of different "reaches" [*Reichweiten*] (Schütz and Luckmann, 1973, 36–40). The pressure to extend the reach of social actors and institutions - or in my terms, the pressure to extend the petri-dish model of human being – has grave consequences in diminishing or sidelining the spaces, times and dispositions necessary for experiences of resonance (Rosa, 2016, 661–662, 690).

Rosa's concept of resonance can be seen as partly complementary to Jaeggi's notion of appropriation. In both cases it is broadly a question of whether some aspect of self, others or the world can be *animated by a sense of meaningful connection to oneself.* But whereas Jaeggi's analysis is avowedly formalistic, Rosa focuses more upon the qualitative character of the animated connection itself, arguing that the acoustical or musical metaphor of resonance is the best way to understand it. One of his fundamental assumptions is that "[p]eople yearn to experience the world as supportive [*tragend*], nourishing, warming and responsive, and themselves as effectual in it, and they fear a silent, pitiless world to which they are helplessly delivered up" (Rosa, 2016, 748). Resonance is defined as a mode of being-in-the-world in which the relation between a subject and some aspect of the world is experienced as "something like a vibrating wire" (Rosa, 2016, 24). Such a relation manifests itself in dispositions of connection and openness on the part of subjects (Rosa, 2016, 53), but also presupposes a "resonance-space" capable of "vibrating" (Rosa, 2016, 285). If a relation of resonance can establish itself over time with a particular person, activity or place, it can become a more durable "resonance-axis" for live, rewarding relations to the world (Rosa, 2016, 26). Relatively stable resonance-axes and resonance-spaces, and the accumulation of memories attached to them, can differentiate the world for us into resonance "oases", and by contrast, "deserts" (Rosa, 2016, 196). Citing Bernhard Waldenfels, Rosa theorizes resonance as an inherently embodied and affective experience based fundamentally upon the pathic "answerability" [*Antwortlichkeit*] humans have to our worlds (Rosa, 2016, 67). More specifically, the idea of a vibrating wire can be seen as:

> an experience or a state in which the subject is affected, that is, touched and moved, by a part of the world, on the one hand, while it reacts, on

the other hand, through an accommodating, outwardly directed emotional movement, with intrinsic interest (*libido*) and corresponding expectations of effectivity. *Af←fect* [...] and *e→motion* [...] thus compose the "wire" whose bi-directional vibration can perhaps be represented in playful form as affect and emotion.

Rosa, 2016, 279

Rosa identifies three "dimensions" of resonant relations: the "horizontal" forms of resonance with other people typical of love and friendship but also potentially including politics and other collective relations; "diagonal" resonance with the world of material things and representations; and finally, the "vertical" dimension in which the "world itself" is experienced as having a voice. This last is the dimension of resonance evoked in art, religion and spirituality, or in encounters with the vastness of nature (Rosa, 2016, 73–75). In all of these dimensions, however, resonance is not only a matter of affect and emotion: Rosa points out that our relations with the world have cognitive and normative or evaluative dimensions as well, and argues that resonant experiences often involve feelings of the *convergence* of our "cognitive maps" and "evaluative maps" with the affective and emotional aspects of our engagements (Rosa, 2016, 291). More generally:

resonance is a concept of *connection* between the moments, strictly separated in the enlightened-rationalist concept of the world, [of] mind and body-as-object [*Körper*] (or lived body [*Leib*] and soul), feeling and understanding, individual and community, and lastly, spirit and nature.

Rosa, 2016, 293

Alienation is, for Rosa, the opposite of resonance. Remaining with the acoustic metaphor, Rosa characterizes alienation as a "mute" or "silent" relation to the world, one in which animating vibrations are absent or have ceased. Rosa draws explicitly upon Jaeggi to characterize an alienated relation as involving a failure of assimilation. "Depression/burnout is the name of the state in which all resonance axes have become mute and deaf" (Rosa, 2016, 316). Whether it is a matter of, for example, a family, a party membership, a hobby or a religious confession, in an alienated relation, these things "don't speak to us anymore, they confront us as mute and/or threatening" (Rosa, 2016, 305). But alienated relations are not simply negative. Both Jaeggi and Rosa emphasize that actions and states of being which might be characterized as instrumental or alienated are an unavoidable, indispensable part of life, and are often necessarily connected with successful appropriation or resonant relations (Jaeggi, 2014, 207–208). Thus, the yardstick against which to evaluate possibilities for the achievement of resonant world-relations cannot be "that as many experiences as possible should be resonant experiences" (Rosa, 2016, 295; cf. 325).

Here it is worth pausing again, briefly, to make a similar point with respect to resonance as that made above with respect to Jaeggi's concept of alienation.

If resonance is a relation of connection in which matters of concern "speak to us", and if our lives are shaped in part by different arrangements of "oases" and "deserts" of resonance, it stands to reason that the possibility of and the preconditions for resonance will vary systematically for differently positioned groups in any social formation. Resonance in what Rosa terms "horizontal" relations with other people, as well as in "diagonal" relations with the material world and perhaps "vertical" (for example, spiritual or religious) relations with the world as a whole, is undoubtedly a more difficult and rare achievement on average for disadvantaged and oppressed groups than for the privileged (Rosa, 2016, 73–75).

Turning relations to the world

It should be clear why the idea of resonance might be relevant to my interest in the directedness of practice. While Rosa stresses the metaphorical character of his concept of resonance, it nevertheless does heavily imply directedness, in part through the imagery of "vibrating wires". Merleau-Ponty's notion of our connection to our surroundings by "intentional threads" comes to mind here (Merleau-Ponty, 1962). The kind of resonant experiences Rosa describes could be understood as the "vibrating" of some of these threads. Many of the fundamental affective and emotional relations we have with the world, such as anxiety and desire, are "directed forces" (Rosa, 2016, 195; cf. 200–201). In line with the notion of corporeal organization developed in the previous chapter, I want to suggest that the coexistence or even dialectical dependency of resonant and non-resonant relations to the world can be "rotationally" differentiated. That with which we are dealing "resonantly" is often, though not always, in front of us, centered on or in our anterior relational fields. The exceptions to this are to be sure not trivial. Resonant relations with affective "atmospheres" are of increasing interest to human geographers and other social scientists (Böhme, 2013). Rosa himself returns repeatedly to music as a vehicle of resonant experiences, and of course acoustic experience is not physically "frontal", though in the partly figurative sense of direction I seek to develop here, concentrating on music does involve "having it in front of us". These kinds of experiences notwithstanding, in many everyday practices to which we can have a resonant relationship, whether at work or in other contexts, we are in fact directed in a bodily and attentional way. As laid out in Chapter 3, the relation between the embodied direction of our doings and sayings and the direction of our attention may vary. Either or both of these dimensions of directedness may be the primary source of resonant experiences, and the two may "resonate" with each other, as for example when listening to music we love helps us tune in to the rhythms of a physical task.

I would like to argue as well that the directionality of resonance is closely related to "critical-creative engagement". By this I mean a relation to matters of concern in which we are able to treat them, in a "live" way, as fluid, contingent, subject to our shaping activity and involving care in the broadest sense. Critical-creative engagement can be seen as the core of much directed practice. Not every critical or creative engagement is necessarily also "resonant" in Rosa's sense. But many resonant experiences presuppose critical-creative engagement. It is easy to imagine artistic creative activity as a sort of paradigm case for this concept. But by placing the term "critical" at the beginning I wish to stress that such a relation need not only be "productive" or "constructive" but can also be "deconstructive", can involve the analysis, dissolution or disassembly of whatever we have before us. The crucial point is that *much of our critical-creative activity can only take place in front of us, when we are pointed toward it (and not toward other things)*. The schema adapted from David Wills, comprising frontal, lateral and dorsal relational fields, is thus a crucially important context for the possibility of "fluidizing" our experience of the world. I will return to this claim in discussing reification in Chapter 6, and also in the concluding chapter. The general point being urged here is that the phenomenon of resonance is configured to a significant – if variable – extent by "critical-creative engagement" and the basic schema of corporeal organization in which it is anchored. If this claim is provisionally accepted, we can turn to look more closely at what kinds of more or less alienated relations to the world take place within this spatially structured zone of live engagement. Here Jaeggi's approach to alienation will be brought into contact with writings on experiences of advanced capitalist life as "cinematic".

Montage, appropriation and will

As noted briefly in Chapter 1, some writings on the political economy of attention approach the problem of attention, in the tradition of Benjamin, in cinematic terms. Jonathan Beller argues that capitalism should be understood as a "cinematic mode of production" in which not only workers but consumers are exploited, the latter precisely in being induced to donate their attention to the realization of value (Beller, 2006). According to Beller, montage has been an organizing principle of capitalist value creation at least since the heyday of mechanized industrialism a century ago. Citing the Soviet filmmaker Vertov, Beller conceives of "cinema" as "a result of the extension of industrial processes to the senses" (Beller, 2006, 39). If montage means "organizing film fragments (shots) into a film-object" (Vertov, cited in Beller, 2006, 39), "the consciousness characteristic of montage is the consciousness endemic to modernity's assemblage process, from the assembly line to constructivism" (Beller, 2006, 39). He argues that montage was the method common to the psychological researcher Pavlov, the founder of industrial rationalization Frederick Taylor and the filmmaker Sergei Eisenstein in the early 20th century (Beller, 2006, 133). Taylor's method for dissecting and optimizing the labor process can, for example, be seen as "editing" fragments of physical movements into optimized schemata for labor processes (Beller, 2006, 134). More recently, immaterial processes of montage have gained prominence in postindustrial workplaces: "Instead of striking a blow to sheet metal wrapped around a mold or tightening a bolt, we sutured one image to the next (and, like workers who disappeared into the commodities they produced, we sutured ourselves into the image)" (Beller, 2006, 9).

Christoph Türcke (2016) and Bernard Stiegler (2011), also portray our conscious relations to the world as a matter of montage. The materials that feed into our ongoing work of montage come, in Stiegler's view, from immediate, distant and social forms of recall: "Consciousness is always in some fashion a montage of overlapping primary, secondary and tertiary memories" (Stiegler, 2011, 27–28). Again, although tertiary memories are not in any simple sense "ours", they enable us to become ourselves through processes of transindividuation. For Beller, the picture is bleaker. The materials we are now given to work with are increasingly alien and indifferent to our interests:

> They are an intensification of separation, capital's consciousness, that is, human consciousness (accumulated subjective practices) that now belongs to capital. [...] Entering through the eyes, images envelop their hosts, positing worlds, bodily configurations, and aspirations, utilizing the bio-power of concrete individuals to confer upon their propositions the aspect of reality.
>
> Beller, 2006, 247–248

Generally speaking, the work of montage takes place within the zone of critical-creative directed engagement. But the degree to which this work involves anything like "autonomy" or "resonance" is a complicated question. On the one hand, there is the issue – already discussed above – of where the materials feeding into our ongoing, directed work of montage come from, the extent to which they are "ours". On the other, there is the question of the breaks or "intervals" that require us to do the work of montage. To what extent are these intervals occasions for appropriation or the construction of resonant experiences, or alternatively, sources of alienating discontinuity and "shock"?

Here Stiegler's discussion of "adoption" can point us toward an important issue relating to direction. As discussed in Chapter 1, Stiegler's political analysis of attention has as its context the larger question of how it is that modern human beings become relatively competent adults. Through processes of transindividuation, we incorporate and integrate capabilities, traditions, and knowledge sedimented by earlier generations in the form of "tertiary memories". We access these memories through "adoption", "a process of protean interiorization" (Stiegler, 2011, 176). Much in the way Jaeggi describes appropriation, for Stiegler, adoption is not merely passive adaptation, but also involves invention (Stiegler, 2011, 176). And yet, Stiegler notes:

> an obvious question here has to do with the extent to which this inheritance is *transferable* on conditions allowing it to remain *adoptable* [...], to

what extent the individuation process of all kinds can be maintained without radical disruption by modifications that have become general and are now enormous, brutal conditions of adoption.

Stiegler, 2011, 223

By "brutal conditions of adoption" Stiegler means the accelerated, image-saturated world of technologically-enhanced neoliberal capitalism. Again, the chief way in which these brutal conditions endanger processes of adoption and render them precarious is through the destruction of *attentional capabilities* (Stiegler, 2010). Through constant confrontation with fast-moving and easily switchable media, according to Stiegler, we are losing the ability to sustain "deep attention". This raises the important question of whether the pace and nature of breaks or intervals between relatively continuous chunks or spans of concentration or activity impacts our ability to appropriate the world, in Jaeggi's sense.

> The interval, a term derived from music that specifies the space/time between notes or passages, names the cinematic juxtaposition of two social moments between which the viewer must supply the intervening elements. Thus, it is a philosophical and conceptual term, specifying a construction through the shaping of hollows or empty spaces or absences.
>
> Beller, 2006, 80, note 3

Our means of dealing with the demands of montage, with the need to fill the intervals, can likewise be more or less "ours", and here, as well, Beller sees heteronomy at work: "new forms for the imposing of continuity are created that modulate and indeed extend the shattering of reality into fragments by capitalized machinery" (Beller, 2006, 158).

The full significance of these analyses of interruption only becomes clear once we realize that *montage is sequential but not linear*; montage is *rotational*. Contrary to the image of a film-strip composed of a linear chain of still images, the intervals with which we must work in appropriating the material of our lives are moments of *turning*, however slight this turning may be in any instance. The sequence of matters we are engaged with involves changes of direction, both in attentional and practical terms, so that incorporating intervals means establishing "transverse" links. This suggests that the problem of alienation, the problem of the "inappropriable" (Jaeggi) heightened by increasingly "brutal conditions of adoption" (Stiegler) may have as much if not more to do with questions of the nature and frequency of disruptive turnings, with formal questions of the rhythms of what confronts and solicits us, as with issues of substantive content. In the final section of this chapter, I suggest some ways in which this hypothesis might be fleshed out. In keeping with the essay-character of the argument as a whole, this must remain relatively schematic.

Rupture, rhythm and alienation

Sara Ahmed's evocative phenomenological description of turning from one matter of concern to another suggests what a "rotational" account of alienation could bring to the fore:

> Say, for example, that you are concentrating. You focus. What is before you becomes the world. The edges of that world disappear as you zoom in. The object – say, the paper, and the thoughts that gather around the paper by gathering as lines on the paper – becomes what is given by losing its contours. The paper becomes worldly, which might even mean you lose sight of the table. Then, behind you, someone calls out your name. As if by force of habit, you look up, you even turn around to face what is behind you. But as your body gestures move up, as you move around, you move out of the world, without simply falling into a new one. Such moments when you "switch" dimensions can be deeply disorienting. One moment does not follow another, as a sequence of spatial givens that unfolds as moments of time. They are moments in which you lose one perspective, but the "loss" itself is not empty or waiting; it is an object, thick with presence.
>
> Ahmed, 2006, 157–158

I want to suggest that the "loss" of the previous world, as "an object, thick with presence", is how the "interval" is initially encountered, and can be thought of as the starting point for the necessary labor of montage. The loss, which at first keeps us tethered to what we have been torn away from, must itself be released so as to make room for the assembly of a new context of intelligibility – or world – around the appeal coming from without. The assembly itself, then is the actual work of connection or suture at the heart of montage.

Ahmed's description is a good place to offer a graphic illustration of turning based upon the images of the directionally asymmetrical body introduced in Chapter 4. Figure 5.1 shows Ahmed's individual engaged in one matter when a new solicitation appears (in this case in the form of a personal address, represented by the star shape).

What Ahmed describes as the experience of disorientation, and what I am suggesting is the occasion for montage, can then be represented in Figures 5.2, 5.3 and 5.4. In Figure 5.2, the person turns her body toward the address, but since she has not yet been able to rearrange her world around the new matter of concern, her lived direction "splits". The dotted outline of the lived body "left behind" retains the earlier direction, in contrast to the physical body already turned. The work of montage is then – although of course this is a simplification – depicted in Figure 5.3 as the process of realigning the lived with the physical body. Once this is accomplished, the person is fully pointed toward the source of address (Figure 5.4).

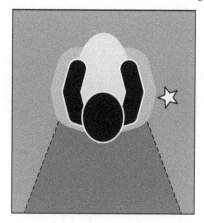

Figure 5.1 Appearance of a new solicitation

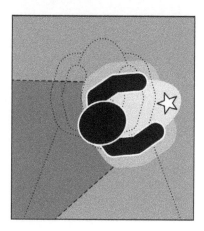

Figure 5.2 Initial bodily turning

This scene of "disorientation" in turning to address a new solicitation clarifies an important connection between time as a scarce resource for which practices "compete" (Shove, Pantzar and Watson, 2012, 127) and time as lived experience. The tension between these two temporalities invites us to linger longer over what is involved in the process Husserl calls "releasing from grasp". In *Ideas I* he writes of attending to something metaphorically in terms of the sequential process of "holding in grasp", "maintaining in grasp" and "releasing from grasp" (Husserl, 2012, 253–255; cf. Gurwitsch, 1964, 350–351). To see what is involved in releasing from grasp, it is useful to consider Gurwitsch's distinction between "continuity of consciousness" and "continuity of context" in the movement of attention (Gurwitsch, 1964, 347). "Continuity of consciousness" rests primarily on the continuity of temporal experience, the interwovenness of each present moment with retentions and protentions. Thus every conscious act which involves a theme "coming into

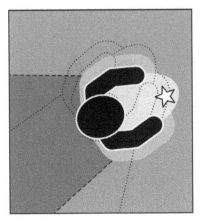

Figure 5.3 Process of realignment

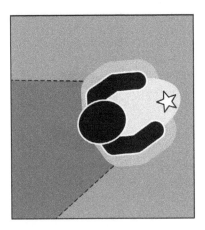

Figure 5.4 New orientation

grasp", being held onto or being released from grasp has this kind of continuity as a necessary condition (Gurwitsch, 1964, 350). "Continuity of context" additionally implies a connection of thematic relevance between one act of apprehension and the next. On the basis of this distinction there is a difference between the process of turning, on the one hand, from one theme to another theme *within the thematic field of the first theme,* and on the other, from one theme to an entirely unrelated theme. In the first case, the process of turning shows both continuity of consciousness and continuity of context; in the second case, only continuity of consciousness (Gurwitsch, 1964, 346–347). The scene described by Ahmed is of the latter type: there is only continuity of consciousness to hold onto, while continuity of context must be reassembled or built up in a process that could be more or less difficult. Insofar as recent changes in technologically mediated neoliberal capitalism are multiplying interruptions of one thematic context by elements of another, it is possible to suggest speculatively that the "rebuilding effort" involved in the work of montage will become more strenuous.

"Releasing a theme from grasp", or ceasing to carry out some step in a practice, can occur in more or less deliberate ways. At the more deliberate end of an imagined spectrum, a thought or an activity can be "set down" before we turn to another one. Ideally, setting something down involves a lack of excessive urgency or hurry, so that one can reach a "good stopping point" before turning away from the matter at hand. A good stopping point may be dictated by the matter itself, for example by the need to stir a pot so the newly added ingredients get mixed before they simmer for a few minutes unattended, or the need to complete an online purchase before the system kicks us out and forces us to start over. A good stopping point may also be determined by our own needs as those carrying out practices, for example, the need to complete a sentence or a thought before moving on to the next thing. A second feature of deliberately "setting something down" is that it makes sense to set it down in an appropriate literal or figurative place, that is, to place it in its proper context. As with finding a good stopping point, setting something down in an appropriate place may be required either by external or internal factors. A hot pot or a freshly-painted piece of furniture cannot be set down just anywhere. Internal reasons often have to do with making it easier for oneself or others to find or pick up the matter or the thought again later. For example, a half-finished document should be saved in the right folder if we want to find it easily later. Such forms of "setting down" can occur as a result of solicitations arising within the thematic field of a topic, or the pragmatic field of a practice, or alternatively from outside the current fields of concern. Broadly speaking, setting something down tends to require at least some additional time beyond the moment at which we stop dealing with it directly.

At the other end of the imagined spectrum, releasing from grasp is not at all a deliberate "setting down" but rather something more like suddenly "dropping" a matter of concern, or having it "torn from one's grasp". This may not be an unpleasant experience: the receipt of an unexpected call from an old friend, or a feeling of suddenly noticing the beauty of one's surroundings in the middle of thinking about something else, may be welcome. The disorientation evoked in Ahmed's scene, for example, may be directly followed by positive or negative experiences. Surprise, a break in the continuity of expected events, is at the heart of comedy, for example, and can be as easily followed by delight as by chagrin. Being seized by a sudden urge can often be pleasurable. Crucially, responsiveness to the needs of others, a core prerequisite for caring relationships, depends upon our ability to be interrupted unexpectedly (Held, 2006). More unpleasant or unwanted interruptions or distractions might include sudden, loud sounds, physical pain or commercial interruptions while watching a film. These examples share a certain suddenness or urgency, but it is also possible to imagine, for instance, a slowly building pain or low-level irritant that at some point reaches a threshold beyond which it can no longer be ignored.

Whether sudden or more gradual, whether pleasant or unpleasant, solicitations that lead to our dropping something in a non-deliberate way generally do not give us as much of a chance either to bring what we're doing to a good stopping point or to set it down in its appropriate context. This can lead to problems with the abandoned matter of concern (burned food, aborted transactions, lost files, etc.) as well as with our own ability to return to it later. Ahmed suggests a third result of this kind of unexpected abandonment: that the lost continuity of context noted above requires time and effort to overcome, a new act of assembling the world or context within which the obtrusive theme or matter of concern can be placed. Montage, in other words, can involve very different processes requiring different levels of effort, depending upon the extent to which the sequence of "clips" to which we turn are expected, thematically related, amenable to fusion. To tie this back to Schatzki's practice theory, it is worth pondering whether more fragmentary, less deliberate demands upon our capabilities of montage have the effect of forcing what were lived previously as more continuous, "integrative" practices into artificially modularized "dispersed" practices, and thereby degrading them (Schatzki, 1996, 91–92, 100). This could be seen as the practical analogue to the shift from "deep" to "hyper" attention highlighted by Stiegler. This is an important issue in approaching the question of how appropriable our social worlds remain, and how likely they are to be experienced as alienating. In thinking about all of this, though, it is important to bear in mind the figure of thought Jaeggi adapts from Tugendhat, namely, that the issue isn't so much simply whether our worlds remain appropriable because we can in some sense "keep up" with the demands for montage that they present. Rather, the issue is a second-order one: *whether the mix of the appropriable and the less-appropriable we experience is itself something we can appropriate or adopt as our own.*

The aggregate effects of new media, operating in the context of the increasing pressures of neoliberal capitalism, heighten the frequency and intensity of demands and solicitations placed upon our faculties of montage (Rosa, 2015). This is a matter not only of the pace and rhythm of solicitations but also of the fact that the proportion of our turnings located toward the deliberate end of the spectrum will tend to shrink, and the proportion of turnings that involve dropping an engagement unexpectedly because of a powerful solicitation will tend to grow. Thus we are ever more often thrown back upon mere continuity of consciousness as a basis for suturing together experiences as continuity of context is less often maintained. Henri Lefebvre's preliminary and schematic thoughts on "rhythmanalysis" can serve as a helpful frame for thinking about these issues (Lefebvre, 2004). Lefebvre sees modern Western capitalist life as shaped in important ways by ongoing tensions and struggles between long-standing quasi-natural rhythms such as diurnal, seasonal, life and bodily cycles, on the one hand, and imposed, artificial temporalities arising from capitalist work and consumption regimes on the other. Both bodies and their environments give forth what Lefebvre nicely terms "garlands" of rhythms, and the key question is whether the interaction, the existing "polyrhythmia" between and within these two produces "eurhythmia", a harmonious integration of rhythms, or pathological and discordant "arrhythmia" (Lefebvre, 2004, 20, 16). "In arrhythmia, rhythms break apart, alter and bypass *synchronization*", possibly leading in extreme cases to "morbid and then fatal desynchronization" (Lefebvre, 2004, 67, 68). The "living body" is the site where these issues play out (Lefebvre and Régulier, 2004, 81).

Eurhythmia is not necessarily a normal or stable state, since different rhythmic orders are always converging in, on and through the living body. But the chances of disruption and discordance are heightened according to Lefebvre, by our increasingly comprehensive and incessant exposure to, our "occupation" by, "the media day":

> Who can hold back the flows, the currents, the tides (or swamps) that break over the world, pieces of information and disinformation, more or less well-founded analyses [...], publications, messages – cryptic or otherwise[?] You can go without sleep, or doze off [...].
>
> Lefebvre, 2004, 46

The media day "fragments" by relentlessly presenting us with choices (Lefebvre, 2004, 47). This way of framing the issue of disruption and redirection of our attention and activities clearly connects with the outlines of a political economy of attention sketched in Chapter 1, but also suggests a new way of understanding alienation in terms of the frequency of disruptions and interruptions and the resulting "arrhythmic" desynchronization of lived experience. In a paper giving an overview of the "rhythmanalytical project", Lefebvre and Catherine Régulier reflect upon the question of whether there might not be a "third time" in addition to the cyclical-natural and the (capitalist) linear-artificial temporalities whose clash lies at the center of rhythmanalysis. It seems to me not at all accidental that they identify this third temporality as "appropriated time":

> Whether normal or exceptional, it is a time that forgets time, during which time no longer counts (and is no longer counted). It arrives or emerges when an activity brings plenitude, whether this activity be banal (an occupation, a piece of work), subtle (meditation, contemplation), spontaneous (a child's game, or even one for adults) or sophisticated. This activity is in harmony with itself and with the world. It has several traits of self-creation or of a gift rather than of an obligation or an imposition come from without. It *is* in time: it *is* a time, but does not reflect on it.
>
> Lefebvre and Régulier, 2004, 76–77

Such "appropriated time" conforms in this description to the basic sense of appropriation Jaeggi puts forward as the basis for non-alienated relations with the world, and suggests Rosa's state of resonance as well. It is also strikingly similar to the concept of "deep attention" foregrounded by Stiegler as that capacity of appropriating tertiary memory which is placed increasingly under threat.

To round out the argument of this chapter, it makes sense to ask and provisionally answer one final question. My argument up to this point is intended to suggest that an alienated, non-resonant relation to the world is in part caused by excessively frequent and discordant interruption, requiring too-frequent turning from one matter to another, too much montage-work, too much fragmentation of integrative practices into dispersed modules, and tending to produce a state of disorientation that renders effectively engaging in an activity or maintaining a focus of attention or an integrated practice difficult. All of this has at least as much to do with direction as it does with distance. Accepting this proposal for the moment, what is it that has caused the much-remarked increase in the frequency of solicitations? One part of the answer is clearly the proliferation of choices for denizens of the Global North, whether through the invention of an ever more vast range of products (Schwartz, 2005; Zerubavel, 2015) or the marketization of formerly state-provided goods and services under neoliberal logics of governance (Peck, 2010; Dardot and Laval, 2014). Another related but more proximate cause driving this pattern, especially for the digitally connected, is identified by the neurologist Adam Gazzaley and the psychologist Larry Rosen (Gazzaley and Rosen, 2016).

The basic framework Gazzaley and Rosen set out is structured around the relationship between what the cognitive science and psychology literatures call "executive functions" such as evaluation, decision-making and planning, and a related but distinct set of functions of "cognitive control" through which the decisions and judgments reached executively must be realized or carried out. Cognitive control functions include attention, working memory and "goal management" or prioritization. Gazzaley and Rosen's hypothesis about human evolution is that:

> our cognitive control abilities that are necessary for the enactment of our goals have not evolved to the same degree as the executive functions required for goal setting. Indeed, the fundamental limitations in our cognitive control abilities do not differ greatly from those observed in other primates, with whom we shared common ancestors tens of millions of years ago.
>
> Gazzaley and Rosen, 2016, 9

Basically, Gazzaley and Rosen assert, humans have long been "information-foragers" evolved to be easily distracted by novel information, a trait which in evolutionary terms conferred survival advantages (Gazzaley and Rosen, 2016, 12, 13–14). Put differently, the omnidirectional vulnerability and openness that forms one half of our directional asymmetry has been important in human evolution. Executive and cognitive control functions have been crucial because their gradual emergence allowed our distant ancestors to break what in most animals is a relatively immediate and reflex-like, non-deliberate sequence linking perceptual or sensual stimulation to responsive action (see also Bergson, 1991, 95ff). In the course of evolution a space was opened up or a buffer established in which the constant solicitation of bottom-up impulses from the environment, to which we are highly attuned, could be sorted for relevancy, urgency, etc. and connected more deliberately to selective responses. Our faculties of cognitive control, though, because less well-developed than executive decision-making, have left us fundamentally vulnerable to distraction from carrying out intended goals. This is of course a simplified model of only one aspect of human evolution. Nonetheless, it comports with some results of phenomenological and practice-theoretic research (for example, Ricœur's 2007 argument placing "hesitation" at the heart of a phenomenology of human freedom).

With respect to the "high tech world" of 21st century information society, Gazzaley and Rosen's general argument is not new: the stimulus-rich artificial environments we are building for ourselves heighten our susceptibility to unhelpful distraction. This point is made also by many of the authors discussed in Chapter 1. What is new and interesting about Gazzaley and Rosen's argument is the specific model they develop to explain the processes through which recent technological changes have come tendentially to overwhelm our cognitive control functions. Their model is an adaptation of the "Marginal Value Theorem" (MVT) used by biologists for decades to explain the foraging behavior of animals. If humans are defined as information foragers, they reason, it makes some sense to translate models of foraging into informational terms. The basic scenario of the MVT is constructed around the behavior of an animal, say, a squirrel foraging for nuts in a particular tree or patch of forest. The question is, how long will the squirrel remain in the same tree or patch, given the diminishing ease of finding additional nuts, before it decides to abandon the tree or patch it is in and move to another one? The MVT assumes that the diminishing benefits of staying in the same tree or patch can be calibrated by a stable relationship linking the time required to find additional nuts where the squirrel already is to the time required to travel to the next tree or patch. Experimental results show that foraging animals appear to be innately aware of the relation between these two times, and the increasing time between finding nuts triggers a move at a relatively predictable point. The analogous process for humans would involve a felt comparison between the rewards of continuing to concentrate on the current theme or matter of concern and the rewards of moving to a different focus.

Of course, many additional factors, for example, perceptions of danger from potential predators, intervene even for squirrels. When the MVT is transposed to humans in an information environment, the picture is yet far more complicated. Gazzaley and Rosen note as important internal or dispositional factors that arise for humans boredom and anxiety, the latter including the newly identified "fear of missing out" (FOMO) that seems to be more frequent among heavier users of social networking sites (Gazzaley and Rosen, 2016, 163–164, 171). Their core argument, though, is that the technologies of the information age are artificially and drastically reducing the physical and time-costs of shifting our attention and engagement. The perceived, and the real, physical distance, or "expected transit time", to the next patch of novel information is rapidly shrinking (Gazzaley and Rosen, 2016, 164). To stick with the squirrel analogy, new attention-capture technologies have brought about a situation where "a neighboring tree could [...] throw a nut at a squirrel any time it was interested in being fed upon" (Gazzaley and Rosen, 2016, 176).

Here we can draw a connection to the spatial complex composed of anterior, lateral and dorsal fields. The reason the ever-more-numerous electronic screens occupying people especially in wealthy societies seem to exercise such a powerful pull on our attention and activities is that "the next patch" is increasingly available in the same intensively monitored core of our anterior relational field where ever more of our activities take place. We still receive bottom-up solicitations from the full spatial and thematic range of possible sources, behind us, nearby, from within the body, and so on. But many of our activities are carried out in the convergence zone of our hands, voices and visual gazes in our near frontal space, and on *multifunctional devices* that are often simultaneously our instruments of labor and potential sources of interruption and distraction. There is hardly any cost in time or effort in turning from one matter to another, and turning itself becomes a movement of infinitesimal smallness. In this light, the rather laborious physical process of turning described by Ahmed (see above) seems almost quaint.

Stiegler and other authors discussed in Chapter 1 suggest that "attention deficit disorders" may fairly be seen to characterize not individuals but increasingly larger social formations as well. In line with the insights of critical disability studies, we can see this as a form of relational disability. The capturing and commercial exploitation of attention, and the associated impacts upon our ability effectively to carry out tasks of increasingly feverish montage-work, is a socio-technical development, closely connected to advanced neoliberal capitalism. We may be sanguine about it, and trust that young people's learned ability to exercise what Hayles calls hyper attention comes with larger social benefits such as an increasing collective ability to make quick decisions based upon meager information (Hayles, 2012). But the clinical evidence of pathologies reviewed by Gazzaley and Rosen is quite clear: whether in the realm of education, safety, the workplace, relationships, or mental and emotional health, the vast bulk of research they summarize shows a clear erosion of effectiveness, satisfaction and success with increasing bottom-up solicitation pressure from and engagements with electronic devices in attempts to "multi-task" (Gazzaley and Rosen, 2016, chapters 7 and 8). Cognitive control functions are only very modestly elastic: "Our brains do not parallel process information, as demanded by many of our daily activities, if those activities both require cognitive control" (Gazzaley and Rosen, 2016, 77). We delude ourselves if we believe in an upwardly elastic capability to "multi-task" without loss of effectiveness (Gazzaley and Rosen, 2016, 177).

The question of disorientation raised by Ahmed, and its relation to the possibility of establishing resonant, non-alienated relations with the world through appropriation, as these processes are conceived by Jaeggi and Rosa, is inherently related to the rhythms through which we are solicited and addressed by internal and external matters. The ongoing proliferation of choices confronting increasing numbers of people, beyond as well as within the Global North, is being mediated to an increasing extent by technologies that allow ever more carefully calibrated presentation of options within the core of our anterior relational fields. In a physical sense, dropping whatever we were doing to turn to something else is getting steadily easier. But the accelerated demands upon our capabilities of montage places our ability to appropriate and focus upon tasks and themes under ever more pressure. Alienation defined in this way, however, is far from the only sense in which phenomena of turning shape or are shaped by social processes. As noted at the beginning of this chapter, critiques of alienation are closely related to, and often paired with, critiques of reification, in which the accent is on how aspects of the world, including ourselves, are objectified, hypostatized or otherwise deanimated. Chapter 6 argues that a sensitivity to the dynamics of turning can also shed a new light upon issues of reification and the role of reification in socio-spatial processes.

References

Ahmed, S. (2006). *Queer Phenomenology: Orientations, Objects, Others*. Durham, NC: Duke University Press.

Beller, J. (2006). *The Cinematic Mode of Production: Attention Economy and the Society of the Spectacle*. Dartmouth, NH: Dartmouth College Press.

Bergson, H. (1991). *Matter and Memory*. Brooklyn, NY: Zone Books.

Bewes, T. (2002). *Reification, or the Anxiety of Late Capitalism*. London: Verso.

Böhme, G. (2013). *Atmosphäre: Essays zur neuen Ästhetik*. Frankfurt am Main: Suhrkamp.

Dardot, P. and Laval, C. (2014). *The New Way of the World: On Neoliberal Society*. Trans. G. Elliott. London: Verso.

Gazzaley, A. and Rosen, L. (2016). *The Distracted Mind: Ancient Brains in a High-Tech World*. Cambridge, MA: MIT Press.

Gurwitsch, A. (1964). *The Field of Consciousness*. Pittsburgh, PA: Duquesne University Press.

Hayles, K. (2012). *How We Think: Digital Media and Contemporary Technogenesis*. Chicago, IL: University of Chicago Press.

Held, V. (2006). *The Ethics of Care: Personal, Political and Global*. Oxford: Oxford University Press.

Husserl, E. (2012). *Ideas*. Trans. W.R.B. Gibson. London: Routledge.

Jaeggi, R. (2014). *Alienation*. Trans. A. Smith. New York: Columbia University Press.

James, W. (1950). *The Principles of Psychology.* 2 Volumes. New York: Dover.

Kirsch, S. and Mitchell, D. (2004). The nature of things: dead labor, non-human actors, and the persistence of Marxism. *Antipode,* 36(4), 687–705.

Lefebvre, H. (2004). *Rhythmanalysis: Space, Time and Everyday Life.* Trans. S. Elden and G. Moore. London: Continuum.

Lefebvre, H. and Régulier, C. (2004). The rhythmanalytical project. In: H. Lefebvre, *Rhythmanalysis: Space, Time and Everyday Life.* Trans. S. Elden and G. Moore. London: Continuum, pp. 71–83.

Merleau-Ponty, M. (1962). *Phenomenology of Perception.* Trans. C. Smith. London: Routledge and Kegan Paul.

Mészáros, I. (2006). *Marx's Theory of Alienation.* Delhi: Aakar Books.

Ollman, B. (1976). *Alienation: Marx's Conception of Man in Capitalist Society.* 2nd ed Cambridge: Cambridge University Press.

Ricœur, P. (2007). *Freedom and Nature: The Voluntary and the Involuntary.* Trans E. Kohak. Evanston, IL: Northwestern University Press.

Peck, J. (2010). *Constructions of Neoliberal Reason.* Oxford: Oxford University Press.

Rosa, H. (2015). *Social Acceleration: A New Theory of Modernity.* Trans. J. Trejo-Mathys. New York: Columbia University Press.

Rosa, H. (2016). *Resonanz: eine Soziologie der Weltbeziehung.* Frankfurt am Main: Suhrkamp.

Schatzki, T. (1996). *Social Practices: A Wittgensteinian Approach to Human Activity and the Social.* Cambridge: Cambridge University Press.

Schütz, A. and Luckmann, T. (1973). *Structures of the Lifeworld,* Vol. 1. Trans. R.N. Zaner and H.T. Engelhardt, Jr. Evanston, IL: Northwestern University Press.

Schwartz, B. (2005). *The Paradox of Choice: Why More is Less.* New York: Harper Perennial.

Shove, E., Pantzar, M., and Watson, M. (2012). *The Dynamics of Social Practice: Everyday Life and How It Changes.* London: Sage.

Stiegler, B. (2010). *Taking Care of Youth and the Generations.* Trans. S. Barker. Stanford CA: Stanford University Press.

Stiegler, B. (2011). *Technics and Time, 3: Cinematic Time and the Question of Malaise.* Trans. S. Barker. Stanford, CA: Stanford University Press.

Türcke, C. (2016). Aufmerksamkeitsdefizitkultur. In: J. Müller, A. Nießeler and A. Rauh, eds., *Aufmerksamkeit: Neue Humanwissenschaftliche Perspektiven.* Bielefeld: Transcript, pp. 101–114.

Zerubavel, E. (2015). *Hidden in Plain Sight: The Social Structure of Irrelevance.* Oxford: Oxford University Press.

6 Turning and reification

Embodied subjects are both fundamentally open and fundamentally directed (Chapter 4). Through our directedness we can be related to the world in more or less resonant or alienated ways (Chapter 5). The concepts of montage and rhythm were raised in the last chapter to suggest a way of understanding world relations in terms of turnings or changes in the direction of practice rather than in terms of the more common trope of distance or separation. Disorientation and desynchronization attendant upon too-frequent or disruptive turnings can, so I argued, be important sources of an alienated relation to the world. This chapter completes the trajectory of the previous two chapters by addressing the ways in which turning contributes to the construction of the world (of objects, other people, relations, etc.). The last chapter focused primarily upon alienation, that is, subjective experiences of world-relations; the main theme here will be the related phenomenon of reification.

Again, a central claim anchoring this entire book is that embodied human beings are directionally asymmetrical. This means, on the one hand, that we are inherently open or vulnerable to being addressed, appealed to, or solicited from *all directions*, and on the other, that we carry out many of our active practices in a more directionally limited way. In performing active practices, every time we turn toward a new matter of concern, we necessarily turn away from others. As argued in Chapter 4, the zone of our active, potentially creative and critical engagement with the world is often in the anterior relational field ensconced within the lateral field of our combined manual, visual and oral skills and capabilities. Even when we are "just thinking" about something, as William James already noted, our engagement is directed in a way that deactivates other potential matters of concern. New themes and matters of concern can emerge to solicit our attention and agency from all directions, both within and outside our bodily boundaries. But when we turn to one of them, we necessarily drop others. This utterly mundane process, I want to argue here, is every bit as important as, if not more important than, the more familiar processes of stabilization that have long occupied critical social theory under the headings of reification, fetishization, essentialism, hypostatization or naturalization. Turning away from matters of concern itself constitutes an independent form of reification. Or better, a consideration of turning away deepens our sense of what reification means.

This chapter proceeds as follows. First, I briefly summarize some of the main features of the concept of reification as it has been developed on the basis of the work of Marx and Heidegger. To throw the directional approach to reification into sharper relief, the second section discusses Sara Ahmed's insightful analysis of Husserl's writing table scenario, a particularly clear account of reification as a matter of directional positionality. As noted in the Introduction, however, positionality does not fully explain the role of direction in the politics of attention and practice. The third section seeks to illustrate this claim by building upon Ahmed's account to identify a more temporal and performative directional dimension of reification. This is manifested not in the positional state of *being turned away* but in the *process of turning away* from a matter of concern with which we have been engaged. A focus upon turning away brings into relief the way in which not only what is foregrounded in reification but also what is ignored or backgrounded is in a specific sense immobilized or "re-reified". The concept of re-reification is introduced by means of Husserl's graphical illustrations of retention and time-consciousness. The fourth section sketches two kinds of implication of the analysis of re-reification. On the one hand I further elaborate Husserl's graphics in order to suggest how the fragmentation of experience can be grasped. Secondly, and most importantly, I argue that re-reification applies to publicly observable practices in general, not just to our personal memories. I support this claim by referring to Schatzki's discussion of the "segmentation" and the event-character of temporal-spatial practice. Re-reification is also illustrated in the context of intersubjective interactions. The final, brief coda brings the argument of Part II to a close.

Reification and the as-structure

As noted in Chapter 5, Marx and Heidegger can justifiably be seen as the founders of the two most influential approaches to problematic aspects of our relations to the world. Despite different theoretical starting points, both Marx and Heidegger "thematize the dominance of modern individuals' reified relations to world and self [...], a situation in which individuals mistakenly view the world as given rather than as the result of their own world-creating acts" (Jaeggi, 2014, 11). In Marx's formulation in the first volume of *Capital*, it is a matter of a "definite social relation" between individuals assuming "the fantastic form of a relation between things" (Marx, 1967, 77). The critique of reification is most elaborately developed by Lukács in his *History and Class Consciousness* (Lukács, 1971). The historical materialist analysis of reification describes it in terms of the misrecognition of social relations as relations between objects, a misrecognition encouraged by and manifested in the capitalist commodity form (Lukács, 1971, 86–87). The commodity form enshrines "dead labor" in a seemingly inert material object (Kirsch and Mitchell, 2004).

Heidegger's analysis of reification is based upon the famous distinction developed in the workshop scenario in *Being and Time*, between the "readiness to hand" [*Zuhandenheit*] of tools in their normal use and the "presence at hand" [*Vorhandenheit*] they may suddenly acquire if they break (Heidegger, 1962, 67, 98ff). Present-at-hand objects, like reified commodities, appear as separate and inert things, artificially divorced from the processual involvement in equipmental contexts and in human being-in-the-world that constitutes their meaning. Human beings, as well, may be reified, whether as subjects simply assumed to be present (Heidegger, 1962, 72) or as labor-power (Lukács, 1971). Both the Marxist and the Heideggerian traditions of critique perceive reification not only at the level of individual understandings of the world but also at more world-historical timescales. For Lukács, following Marx, it is only once the commodity form has become pervasive with the historical pre-eminence of capitalism that reification becomes the dominant mode of relating to the world (Lukács, 1971). For Heidegger, the historical advance of the understanding of being in terms of presence-at-hand can be seen in the increasing dominance of technology, which transforms the world into "standing reserve" (Heidegger, 1977).

In the most general sense, reification involves the substitution of a mistaken understanding of something for a more accurate understanding. Central to this mistaken understanding is a referential "as-structure": human relations are mistakenly identified *as* relations between things (Lukács, 1971, 86–87); a broken hammer is mistakenly perceived *as* an isolated object (Heidegger, 1962, 102–103). In analyses of reification, it is not only a question of getting the "as-reference" wrong; the as-structure itself is part of the problem. Graham Harman paraphrases the implications of Heidegger's argument regarding the inadequacy of the as-structure as an account of the existence of beings:

> A thing appears as what it is; entities are encountered on the plane of the as-structure. Phenomenology has long focused our attention on this basic appearance-character of reality, which precedes any distinction between correctness, semblance, and falsity. Every phenomenon is necessarily an appearance taken "as" something, whether it be empty hallucination or unshakeable fact. But the thing "as" thing is not the same as the thing itself, which can *never* be openly encountered.
>
> Harman, 2002, 69

The problem with the as-structure in Marxist accounts is not that "the thing itself" can never be "openly encountered". It is that the as-structure reinforces the tendency to see relations or products of human labor as objectified and inert.

Timothy Bewes, in a subtle dialectical elaboration of the Marxist tradition, defines reification more broadly as "the moment that a process or relation is generalized into an abstraction, and thereby turned into a 'thing'" (Bewes,

2002, 3). Thus, reification is at work not only in the economic realm or in our understanding of beings but, for example, in "the broader socio-political sphere […] in every instance of racism and sexism" (Bewes, 2002, 4). Bewes draws upon postcolonial theory, the Frankfurt school and other critical literatures to support his contention that the problem of reification continues to be a major reference point even where it is not explicitly acknowledged as such. Reification was presumed in some corners of critical discourse to have been superseded by the poststructuralist and postcolonial critiques that denounced the inherent dualism of the term, its clear intimation of an other, non-reified state now threatened or entirely lost. However, Bewes argues, reification continues to haunt these discourses, as well, in the form of a pervasive anxiety and an implicit allegiance to a non-reified "other" form of social life of the sort they claim to abjure (Bewes, 2002, 58, 69, 112ff.). Despite protestations to the contrary, "[a]ll the signs are that the overriding characteristic of contemporary consciousness is precisely the *fear of reification*" (Bewes, 2002, 173). In my view this is a broadly valid conclusion for critical social and cultural scholarship, if not for the larger socio-political and economic context of the 21st century Global North.

Anxiety regarding reification cannot be dismissed as irrational or misguided, of course, for reifications of racial, gender or sexual identity, "the poor", and any number of other categories have played a major role in systematic violence, exploitation, and discrimination against countless groups throughout human history. And yet "[t]here are no theories which escape reification" (Bewes, 2002, xvi). This appreciation of the difficulty of escaping or avoiding reification, even in critical theories aimed at exposing it, is a useful frame for the argument presented here. I, too, am interested in reconciling what I believe to be the unavoidability of reification with what I am equally convinced is an absolute necessity to analyze it critically. Yet the ambition of this chapter is to offer a somewhat different understanding of reification than those familiar from the Marxist and Heideggerian traditions. To introduce this alternative approach it is helpful to give a particular twist to an oft-repeated phrase from Marx. In the first chapter of the first volume of *Capital*, Marx explains the way qualitatively different kinds of labor can be reduced to equivalents of quantitatively different amounts of unskilled labor. He goes on to bracket such qualitative differences and assume that all labor is generic unskilled labor in his subsequent discussions. But first he sketches the establishment of these equivalences with an arresting formulation: "The different proportions in which different sorts of labor are reduced to unskilled labor as their standard are established by a social process that goes on behind the backs of the producers, and, consequently, appears to be fixed by custom" (Marx, 1967, 51–52). The idea of social processes going on "behind the backs of the producers" has been adopted and adapted by many critical scholars to describe both specific and general aspects of social reproduction and structural causation. I would like to suggest that reification can be more completely understood if we supplement existing accounts of it with a perspective in which "having one's back turned" toward a potential matter of concern is understood as itself a form reification.

The backside of the world: Husserl at his table

We can begin to get a sharper directional sense of reification through Sara Ahmed's reflections on the "backside" of Husserl's phenomenology. Husserl's foundational thoughts on attention were introduced in Chapter 2 through an illustrative scenario from *Ideas I* that has him sitting at his writing table. The table itself supports a range of objects (papers, an inkwell) between which he can move his attention (Husserl, 2012, 65–66). Husserl had already introduced this tableau of the writing table in an earlier section of *Ideas I* in the process of explaining the "natural standpoint" in which a many-layered "world" is present to us unreflectively in the course of daily life (Husserl, 2012, 51–52). In a subtle reading of this scenario, Ahmed teases out the ways in which what is bracketed from consideration in Husserl's idyllic writing table scene functions as an unacknowledged support for its reification. "Being orientated toward the writing table", Ahmed observes, "not only relegates other rooms in the house to the background, but also might depend *on the work done to keep the desk clear*" (Ahmed, 2006, 30). Referring to the long history of feminist scholarship on the subject, she suggests that it is often women who "do the work required to keep such spaces available for men and the work they do" (Ahmed, 2006, 30–31). All of this work is invisible. Children, for example, remain in the background of Husserl's active concerns as he sits at his writing table. Children are a possible stopover for his freely wandering attention and nothing more, "because others (wives, mothers, nannies) care for them" (Ahmed, 2006, 31). Ahmed juxtaposes to Husserl's serene and reflective situation the harried experiences recounted by the feminist theorist Adrienne Rich of trying to write a letter but being repeatedly pulled away from her table by the demands of a child (Ahmed, 2006, 32). The children Husserl need not concern himself with have been bracketed in an "act of relegation" it is his privilege to make, a privilege many working women still do not share even today (Ahmed, 2006, 31). Seen in this way, the phenomenological "method" of bracketing or *epoché* no longer appears as a technical procedure for transcending the empirical world, as Husserl had wished it to be.

> Perhaps to bracket does not mean to transcend, even if we put something aside. We remain reliant on what we put in brackets; indeed the activity of bracketing may sustain the fantasy that "what we put aside" can be transcended in the first place.
>
> Ahmed, 2006, 33

To pick up a metaphor from the previous chapter, this bracketing as analysed by Ahmed can be thought of as the scenes cut out of a movie in the process of montage.

Ahmed's larger point is to advance a program of "queer phenomenology" centered on the problem of "orientation", a phenomenology which "faces the back, which looks 'behind' phenomenology, which hesitates at the sight of the philosopher's back" (Ahmed, 2006, 29). Thus her analysis complements that of David Wills discussed in Chapter 4 (Wills, 2008). Both authors haul the backside of human embodiment and human relations with the world into view and thus reveal corporeal, affective and discursive directional selectivity as a distinctive medium of naturalizations or reifications. They focus, that is, upon the clips left lying on the cutting floor in the process of montage, and upon how it is that we don't attend to them. Being turned away is in an important sense a zero-sum game. If we are oriented toward a matter of concern, we may relate to it in a reifying or a non-reifying way, according to whether and how our critical-creative focus is brought to bear upon it. Not being oriented toward it, though, at least temporarily rules out critical-creative engagement. Ahmed, paraphrasing Linda Akoff, brings this insight to a fine point: "If race is behind what we do, then it is what we do" (Ahmed, 2006, 131). This is an efficient summary of the first "rotational" sense of reification I want to highlight.

In effect, Ahmed's argument is a directional version of more familiar analyses of positionality. As mentioned in Chapter 4, Ahmed also designates the "phenomenology of the 'I can'" a "white" phenomenology (Ahmed, 2006, 138). Challenging white phenomenology means, in part, bringing into view what it ignores, what is "behind" it. The core insight of feminist and anti-racist standpoint epistemologies, namely that oppression is more apparent to the oppressed than to the oppressors, is one important basis upon which to bring previously invisible relations into view, and this is in effect what Ahmed does with Husserl (Haraway, 1988). This directional view of positionality is valid and important as far as it goes. Indeed, it suggests that the present book itself "does race" by the simple fact of not being turned toward genealogies of hierarchical difference. However, I would argue that it also contributes to the "undoing" of race. Building upon Ahmed's analysis, I seek to challenge the figure of general possibility, the "I can" central to white phenomenology, in a different and complementary way. My argument is that the "I can" is deceptive not only because it obscures others whose "I cannot" forms the unacknowledged foundation for the "I can" of the privileged. It is also deceptive because, even for the relatively privileged, the "I can" is constantly and intimately linked to an insufficiently acknowledged "I cannot". The argument here thus attends to the dynamic, performative process of turning toward and away from matters of concern. Our turning *always has two sides: destabilization and (re)stabilization.* We are directionally asymmetrical beings (see Chapter 4). Whatever we turn away from thus necessarily sinks into a state of attentional and practical abeyance *for us.* This restabilization is never complete: destabilization of what has previously been taken for granted does make a lasting difference. But the difference it makes is perhaps more modest and more complicated than we tend to assume.

Turning, retention and re-reification

This section identifies an additional, hitherto unremarked directional dimension of reification that emerges from the *movement* of attentive and practical engagement. Quite apart from whether or not we experience something in a reified way, turning away from it, so I will argue, "re-reifies" it. In the language of montage, not just the clips we never included in the film, the clips left lying on the cutting floor, but the clips retained and integrated into our filmic experience are deanimated, re-reified, when we turn away from them. To bring the contours of this additional form of reification into view, it is useful to turn to a different line of thinking developed by Husserl in his writings on time consciousness and memory. The terminology of memory and forgetting is central to many discussions of reification. Forgetting can be seen here as the process by which mis-recognition leads to not noticing the contingent or processual character of something any longer (Massey, 2005, 151). As Adorno would write to Benjamin, "all reification is a forgetting, objects become purely thing-like the moment they are retained for us without the continued presence of their other aspects: when something of them has been forgotten" (Adorno, quoted in Bewes, 2002, 208).

But forgetting is central to reification also in another way, at the micro-level of our daily engagements. In Chapter 1 Husserl's concept of retention was briefly introduced to help explain Bernard Stiegler's notion of "tertiary retentions", the long archive of memories and traditions humans have learned to externalize in tools and inscriptions (Stiegler, 1998). Here it is worth returning to the concepts of primary and secondary retention Husserl had distinguished in his lectures on time consciousness (Husserl, 1991). These concepts will be the basis for a way of visualizing and thinking about re-reification. Husserl develops his distinction between retention and recollection or secondary memory around a hypothetical account of the experience of hearing a tone in the context of a musical melody. The hypothetical tone

> begins and ends, and after it has ended, its whole duration-unity, the unity of the whole process in which it begins and ends, "recedes" into the ever-more-distant past. In this sinking back I still "hold onto it", have it in a "retention". And as long as the retention lasts, the tone has its own temporality; it is the same, its duration is the same.
>
> Husserl, 1991, 25

Thanks to this retention "a looking-back upon what has elapsed is possible. The retention itself is not a looking-back that makes the elapsed phase into an object" (Husserl, 1991, 122).

Retention, in other words, is a form of memory seamlessly attached to and trailing out behind the presently perceived moment, not a distinct, referential memory "of" something that has ended and is now being recalled. Only once a retention has ended, only once it is no longer a seamless part our lived present, does it become potentially available for recollection. Secondary retentions or recollections are what we typically think of as "memories" in the everyday sense, that is, as experiences, events or episodes that we can recall. Primary retention is the condition of possibility of these everyday memories. It is also the basis of the continuity of intentional consciousness. For if each instant of experiencing something, for example a tone, did not in some way retain the previous instants and at the same time look forward to coming development or continuation, it would be impossible to recognize any connection between them, any temporal unity of the experienced phenomenon. Formulating the distinction between ordinary recollections and retentions proper, or primary memories, and the analogous distinction between ordinary expectations and "protentions", was one of Husserl's important conceptual advances. The idea of a present involving both retentions and protentions was a crucial antecedent to Heidegger's development of the temporal ekstases of *Dasein* (Heidegger, 1962).

One of the most interesting aspects of Husserl's account of retention is the set of diagrams he develops to illustrate it. I will adapt these diagrams as a way of illustrating the claim made here that an additional kind of reification is at work in our everyday lives beyond what has already been discussed in the critical literature. The adapted diagrams will, in effect, depict the process of montage-as-turning introduced in the previous chapter, but will emphasize issues of reification of the world rather than alienation as a mode of experiencing it. Exactly what Husserl's diagrams were designed to represent, and the role they play in the development of Husserl's conceptualization of temporality, are complex questions. James Dodd argues that they can best be understood as "a graphic representation of the inner perspective consciousness has on the temporality of its own object-saturated intentionality" (Dodd, 2005, 8). In this sense the diagrams depict memories and retentions of a perceptual and conscious kind, and thus it is no great leap to interpret them in terms of attention. However, relieved of the technical function they have in Husserl's philosophy, they can be used more loosely and heuristically as well to represent our practices more generally, as I will do further below.

Figure 6.1 is a slightly altered adaptation of the initial diagram Husserl provides (Husserl, 1991, 29). He would progressively complicate this diagram

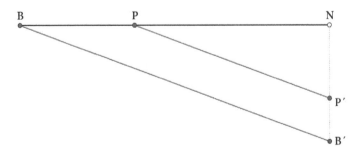

Figure 6.1 Primary retention of an experience

to bring in ever more nuances (Husserl, 1991, 98, 238, 243, 342, 343; see Dodd, 2005). But these nuances need not concern us in the present context, so the basic scheme shown in Figure 6.1 is already sufficient.

The horizontal line extending across the top of the diagram should be read from left (point B for beginning) to right (point N for "now"). Everything to the left of the now-point N is in the past, and temporal experience can be thought of as steadily trailing out to the left of, "behind", the now-point. This basic timeline of experience is composed of segments (B-P and P-N) corresponding to two successive experiences: during the first – earlier – segment B-P the tone Husserl is listening to is still sounding. The tone ends at P, and then during the segment P-N there is no tone. The vertical dimension represents the retentional "depth" of temporal experience. The diagonal line slanting downward and to the right from B to B' represents the unfolding of a retention corresponding to the first phase of this experience. Starting at P, the retention of the tone ceases to grow, and a subsequent retention of the absence of a tone starts sloping downward in parallel toward P'. Both the tone segment and the segment without a tone are retained as primary memory. The vertical line from N down to B' represents the retentions accompanying the present moment in the experience of the now-point. That is, along the horizontal line at the top of the diagram, new experiences continue to be had at the moving point N. But hanging down from this live, moving now-point is a "trail" of retentions of previous phases of experience. The older retention B' is farthest below N, the more recent P' is closer to N. The segment B'-P' is the retention at the now-moment of the past experience of the tone; segment P'-N is the retention at the now-moment of the subsequent phase in which there was no tone. It is these retentions that allow the stream of consciousness to be experienced as continuous.

By depicting the flow of time and the development of retentions in two dimensions rather than just one, Husserl's diagramatic conception offers a neat visualization of the retentional "depth" of our time-consciousness. At the same time, as he readily admits, it is a highly simplified graphical device. Not only does it bracket all qualitative aspects of experience save the presence or absence of a tone, it also visually suggests that retentions can be added on without limit to the string hanging down from the now point, that retentions do not fade or disappear (Husserl, 1991, 32, note 14). Additionally, the auditory scenario suggests a steady and uninterrupted attention, a continuous auditory experience. Yet, as the argument here has highlighted repeatedly, turning from one matter to another, whether deliberately or as a result of interruption or distraction, is a central and common feature of our experience. Although they do not depict this fact, however, Husserl's diagrams can be enhanced without great difficulty to incorporate the phenomenon of turning. This enhancement then opens up a series of additional possibilities for visualizing and thinking about the process of montage. Again, the point of this graphical exercise is ultimately to provide a way of visualizing what I term re-reification.

Figure 6.2 places Husserl's two-dimensional diagram in three dimensions, which allows the process of turning to be visualized as rotation around the time-axis represented in the original diagram by the horizontal line at the top. Now this time-axis is running at an angle out of the perspectival background towards the viewer, and the view back along it is a view into the ever more distant past. The sequence of events and experiences can now be represented not only as a linear series but as a series of engagements of attention or practice in which we *turn toward* new matters of concern. The triangular figure in Husserl's original diagram, which represented the retentions in a listening experience, is visible toward the upper left of Figure 6.2. At the "front" or most recent end of this experience, the hypothetical listener then turned briefly to another matter, let us say, the interruption caused by an unrelated sound, to which the person attends long enough to establish that it is unimportant. The smaller triangle that begins where the previous one ends represents this new engagement. After a short while the listener then turns back to the original auditory experience, and this third phase is represented by the larger continuation of the original retention up to the front end of the diagram.

This is of course still a highly reductive and simplified graphic. It is not capable, for example, of visualizing the qualitative differences between different specific retentions (whether primarily of perceptual, emotional, bodily or other sorts). It also suggests that retained experiences of whatever kind can always be neatly and exactly circumscribed, when in fact the boundary zones and transitions through which experiences bleed into each other can be highly complex and inexact. Another graphical simplification can be seen in the fact that the different triangles extend outward from the central line only in the four cardinal directions. This is done to make recognition of directional difference as easy as possible for the reader, but in principle a triangle of engagement could set off at any of the specific angles in between the four cardinal directions. Finally, the diagram does not actually depict turning as a process. One segment merely ends at a point in time and the next one, oriented in a different direction, begins. Nevertheless, we can and do interpret our experiences as forming a more or less clearly describable sequence, as for example when recounting a day's events to a friend or

Figure 6.2 Retention and turning in three dimensions

family member (more on this below). The triangular segments in Figure 6.2 can thus be understood to represent the "film clips" we tie together in the process of montage.

In Husserl's terms, both of the earlier retentional segments in Figure 6.2, since they have been brought to an end by turning away from them, cease to be primary memories or retentions proper, seamlessly connected to the present moment, and become candidates for secondary memories, capable of recognition and recollection *as something*. It is precisely this delimitation, this ending, the bounding or definition of a retention, caused by turning away from it, that constitutes a re-reification. It is not only the more familiar processes of hypostatization and objectification, for example through naming something, assigning it to a category, or giving it a number, that reifies the world. In addition, the basic segmentation of experiences and activities of all kinds by the ongoing series of turnings-away from matters of concern "reforms" the world into more easily reifiable chunks or stretches – "profiles" – of experience, even if some or many of these chunks are never actually drawn into more explicit reifications involving a full-blown as-structure. The rotational montage of turning toward and away from matters may work with all sorts of raw materials, both of "our own" and of external origin. But in either case the basic experiences delimited by each new turning-away are always potentially reifiable, whatever their qualitative content.

I call this "re-reification" because turning away from something presupposes that one has already been explicitly engaged with it. Since the realm of what we have never been turned towards is far vaster than the things we have at one time or another turned away from, re-reification represents a relatively limited subset of the range of non-engagements with the world at any moment. On the other hand, it is composed of all the identifiable acts and experiences that have gone to make up our biographies, so it is of central significance to an understanding of how an individual's engagements relate to social reproduction and transformation. As Sara Ahmed so perceptively puts it, *"We accumulate 'behinds,' just as what is 'behind' is an effect of past accumulations"* (Ahmed, 2006, 137). Re-reification is distinguished by an intermediate, weak or spectral kind of as-structure. This is not the strong as-structure of traditional accounts of reification, for example, Heideggerian presence-at-hand, wherein something or someone is understood as a specific, identifiable object divorced from its immersive context. The weak as-structure can be characterized provisionally in terms of re-reifying a matter of concern *as something we have turned away from*. This "something we have turned away from" is delimited only by our having turned away from it. It is not delimited with explicit, nameable boundaries or identified as belonging to a specific category, though it can be subsequently. It is given a "terminus" just by our having turned away, but it is not necessarily given a "term", that is, retained as anything more coherent or strongly identified than that.

Segmentation, fragmentation and practice

I would now like to explore two implications of the analysis of re-reification sketched in the foregoing section. First and more briefly, I will suggest that the diagrammatic elaborations of Husserl's depiction of memory may be able to help us understand the fragmentation of experience as one possible source of alienation. Second, I argue that the three-dimensional image of the sequence of retentions composing memory can be used also as a heuristic for considering not just how our memories are re-reified but also how our practices more generally are re-reified when we turn away from them. Broadly speaking, the more rapid the rhythm of turnings punctuating our experience, the smaller and more numerous the profiles we trail out behind us, and the more fragmented our sense of the world. This notion of fragmentation can be thought of as the rotational analogue of the fragmentation and loss of the ability to think totality which Lukács saw as a major component of reification through the commodity form (Lukács, 1971, 120–121). Fragmentation in the rotational sense sketched here is not necessarily a bad thing in and of itself, although it seems reasonable to suppose that since it requires more frequent montage-work, it can be a source of strain or disorientation. We can use the visualization scheme introduced above to depict it. Figures 6.3 and 6.4 represent two markedly different rhythms of turning from one matter to the next.

In Figure 6.3, most of the pictured engagements are relatively sustained, and thus leave visually prominent profiles behind for possible recollection. For simplicity each profile is depicted – other than in Figure 6.2 – as a simple, uninterrupted triangle. The material giving purchase to recollection is conceived here as roughly proportional to the length of continuous engagement that generated the original retention. That is, the variable intensity of different experiences is left aside. By contrast, Figure 6.4 imagines a much more rapid rhythm of changing directional engagement. If we think of the overall

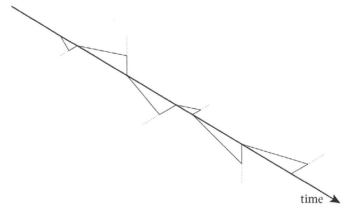

time

Figure 6.3 Sequence of more sustained engagements

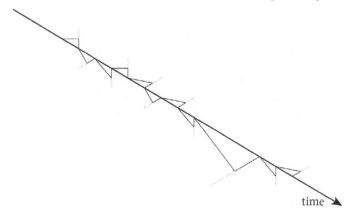

Figure 6.4 Fragmentation

patterns of profiles around the respective central time-axes as "fletchings" on metaphorical arrows, there is a double sense in which Figure 6.4 suggests a fragmented relation to self and world. On the one hand, the rapid rhythm of change itself could reasonably be expected to engender a more fragmented experience. But secondly, the fast pace of turnings leaves less developed retentional profiles. In other words, I want to suggest that re-reification can vary in qualitative terms, in the sense that the longer and more sustained an activity, the more depth and internal differentiation it acquires. By contrast, very short engagements may be in a sense easier to re-reify since they lack internal differentiation. Insofar as this is true it may also make it more difficult to stitch together recollected scenes into a continuous and coherent "filmic narrative" with any extended scenic anchors to supplement the bare continuity engendered by the felt passage of time alone (Gurwitsch's "continuity of consciousness") (Gurwitsch, 1964). This is just a speculative suggestion, and will simply be left hanging here without further development. But it may support the account of rotational alienation sketched in the previous chapter.

My second claim here is that re-reification applies just as much to publicly observable practices as to memories, just as much to things others perceive us to be doing as to our own retained experiences of our activities. The profiles pictured in Figures 6.2, 6.3 and 6.4 do not necessarily only represent private memories but also intersubjectively or publicly observable episodes of engagement. The social life of practice, like that of embodied memory, is segmented. As in the case of personal memories, my argument here is that the segmented character of practices, their punctuation into a series by moments of turning, has a re-reifying effect independent of the content or substantive "meaning" of those practices. Public traces of segmented practice may take a variety of forms, perhaps most importantly in the memories of other people. They can also subsist in more durable inscriptions such as entries in daily planners, in- and out-times in guest registers, or the exploding array of data trails generated by security cameras and electronic media. Other material traces of having turned away from a practice may include configurations of tools set down on a work-surface, a half-finished – or empty – coffee cup, a blinking light on a telephone indicating that someone is on hold, a bookmark in a book, a parked car, indeed an infinite number of possible material constellations. Such traces can be understood as part of Stiegler's "tertiary retentions" (Stiegler, 1998). Probably the most potent kind of trace of what we have turned away from is the continued physical presence of another person or people (more on this below). These traces usually function for us as triggers for the memory of what we were doing and possibly also as anchors for the eventual resumption of what we were doing. For the person who had to set down the cup of coffee to attend unexpectedly to something else, seeing the half-empty coffee cup later may lead not only to the recollection that they were drinking coffee but also to a renewed grasp of what they were doing or thinking while drinking the coffee. In effect, the half-empty coffee cup or the arrangement of tools set down on a work surface is what is represented by the front edge of the segments in Figures 6.2, 6.3 or 6.4: it is a trace of the suspension of a practice cause by having turned away from it.

Here I offer two illustrations of the sequential, relatively "chunky" character of practice. The first is based upon a passage from Schatzki's *The Timespace of Human Activity* (Schatzki, 2010). The context for the passage is a critique of Bergson's claim that temporal duration is to be understood as uninterrupted transition and change. I agree with Schatzki that Bergson's notion of duration as constantly transforming flux is not a realistic representation of concrete temporal experience. Schatzki's explanation of why this is so is excellent:

> I'm sitting at my desk reading. The phone rings. I turn toward the phone, lift the receiver, and answer it, noticing, as I turn, that a pile of paper is about to fall and thinking to myself, "If only the phone would stop ringing." This description of my recent past suggests that the "flow" of activity possesses significant segmentation. I'm performing one action, a perceived event leads me to abandon this action and to take up others, in the process of which I notice something about the world and think something. Any passage of moment-to-moment life has a parsing similar to this one. As indicated, Bergson would have argued that this segmentation of my life was a product of memory and intellect; as it unfolded, it was a thick duration, an undivided amalgamation of action, sensation, and memories. As Deleuze might have put it, my life, as it unfolds, contains differences, but none of the named actions and perceptions as distinct moments. It seems to me, however, that the job of memory in this context is to preserve and to re-member the segmentations that were there in my life, not to introduce ones or to articulate ones that were "latently", "virtually", or [...] "implicitly" there. Breaking off from reading, turning to the phone, and answering it were set out as such in my activity prior to

my attending ex post facto to what I had been doing. [...] I do not attend to, and am not thematically aware of, the segmentation of my ongoing life as it transpires. I know of it, however. It is available to me as my life transpires (if you ask me, I can tell you).

Schatzki, 2010, 193

The first part of this passage, Schatzki's brief description of the sequence of his engagements, illustrates very well the complex interplay of attention and practice I sought to outline in Chapter 3. It is possible to imagine graphically depicting both practical and attentional segments along the same path, perhaps in two different colors. Where the attentional focus is the same as the practical focus, the two segments would be perfectly superimposed; where attention is on a different theme, there would be two diagonal lines growing off of the same segment of the central axis but separated by an angle. What concerns me here are the traces left by Schatzki as a result of turning away from a sequence of matters of concern. The first thing he turns away from is reading. Assuming he is reading a book, he probably sets it down, either facedown and open on his desk or with a bookmark. Then, as he turns, he notices that a pile of paper is about to fall. Since he is turning to answer the phone, it is reasonable to assume the pile of papers does fall, fanning out on the office floor. While turning, Schatzki reports also thinking that he wished the phone would stop ringing. Turning away from this thought leaves only a memory trace, while turning away from the reading and from the papers poised to fall leave both material and memory traces. All of these traces are re-reifications. They become inert or dormant for Schatzki when he turns away from them, but they support his future recollection of the doings, sayings or thinkings he was engaged in. So, for example, the book lying on his desk with a bookmark may soon trigger the recognition, "That's right, I was reading." The papers lying on the floor might likewise lead him to think, "That phone call came at a bad time!" In such cases the trace invites the development of a full as-structure.

The second illustration of the segmented character of practices picks up the claim made earlier that other people are often the most potent traces of what we have turned away from. Perhaps the clearest example of re-reification is the act of turning away from another person with whom one has been interacting in order to take a call or read an incoming text on a smartphone. Anyone who uses such a device regularly will have experienced the sense of guilt, or at least sheepishness, that accompanies turning away from another person to take a call. To parse this process, it is helpful to return to a distinction Michael Tomasello makes in his accounts of the evolutionary origins of humanity in cooperative practice (Tomasello, 1999, 2014). In these studies he distinguishes two levels of human interaction and cooperation. His evolutionary argument, though compatible with Stiegler's views (see Chapter 1), need not concern us here. The two levels of interaction he identifies, however, are analytically helpful. The first, "joint attention", is his term for a situation in which two individuals in a shared cognitive context comprehend each other as "intentional agents", that is, as agents acting and pursuing goals in a manner directed toward a shared matter of concern (Tomasello, 1999). The second level of interaction involves the individuals viewing each other not just as intentional agents but as "mental agents". Tomasello means by this that they understand each other not just as oriented toward the same issues but as cognitively competent partners and independent centers of experience in cooperation and communication. At this second level each participant is able to simulate the other person's perspective, to impute to the other person relations of differential relevance, to understand that the other can do the same regarding oneself, and on the basis of this deeper understanding, to communicate cooperatively in the interest of pursuing joint projects (Tomasello, 2014). Below these levels Tomasello places many animal species, who are capable of recognizing other individuals as active beings that have effects but not capable of putting themselves in their positions in the kinds of ways humans can do this.

To illustrate the re-reifying effects of turning away from another person to take a phone call, I will draw upon Tomasello's distinctions to couch the event of turning away in terms of evolutionary regression. This may seem a bit over-dramatic, but it helps to highlight what is at issue. When we take a call while a person we are with is talking to us, we are forced to interrupt the other person. In the Global North at least, this usually involves some combination of raising a hand, adopting an apologetic grimace and perhaps offering a quick verbal apology while covering the phone with a hand. A particularly considerate conversational partner may even be the first to signal to the person receiving the call that they should feel free to take it. Once these preliminaries are completed, the demotion of the conversational partner from their previous status as a mental agent begins. Some skilled smartphone users may succeed in limiting the demotion to one level, switching their communicative engagements rapidly and convincingly enough to preserve the impression that they continue to acknowledge a joint attentional situation shared with the physically present person, a joint situation that is thereby only partly suspended. The other person cannot be fully attended to and actively treated as one's primary communicative and cooperative partner at the moment, but they can at least be reassured by the one taking the phone call that their character as goal-oriented agents sharing a common concern has not been completely forgotten or set aside. They remain intentional, if no longer mental, agents.

In other contexts, however, taking a phone call that interrupts a conversation may involve a more complete turning away and a deeper demotion of one's partner. This might be because one is waiting for a call on some urgent matter. In any case, while the preliminary rituals of detachment may be similar to those described above, the detachment itself is more complete. This is often clear in physical manifestations such as turning the body away from the partner and covering the ear not occupied by the phone. In such cases the former conversational partner loses not just their status as a mental agent but also the attribution of intentional agency. The joint attentional scene is dissolved, at least temporarily, and the other person is reduced to the status merely of an active being capable of impinging upon the person taking the call but no longer involved in joint orientation toward a shared matter of concern, and no longer perceived in terms of attributed second-person perspectives, relevance structures and the like. In this case the conversational partner, and the conversation itself, are re-reified. The most important recoverable "trace" of the conversation that has been abandoned is the continued physical presence of the person with whom one was talking.

The re-reification of the person is normally fully reversible, except in rare cases where the person turned away from is deeply offended by the episode and breaks off, or downgrades their commitment to, the relationship. Through mutually acknowledged rituals of apology and explanation, the one taking the phone call can and does "repromote" the other person to full human mental agency, and the other person typically expects this. But it is not always the case that the re-reified conversation can so immediately be de-reified again. The one who was on the phone may not be able reconstruct anything specific about the previous conversation without help from the other person. And even where the reconstruction is successful, the interruption may have disrupted the flow of the previous conversation to a sufficient degree that it prompts a decision on the part of one or both parties not to pursue the conversation any further. In either case, the interruption segments the previous conversation, lending it a weak as-structure and thereby making it more likely that it will be fully reified as a unit of conversation.

One of the key questions raised earlier in this chapter was that of exactly how a transformative issue or focus of engagement changes the pre-existing situation after we have turned away from it. The crux of the answer I want to give is that in directional terms, it *adds a possible theme* – a possible focus of directed engagement – to the thematic or pragmatic field made up of matters related to whatever we were engaged with beforehand. In many cases, repeated engagement with something in our frontal space can alter our habitual behaviors and attitudes, that is, add new vocabularies, patterns of thought, habits and tools to the lateral space that plays a generally unreflected role in much of what we do. Thus, for example, using gender-neutral language or sorting waste for recycling can become habitual only because we have engaged with these issues often enough. But such permanent change, important though it is, is not as continuously effective as we tend to assume, especially in critical social and cultural theory. In a certain sense, even the most potentially transformative experiences are initially "domesticated" by their status as one within a series of engagements, even if they are never incorporated into our practices so deeply as to become habitual and unreflective. However inspiring or motivating an issue is to us, we cannot but experience it at the level of everyday practice as a matter we must sometimes turn away from before we can turn back to it later. The leveling effects of this embedment in the practical "one thing after another" of everyday life must first be overcome if an issue is to become transformative for an individual. The segmentation of experience by turning frames a certain kind of baseline inertia.

The overcoming of this inertia can be more or less radical: inspired, fascinated or outraged by something, we may decide to dedicate ourselves to it through longer-term projects. To stick with the speculation about the scenario in Schatzki's office, if what he was reading strikes him as important enough he might decide he needs to publish a paper discussing its implications for his own account of practice. This means refocusing some aspects of his weekly activities for the next couple of months in order to accommodate the new writing project. In other cases, the overcoming of the baseline inertia may be more radical, as for example in the case of full-time activists whose outrage at injustice at some point led them to reorient not just their weekly calendars but their personal identities and professional lives around a new focus of activity. Even in this case, though, if an issue is actually to have transformative effects, this will not be because of its implications *in principle* but because enough – or, the right – people make it a central and constant enough theme of their own activity to allow it to unfold wider effects. If this happens, it will likewise be in a collectively segmented manner, composed of individual-level segmented practices. In a directional sense, that is, the social significance of any activity is utterly performative because it is circumscribed by the directional commitments of social actors.

Turning, reification and practice theory

The three chapters now drawing to a close have sought to provide a fundament for the initial sketch of directed practice provided in Chapter 3. There I argued that Schatzki's detailed practice theory could be enhanced by attending more systematically to the role of attention in helping to explain the sequences of practices in which embodied individuals are engaged. What Chapters 4, 5 and 6 have been intended to do is to tie the performance of practices in timespace to structures and processes of turning. Among these structures and processes are:

- the directional asymmetry of the human body based physically in corporeal organization and lived in a *leibliche* register through the interplay of frontal, lateral and dorsal zones;
- a directional understanding of more or less successful or alienated relations to the world; and
- a related directional account of how our turning away from matters of concern constantly "re-reifies" the world around us.

These three chapters form the core of my attempt to lay out a directional sensibility. The last part of the book turns to what might somewhat inadequately be called "implications". Chapter 7 deploys the directional sensibility developed throughout the preceding chapters in a reconsideration of some long-standing features of critical socio-spatial theory. Here the concepts and images built up thus far around notions of embodied individuals are finally reinserted within social and political dynamics, and on this basis some rudiments of a political economy of orientation are outlined. Key concepts introduced there will be "occupation", "the body as land", "social dark matter" and "reproduction by neglect". Chapter 8 is, in effect, an annotated graphic summary of most of the argument, using the visual devices developed throughout Part II, in combination with diagrams adapted from time-geography, to construct an overall picture of directed social practice applicable to a range of different empirical settings. The Conclusion links the political economy of oriented practice to more concrete ethical questions of what to do.

References

Ahmed, S. (2006). *Queer Phenomenology: Orientations, Objects, Others*. Durham, NC: Duke University Press.

Bewes, T. (2002). *Reification, or the Anxiety of Late Capitalism*. London: Verso.

Dodd, J. (2005). Reading Husserl's time-diagrams from 1917/1918. *Husserl Studies*, 21, pp. 111–137.

Gurwitsch, A. (1964). *The Field of Consciousness*. Pittsburgh, PA: Duquesne University Press.

Haraway, D. (1988). Situated knowledges: the science question in feminism and the privilege of partial perspective. *Feminist Studies*, 14(3), pp. 575–599.

Harman, G. (2002). *Tool Being: Heidegger and the Metaphysics of Objects*. Chicago, IL: Open Court Press.

Heidegger, M. (1962). *Being and Time*. Trans. J. Macquarrie and E. Robinson. Oxford: Blackwell.

Heidegger, M. (1977). The question concerning technology. In: *The Question Concerning Technology and Other Essays*. Trans. W. Lovitt. New York: Harper Torchbooks, pp. 3–35.

Husserl, E. (1991). *On the Phenomenology of the Consciousness of Internal Time (1893–1917)*. Trans. J. Brough. Dordrecht: Springer.

Husserl, E. (2012). *Ideas*. Trans. W.R.B. Gibson. London: Routledge.

Jaeggi, R. (2014). *Alienation*. Trans. A. Smith. New York: Columbia University Press.

Kirsch, S. and Mitchell, D. (2004). The nature of things: dead labor, non-human actors, and the persistence of Marxism. *Antipode*, 36(4): 687–705.

Lukács, G. (1971). *History and Class Consciousness: Studies in Marxist Dialectics*. Trans. R. Livingstone. Cambridge, MA: MIT Press.

Marx, K. (1967). *Capital, Volume 1*. Trans. S. Moore, and E. Aveling. New York: International Publishers.

Massey, D. (2005). *For Space*. London: Sage.

Schatzki, T. (2010). *The Timespace of Human Activity: On Performance, Society, and History as Indeterminate Teleological Events*. Lanham, MD: Lexington Books.

Stiegler, B. (1998). *Technics and Time, 1: The Fault of Epimetheus*. Trans. R. Beardsworth and G. Collins. Stanford, CA: Stanford University Press.

Tomasello, M. (1999). *The Cultural Origins of Human Cognition*. Cambridge, MA: Harvard University Press.

Tomasello, M. (2014). *A Natural History of Human Thinking*. Cambridge, MA: Harvard University Press.

Wills, D. (2008). *Dorsality: Thinking Back through Technology and Politics*. Minneapolis, MN: University of Minnesota Press.

Part III

Direction, socio-spatial theory and ethics

7 Occupation and directed practice
Outline of a political economy

This chapter draws together many of the arguments and concepts from the foregoing chapters to do two things. The first is to define and explain a type of power relation given the name "occupation". Occupation is a distinct form of power relation articulated with but not reducible to the more familiar array of phenomena such as class rule, patriarchy, sovereignty, biopolitics, discipline or liberal governmentality. Through some of these articulations, occupation will be placed, secondly, at the core of a broader sketch of a political economy of orientation. This political economy extends the analysis of alienation in Chapter 5 and of reification in Chapter 6. But it remains a sketch, one which leaves aside, for example, questions of class. After some further introductory remarks here, the first section gives a broad definition of occupation and lays out some of its most general features. The second section refines the notion of occupation by linking it to concepts in historical geographical materialism. The third section relates occupation to feminist care ethics and Foucault's writings on care of the self. The fourth section reframes these articulations of power within an historical-geographical dialectic centered upon time-space compression and acceleration. The final section develops the analysis of reification introduced in Chapter 6 through the concept of "social dark matter", and uses this concept to argue for the importance of "reproduction by neglect".

Occupation

Our directional asymmetry implies:

- that many different activities and foci of attention may compete for occupation of what Leroi-Gourhan called our "anterior relational fields", our front-spaces (Leroi-Gourhan, 1993, 31ff.); and
- that whatever we are doing in our front spaces, for the most part we cannot be occupied by whatever is in our dorsal or back spaces.

These two circumstances already give a basic idea of what is meant here by occupation, which is in and of itself not particularly difficult to grasp. Something like occupation was already implicit in William James's observations regarding the central importance of control of attention to the question of how autonomously we lead our lives (James, 1950, 447–448). It is no accident that Hartmut Rosa sounds a similar note writing more recently about the control of social time: "The question of *who* determines the rhythm, duration, sequencing and synchronization of activities and events forms a central arena for conflicts of interest and power struggles" (Rosa, 2015, 11–12). Jonathan Beller makes the same argument with respect to bodies: "In the age of the cinematic mode of production, surely the fate of bodies – who occupies them, who thinks or feels in them, what they want – is again in question. If we are occupied by cinematic consciousness, what is the value of our seeing, our thought?" (Beller, 2006, 139). By now it should be clear that attention, time and bodies are all integral to the directionality of practice.

I would like to define occupation as *a form of power centered upon the determination of which activities and attentional themes are able to pre-empt others in absorbing our bodily energies and time, and upon the processes through which this pre-emption occurs.* It would be folly to suggest that the problem of occupation has never been noticed before, but I do want to suggest that it deserves to be understood as more centrally articulated with the operation of many forms of social power than has hitherto been recognized. What is occupied in one way or another is more precisely *embodied, directed time*. Again, I understand directed time – which blends spatiality and temporality – as the micro-level substrate or innermost constituent of what Schatzki calls the "timespace of human activity" (Schatzki, 2010). Here I will largely follow those theories of practice that treat time – reductively – as "a finite resource for which practices compete" (Shove, Pantzar and Watson, 2012, 127). As Postone and many others have noted, the emergence and consolidation of this notion of time has a specific, historical-geographical genealogy (Postone, 1993, 202–216). Yet recognizing this, and recognizing that the "lived time" of embodied being-in-the-world is the existential condition of possibility for our discovering or constructing it, does not free us of our own immersion in and partial dependence upon modern abstract time (Schatzki, 2010, 23).

Sara Ahmed lays out the many levels of association – including spatial and temporal – raised by the term "occupation":

> Whether we "take" up different objects depends on how we are already occupied and on the kind of work that we do. We say that we occupy space; that we have an occupation. We are occupied with objects, which present themselves as tools [...]. We are occupied when we are busy. We are booked up; we are using up time when we are occupied with something. [...] The word "occupy" allows us to link the question of inhabiting or residing within space; to work, or even having an identity through work (an occupation); to time (to be occupied with); to holding something; and to taking possession of something *as* a thing.
>
> Ahmed, 2006, 44

One important feature of many of these typical associations is that they are strongly oriented toward the here and now of practice. Again, the petri-dish model of agency, the "phenomenology of the 'I can'" (Ahmed, 2006, 138), goes hand-in-hand with a devaluation of the present in favor of the possibilities for future activities. Also, it is worth stressing once again the formal connotations of the directedness of practice. In place of "occupation" it might have made sense to consider the term "colonization". Doing so would have been more appropriate had the focus of the book been more upon genealogies of hierarchical difference. However, despite its association with injustice in some usages, "occupation" allows a more neutral interpretation of simply "taking up timespace" that is therefore unavailable for other occupations. It is this more formal sense that I wish to foreground.

Occupation and the body in historical-geographical materialism

At the most basic level, Marx's analysis of exploitation in terms of labor-time, indeed the very possibility of the commodification of labor-time, is built upon the largely exclusive seriality of directed practical engagement (see Postone 1993; Mészáros 2008). The directionality of practice is likewise the basis for what Mészáros characterizes as the tyranny of capital's time imperative, and for his claim that the most fundamental condition of possibility for true emancipation is "free time" (Mészáros 2008, 56–58). Time only has to be "freed" because of the directional exclusivity of most practices, whether economic or non-economic. Exploitation as extraction of surplus labor time presupposes the directional exclusivity of the engagement of workers. "If humankind had an 'infinity of time' at its disposal, then no one could talk about 'capital's abuse of time'" (Mészáros 2008, 25). The finitude of the time at our disposal is translated by our directional finitude into a concretely limited number of things we can be doing.

Some other political insights from the Marxist tradition presuppose the workings of occupation and the directional finitude underlying it, most obviously what Harvey calls "the old Roman formula of 'bread and circuses'" (Harvey 1990, 427). Distraction need not be a matter of anything as grand as "circus" or "spectacle", but the multitude of commercial blandishments that plaster the surfaces of everyday life would not add up to an effective strategy of depoliticization if the direction of our engaged attention and practice were not limited. The analysis of Jonathan Beller discussed in Chapter 1, according to which ever more sophisticated schemes of attention capture solicit consumers to self-exploit through the uncompensated paying of attention, is likewise premised upon the exclusiveness of occupation (Beller, 2006). The ideological interpellation identified by Althusser is an instance of the interpellated individual being occupied by state sovereignty (Althusser, 1971). At the same time as being hailed by a police officer represents the enlistment of the individual as a subject of the state, it also and more concretely places the state in a pre-emptive position in the course of that individual's daily life-path, asserting a claim to prioritize an encounter with the state above other activities. Lastly, a critique of ideology as occupation has also framed critiques of monopolization of media space (Herman and Chomsky, 1988).

How can the concept of occupation add to our understanding of life under capitalism beyond these relatively obvious conditions? Approaching core dynamics of capitalism from the perspective of material bodily life, as David Harvey, Reecia Orzeck, Felicity Callard, Joseph Fracchia and others have done, strikes me as a particularly promising way of discerning points of connection with the issues central to the present book. Harvey's notion of "the body as an accumulation strategy" provides a more specific entry point for delving somewhat more deeply into the issue (Harvey, 1998). The suggestion here is that the directional features of the human body can be understood in political economic terms as analogous to "land". Harvey's 1998 paper begins with an acknowledgement of the twofold character of human bodies. On the one hand, the body is a relational, porous affair, an "unfinished project", and thus historically "malleable", as Harvey asserts; the body "crystallizes out as a 'contingently bounded permanence' within the flows of multiple processes" (Harvey, 1998, 402). The history of capitalism has in part been about "discovering new ways (and potentialities) in which the human body can be put to use as the bearer of the capacity to labor. [...] Older capacities of the human body are reinvented, new capacities revealed" (Harvey, 1998, 406). Orzeck points out that under capitalism, the production of bodies differentiates them in much the same way that the production of space results in uneven development (Orzeck, 2007, 501). This differentiation can shape gender- and race-based patterns of inequality, for example (Orzeck, 2007, 502).

On the other hand, though, human bodies are not "infinitely or even easily" malleable (Harvey, 1998, 402). This was the main point of the work of Joseph Fracchia discussed in Chapter 4 (Fracchia, 2005). Like Fracchia, Orzeck argues that while capitalism has long been engaged in the production of human bodies in a manner analogous to its production of space, human bodies cannot be understood only as "products" but are also natural entities with independent dynamics (Orzeck, 2007, 504ff). The relation between the malleable and the less malleable features of human bodies has long been a site of contradiction and conflict. Because of the specific qualities and inertias that limit their malleability, laboring bodies have borne the scars and injuries of projects for adapting and transforming them in the interest of capital accumulation. "Different types of labour transform the body in different ways. Workers lose limbs, digits, fingernails, eyes; they develop repetitive strain injuries, respiratory diseases, skin diseases, diseases from exposure to asbestos, pesticides, and other hazardous substances" (Orzeck, 2007, 503). Different bodily accumulation strategies may also clash or be incompatible.

Injuries to bodies may emerge not only in the sphere of production but also through consumption. In an insightful argument, Julie Guthman and Melanie DePuis sketch a political economy of body fat, asserting that "the problem of obesity is implicated in how neoliberalism recreates the subject" (Guthman and DePuis, 2006, 429). They frame their argument within specifically neoliberal capitalism, but the underlying logic they describe certainly predates neoliberalism. At the intersection of the core dialectic of capital accumulation and an accompanying dialectic of consumer desire, they place eating as a site at which crises of overaccumulation can be at least temporarily warded off (Guthman and DePuis, 2006, 439). "Fast food becomes a doubly good fix for capitalism; not only does it involve the superexploitation of the labor force, it also provides an outlet for surplus food. Insofar as this surplus manifests in obesity [...], the contradiction is temporarily resolved in the body" (Guthman and DePuis, 2006, 441). Paralleling accumulation by dispossession, this amounts to "accumulation by engorgement in the spatial fix of the body" (Guthman and DePuis, 2006, 442). But the body cannot absorb infinite amounts of excess food. This bodily limit, they argue, illuminates the function of "food products that do not act like food", such as synthetic fat substitutes that simply pass through the body without being absorbed (Guthman and DePuis, 2006, 441). It also helps explain the symbolic significance of bulimia, which, they argue, can be taken as "a way to read the neoliberal economy itself" (Guthman and DePuis, 2006, 442). In all such cases, the needs of capital for transformation of bodily capabilities runs up against biological and physical limits of the body. Straining those limits can shorten lives and impair people's ability to live them in relative health and comfort.

My argument builds upon these insights in a specific way. For analytical purposes it makes sense to think of the directional features of corporeal organization worked out in Chapter 4 as among the bodily characteristics that are not infinitely malleable. Broadly speaking, our fundamental directionality frames or mediates the social significance of our other historically and geographically specific capabilities and needs. The reinvented or newly discovered capabilities of the human body that emerge in a historically and geographically uneven way through the dynamics of capitalism (but also through other processes such as advances in medical knowledge) have not appreciably altered the directional asymmetry intrinsic to our corporeal organization. This is, for example, how we can understand the subtitle of Gazzaley and Rosen's book on new problems of attention in the information age, "ancient brains in a high-tech world" (Gazzaley and Rosen, 2016). I will argue that, understood in these terms, the body is internally riven by an additional contradiction centered on our directionality. This additional contradiction can be approached in political-economic terms by suggesting that directed bodily time occupied by different activities be seen as analogous to land.

Proposing that the body be seen as land may seem strange at first sight, so some detailed explanation is in order. As Harvey argues in *The Limits to Capital*, the question of how to deal with the role of land and land rent in processes of capital accumulation is a difficult one, and Marx himself only advanced some rudiments of an analysis (Harvey, 1982, 330–331). Generalizing

Marx's example of a waterfall as a source of energy for industrial processes, land differs from many other factors in production because it can be seen as a "monopolizable force of Nature" (Marx, quoted in Harvey, 1982, 336). And yet the underlying principle of Marx's political economy is that value is only produced by human labor. Harvey's account of land under capitalism thus lays great emphasis on the historical and analytical question of how land comes to be subsumed completely within the value-producing dynamics of capital accumulation despite its non-capitalist origins. He argues that the crucial step is the complete separation of land ownership from control over what is done on and with land by means of the modern form of land rent. By accepting rent, modern landlords turn over the right to shape activities undertaken on the land thus rented (Harvey, 1982, 345).

Like land, the body originates outside of capitalist production processes in a direct sense. Also like land, the finite directed time of the body is largely "taken up" by its use. As Harvey notes with respect to land, whether it is viewed as absolute, relative or relational space depends on the circumstances of human practice with which it is connected (Harvey, 1982, 339, note 5). A similar point can be made about human bodies: they can be seen as relative, relational or absolute according to the practical context. In its capacity as the locus of finite directed time that can be occupied by one thing *or* another, the body is an example of "absolute space" defined by "exclusivity of occupation" (Harvey, 1982, 338–339). Embodied, directed time, like a long, slender ribbon of land, comprises a "ground" that can largely only be occupied in an exclusive way by different activities and attentional foci. (The imagery of a ribbon or strip should also evoke the discussion of film and montage in Chapters 5 and 6.) The analogy between directed bodily time and land is imperfect, of course. But the basic point may still be useful. If our directed time is a sort of land, then the specific tasks and focused concerns that occupy it can be seen as the "built environment". This built environment not only occupies each here and now but trails out behind us as a segmented, re-reified set of profiles, and thus occupies our past.

In what senses and to what degree can the integration of the directed time of the body into capital accumulation be seen as analogous to the integration of land as discussed by Harvey? Here the limits to the analogy between the body and land become apparent, but in an instructive way. These limits have to do with the moments of production and consumption. In the realm of production, the analogy between directed bodily time and land holds to a certain degree, as the directionally finite time of the body can be "rented" by the payment of a wage. The wage entitles the employer/renter to occupy a certain length of the ribbon of directed time. As in the case of land, capital must try to detach our control over our directed time from our continued ownership of our bodies as "landlords". In the sphere of capitalist production this entails the long-familiar project of labor discipline: through the establishment of separate workplaces, as well as the propagation and enforcement of rules, supplemented by surveillance systems of whatever kind within the workplace, employers have long sought to subjugate workers to work regimes aimed at exclusively occupying their directed time with productive labor. New information technology has expanded the possibilities of surveillance but at the same time enhanced and multiplied the possibilities for non-work activities within the workplace.

This brings us to the moment of consumption. In one sense, the project of realization of value through consumption is analogous to that of value creation in production: separating our control over directed time from our ownership of our bodies. But the circumstances and the strategies involved are different. Capital cannot directly rent our bodily needs, desires and manipulable urges in the way that it can rent our productive capacities. But it can rent stretches and surfaces of our surroundings and perceptual environments, and can seek to attract our desires and urges onto these rented surfaces. Here our omnidirectional vulnerability and answerability comes into play. Advertising, marketing, PR and other genres of manipulative stimulation seek to sever control over our bodies from rational processes of deliberation or steering not through discipline but through indiscipline, through the cultivation of desire and impulse. But this means that the contradiction Julie Guthman and Melanie DePuis ascribe narrowly to "neoliberal governmentality" is characteristic of the construction of laboring and consuming subjects under capitalism more generally: we are urged "to participate in society as both out-of-control consumer and self-controlled subject" (Guthman and DePuis, 2006, 444).

Production and consumption generate contradictory dispositions and compete for our directed time. Capital accumulation depends upon both production and consumption, but the directional exclusivity of these two types of activity means they often cannot be pursued by the same person at the same time. From the late 19th through the late 20th century, an important way of easing this tension, at least among the bourgeoisie, was the gender division of labor according to which men were often the main earners while women became the chief consumers (Domosh, 1998; Domosh and Seager, 2001). In the early 21st century, almost unlimited possibilities of consumption have entered the workplace in the form of computers connected to the Internet and of course smartphones. Spatial segregation of work from consumption has become much less enforceable than it was a generation ago. The fact that the occupation of the "land" of our directed time through hourly wages has become such a precarious and vulnerable affair probably helps explain the return to the piece-wage in "platform capitalism" (Srnicek, 2016, 77). On the production side, our directed time simply can't be fenced off anymore by formal rental agreements from incursions by other prospectors. Paying producers only according to output offloads onto working people the whole problem of juggling competing attempts to occupy our bodies.

Occupation, care ethics and care of the self

With this somewhat speculative discussion of the body as land, I have tried to expand and deepen the concerns already raised in the literature on political economies of attention. Directed, embodied time as a thin ribbon of land that can usually only be occupied in an exclusive way by practices then becomes the context within which the political economy of attention plays an important but not exclusive role. Yet, as in the literature on attention, this way of understanding things tends to encourage a fundamentally defensive attitude toward the appeals, solicitations and impulses with which life confronts us and an attendant desire for increased control. Such a focus on control is incomplete. In part, this is because spontaneity and openness is a precondition for responsiveness to our own desires and needs, and to the vast range of unexpected things that can give pleasure. Of course it is a hopeless task to attempt to distinguish definitively between "authentic" or "genuine", and constructed or manipulated, needs and desires. That said, the two-level approach of Jaeggi, centered on the question of whether we want to want what we spontaneously want, can be helpful. In the context of the argument here, it is especially important to focus upon issues of solidarity with and care for others. I will now pick up on the string of hints and allusions throughout the foregoing chapters and present a somewhat more extensive discussion of feminist care ethics. The point will not be to argue that a feminist perspective in general counteracts the defensive approach suggested by political economy. Some strands of feminist analysis can be seen to reinforce the temptation to seek more control over what occupies directed time. A long-standing concern of feminist critiques is the "double career", the fact that "even when women work outside the home they normally carry the burden of household organization and labour at home as well", such as child-rearing, grocery shopping, cleaning, etc. (Barrett, 2014, 208). At an obvious level, the double career is a form of exploitation, and a gendered pattern of heightened claims by others upon the time, attention and practices of women as opposed to men (Davies 2001). This is an underlying concern in some geographic research, for example, on the "spatial entrapment hypothesis" (Palm and Pred, 1978; Hanson and Pratt, 1988).

But other strands of feminist thinking raise another important possibility, one that fundamentally complicates the defensive, control-oriented approach to problems of occupation. Some, though not all of these strands are connected with feminist care ethics (Tronto, 1993; Held, 2006; Noddings, 2013). Virginia Held frames feminist care ethics as follows: "In contrast with the dominant views that give primacy to such values as autonomy, independence, noninterference, fairness and rights, the ethics of care values the interdependence and caring relations that connect persons to one another" (Held, 2006, 129). Feminist care ethics, like critical disability studies, insists upon a different picture of the human, one in which, "[t]hroughout our lives, all of us go through varying degrees of dependence and independence, of autonomy and vulnerability" (Tronto, 1993, 135). Disability scholars have often been leery of the term "care", which seems to transport associations of passivity and dependency – in the traditional, unwanted sense – for receivers of care (Oliver and Barnes, 2012, 66). But one ambition of feminist care ethics is precisely to dissolve these inherited associations and validate care as something fully legitimate and worthy both to give and to receive (Tronto, 1993, 111–122). Such a rehabilitation faces significant barriers, especially in what Goodley terms "neoliberal-ableist" society, with its extreme emphasis on the ideal of maximal individual autonomy (Goodley, 2014, 33; Tronto, 1993, 117). As a basis for an ethics, care is markedly different from more familiar ethical concepts such as justice and virtue. Liberal ethical theories, whether Kantian or utilitarian, take as their model relations between relative strangers, and assume the only relevant unit is the isolated human agent outside of or "prior to" all social relations. Theories of justice argue "as though social ties did not exist prior to our creating them" (Held, 2006, 84). But these kinds of ethics are ill-suited to cover ethical aspects of particular, often unchosen relations with friends or family members, or indeed, particular aspects of *any* ethical relations.

Feminist care ethics is so important here because it throws the question of our vulnerability to address from others into a decidedly different light, and can thus counterbalance the defensive temptations of a more conventionally political-economic argument. For we are only in a position to provide care for others, or to respond in solidarity to the needs of others, if we are capable of being addressed "heteronomously". The dimensions of vulnerability explored by Butler, Harrison and Schatzki and discussed in Chapter 4 are not only an ineluctable part of embodied human being but the positive condition of possibility for us to act caringly toward others. "Close attention to the feelings, needs, desires and thoughts of those cared for, and a skill in understanding a situation from that person's point of view, are central to caring for someone" (Held, 2006, 31). And these qualities, in turn, are premised upon our fundamental openness to unanticipated appeal, address, solicitation or information whose arrival is not under our control. To return to Waldenfels's terminology, we need to be able to notice (*aufmerken*) when something has become obtrusive or noticeable (*ist aufgefallen*) (Waldenfels, 2004).

If this is the case, then we can no longer view individual autonomy as a general good always to be maximized or defended both for the ethical subject and for those toward whom ethical subjects act. By contrast, Held recommends "mutual autonomy" as a goal. "Mutual autonomy is different from individual autonomy. It includes mutual understandings and acceptance of how much sharing of time, space, daily decisions and so on there will be, and how much independently arrived at activity" (Held, 2006, 55). This meta-level figure of thought, oriented toward a second-order agreement about the appropriate mix of autonomy and interdependence, echoes Rahel Jaeggi's discussion of non-alienated or alienated life, glossed in Chapter 5. Recall that for Jaeggi, the question is not whether we are in complete control of what we do and what we want in life. Inevitably, much of what fills our lives is not of our own making. The question is, rather, whether we are able successfully to "appropriate" what makes up our lives such that we can identify ourselves in it (Jaeggi, 2014). Thus, the maximization of control by itself is neither realistic nor desirable, but rather the goal should be a satisfactory mix of autonomy and heteronomy. The crucial point to make here is that we can think of the problem of occupation in a similar way: the question is not whether we can attain maximal control over what occupies us, but rather the second-order question of whether we have enough of a say in establishing and maintaining a qualitatively and proportionally livable *mix of control and lack of control.* Some, perhaps a great deal, of occupation as a result of unanticipated address from others beyond our control is a good thing.

The expanded political economy of oriented practice that results from complementing the conception of the body as land with these principles of feminist care ethics is thus organized around a core ambivalence stemming from our directional asymmetry. On the one hand, our openness and vulnerability can be the gateway for exploitative occupation driven by the mechanisms of capital accumulation. On the other hand, this same openness and susceptibility to appeals is what allows us to engage in relations of care and solidarity with others. As noted earlier, tensions or contradictions may arise between capitalist demands on bodies as producers and as consumers. These tensions are nested in turn within the more fundamental tension between our occupation by capitalist social relations and our occupation with relations of caring or solidarity that escape the instrumental logic of value production. This fundamental tension between instrumental and non-instrumental relations has in turn been increasingly mirrored, under neoliberal regimes, within the realm of subjects' activities of self-care. Here it is possible to connect political economic and feminist articulations with the problem of occupation to one strand of Foucault's thought.

Feminist care ethics has long recognized the necessity of self-care alongside care for others (Held, 2006, 31). Care of the self, in this context, is to be valued. Foucault's writings on the genealogy of forms of self-government and self-care complicate the picture. In his 1981–1982 lectures, published in English as *The Hermeneutics of the Subject*, Foucault (2005) seeks to understand early forms of the imperative to care for oneself. This is but one of many steps in his long genealogy of modern forms of governance, and in this lecture series he is still a long way from contemporary neoliberalism. Nevertheless, he frames his detailed discussion of the imperative of self-care asserted by Stoics and Cynics with an intriguing qualification that directly implicates occupation in the present day as well. In one of the early lectures setting the frame for his exploration of the theme of self-care in the writings of Stoics and Cynics, Foucault relates the following anecdote:

> Plutarch reports a comment supposedly made by Anaxandridas, a Lacedaemonian, a Spartan, who is asked one day: You Spartans really are a bit strange. You have a lot of land and your territory is huge, or anyway substantial. Why don't you cultivate it yourselves, why do entrust it to helots? And Anaxandridas is supposed to have answered: Well, quite simply, so that we can take care of ourselves.
>
> Foucault, 2005, 31

Foucault returns to this qualification in the following week's lecture, noting again that while a generalization of the imperative to care for oneself can be discerned among Stoics and Cynics, this imperative is not addressed to all. This qualification is not an accident.

> [T]o take care of the self one must have the ability, time, and culture, etcetera, to do so. It is an activity of the elite. [...] Second [...] the effect, meaning and aim of taking care of oneself is to distinguish the individual who takes care of himself from the crowd, from the majority, from the *hoi polloi* who are, precisely, the people absorbed in everyday life.
>
> Foucault, 2005, 75

In the fourth lecture of the term, Foucault again returns to this qualification, and links the possibility of cultivating oneself explicitly with free time or *otium* (Foucault, 2005, 112).

Self-care occupies directed time. This is clear in Foucault's acknowledgment that what was then considered proper care and cultivation of the self depended upon off-loading other forms of activity, and the related recognition that this off-loading both relies upon and reinforces distinctions of class and privilege. The imperative of self-care will resurface in altered form in the culture of neoliberalism that takes shape from the late 1970s onward (Rose, 1999; Ojankangas, 2005; Dardot and Laval, 2014; Brown, 2015). The imperative will no longer be addressed only to the elite, but to all working people. But it will not cease to be the case that self-care is an occupation, a set of directed activities (evening courses, self-improvement programs, special diets, fitness regimes, etc.) that excludes other possible activities while we are engaged in them. And it will not cease to be the case that there are systematic differences in the resources for self-care available to more or less privileged groups. The purpose of these activities under neoliberalism is in many cases precisely to improve the physical and psychological resilience and flexibility of individuals in the face of intensifying pressures to find and hold onto enough work to support oneself and in the face of solicitations and demands from management within any particular employment. As neoliberal subjects, even elite, privileged individuals ignore at their peril the increasingly insistent pressure to live in an ever-more deliberately self-cultivating register.

However, as Alexandra Rau points out, Foucault does not distinguish clearly enough between this kind of self-cultivation for the sake of competitive advantage and healthy self-care more in line with feminist discussions (Rau, 2010, 15). Indeed, as Rau discovers in her research with workers, the latter more positive side of self-care is often a matter of "defense of the self" against occupation by the former kind: the goal is "at the same time to dissolve the obligation or 'chaining' of the self (*die Haftbarmachung des Selbst/Selbstver-haftung*) to work and to occupy in a new and different way the self-relation with other systems, themes and interests". She even calls this project "the re-occupation of the self" (Rau, 2010, 342). Thus, to summarize, in addition to the fundamental ambivalence of our omnidirectional openness to address and appeal, the tension between capitalistic-exploitative and healthy, constructive occupations of our directed practice, it is possible to discern a similar tension nested within practices of self-care that have become an increasingly central site of contestation in neoliberal regimes.

Time-space compression, acceleration and contradiction

If the above can be taken as a plausible initial outline of a political economy of directed practice, on what basis can we say that the issues it raises are becoming increasingly important in the early 21st century Global North? A range of perspectives discussed throughout this book have invoked both neo-liberalism and recent advances in information technology. These phenomena can be placed within the historical-geographic development of practices and conceptions of space and time under capitalism. In particular, they can be seen as the latest stages in the long, uneven and contested process of capitalist "annihilation of space by time" and the associated "time-space compression" or "sense of overwhelming change in space-time dimensionality" (Harvey, 1990, 426). Building upon the discussion above about the increasing impossibility of spatially separating production and consumption, I would now like to reframe the relation between distance and direction in socio-spatial theory. Up to now I have treated them as two competing or complementary lenses upon a range of phenomena. But my contention is that it is possible to see the relation between these lenses as embedded in an historical process of change.

The basic thesis here is that the tendency of much modern socio-spatial theory to place questions of distance at the center of analysis and to sideline direction is appropriate to a stage of time-space compression that is now passing, at least for privileged denizens of the Global North. The shrinkage of effective distance through technological change driven by the dynamics of capital accumulation can in fact be seen as an historical precondition for the new importance of direction. As effective distance shrinks ever more strongly, especially through information and communication technologies, increases in what Anthony Giddens calls the "presence availability" of material and immaterial goods to people, as well as of people to each other, diminishes the significance of physical mobility as a barrier (Giddens, 1984, 122). This much is well known. But my claim is that *the diminishing importance of distance tends to increase the importance of direction*. If we can do a wider range of things anywhere we happen to be, then shifting from one activity to another is less often a matter of moving between places and more often a matter of *turning*. It is no longer a question of being limited by distance in what we can do but by the inherent directedness of our embodied activities. Reduced to an admittedly oversimplified slogan, *turning is the new moving*. Of course moving, too, is becoming easier, as can be seen in the increase of international travel. However, moving is becoming less central as a condition of possibility for switching from one activity to another in the everyday lives of millions.

And even when on the move, our location generally matters less than it used to in determining what we can and cannot do. The process of dropping one matter of concern in order to pick up another is thus becoming all the more salient as an organizing principle for individual lives in the social contexts of the Global North. Thus, too, the political economy of orientation – questions of who or what is able to occupy us, how much control we have over this process, and which interests are served by our turnings, which concerns are relegated thereby to the realm of social dark matter – is becoming more salient.

It is important to stress that this historic – and of course still very uneven and incomplete – shift from moving to turning *is not an emancipation from constraint*. This is because time-space compression *has no directional equivalent*: embodied human beings are for all intents and purposes just as limited in the directional scope of our active engagements as we were hundreds or thousands of years ago (Gazzaley and Rosen, 2016). Thus, while presence availability, or the proximity of potential partners in interaction, has certainly increased in a dramatic fashion through time-space compression, "engagement-availability" has in directional terms not changed much if at all. Put differently, the more possibilities we have to do any of a wide range of things at any point in time and space, *the more starkly we are confronted with the fact that any one engagement is temporarily exclusive of others*. The dialectical movement away from distance and toward directionality is the most important sense in which our universal characteristics as embodied human beings are being strained in a new way by the historical dynamics of capitalism. This dialectical transition from distance to direction is also the key context for understanding the impacts of what Rosa calls "social acceleration" (Rosa, 2015).

One of the dimensions of acceleration Rosa identifies is the increasing pressure for many actors in the Global North not simply to do more in and with time, but to devote ever more time and effort recursively to the problem of prioritizing and planning time and effort (Rosa, 2015). Other scholars have noticed this increasing imperative to choose (Schwartz, 2005). It is possible to think of this phenomenon both as a directional problem and as an increasing "occupation by freedom". It illustrates very well the principle that runs through much of Foucault's work on governmentality, namely that "freedom" is always an historically specific and shifting construct which can function as a means of government. Behind this trend lie some of the central pillars of neoliberal governance, especially the privatization of public goods and services, from health insurance and pensions to public transport and utilities (Dardot and Laval, 2014). Privatization is usually accompanied by the creation of artificial markets for public goods, which forces individual actors to make more choices. At the same time, it contributes to higher unemployment, the precarization of work for those who still have it, and wage suppression within privatized industries, and thus pushes ever larger numbers of workers into taking on multiple jobs.

A second, related dimension of pressure on directed time is what Rosa calls "desynchronization" (Rosa, 2015, 51, 274). By this he means, at the smallest scales, divergence between the demands of institutionally-specific time structures (such as opening times, work deadlines, etc.), on the one hand, and the integrative imperatives structuring agents' time planning (coordinating work and errands with meals, etc.) on the other. This problem can be seen, among other things, as heightening the difficulties of the "double career" for women still battling its demands. Similarly to the effects of increased forced choice, desynchronization also tends to require that more of our attention and practice be directed to issues of coordination more frequently than in the past. In the political economy of directed practice being sketched here, I propose that we think of the three spheres of intensified "work on the self" (that is, the instrumental kind of self-care) in the context of increasingly precarious employment, our increasing responsibility for making forced choices as consumers of formerly public goods, and the heightened pressure of logistical coordination brought on by desynchronization together comprise a sphere of "second order" practices cutting across the spheres of production and reproduction. It is a hallmark of accelerated neoliberal capitalism that these second-order activities occupy an increasing proportion of our directed time.

If, on the one hand, the decreasing importance of distance means that more of the segmentation of activities is accomplished by turning than by traveling, and if, on the other hand, pressures upon finite, directed engagement-time are mounting, it should not be surprising to see an increase in pathologies relating to the over-solicited directedness of our attention and practice. Some cognitive symptoms of this situation have been flagged by Stiegler and others as a collective cognitive disability, a "crisis of attention" (Jackson, 2009) or a "global attention deficit disorder" (Stiegler, 2010a, 2010b; Türcke, 2016). Stiegler claims that this crisis of attention threatens to undermine the flow of ever-renewed desire capitalism needs in order for consumption to continue keeping pace with expanded production. Byung-Chul Han identifies a growing collective exhaustion as a hallmark of neoliberal subjects (Han, 2014, 2015). Earlier stages of the present argument have asserted that such stresses and strains concern not just attention but directed practice more generally. The sketch of a political economic argument presented here should accordingly further ground the analysis of directional alienation given in Chapter 5. A general increase in alienation as an inability to cope adequately with the frequency and uncontrolled external sources of demands upon our finite directed time could signal the emergence or perhaps increasing saliency of a new contradiction of 21st-century capitalism.

Harvey has identified seventeen contradictions that in various combinations may conspire to destabilize contemporary capitalism (Harvey, 2014). The crisis of directed practice outlined here can be seen as a contradiction brought on by increasingly unmeetable demands of production, reproduction, care, solidarity, and second-order activities. Such pressures do not fall upon infinitely elastic embodied human beings who can, through technology or increasingly sophisticated prosthetics, arbitrarily expand our directional capacities. As psychological research has shown, live, focused attention *is not like memory or computing power: it is not something we can outsource* (Styles, 2006; Gazzaley and Rosen, 2016). The same is true, I submit, for active, critical-creative engagement in practices: it is inherently directionally limited. Labor-saving devices, algorithm-driven pre-selection apps, etc. may take a growing number of tasks for which we are responsible off our hands. But whatever tasks are on our hands temporarily exclude the doing of other tasks. And we can only deal with the results of outsourced tasks by, again, turning to engage them. One way for individuals to respond to this situation is through more frequent task-switching. However, this does not increase our practical capacity. And as suggested in Chapters 5 and 6, it may lead to new forms of alienation.

I would like to frame all of this once again within the tremendously powerful social model developed by activists and scholars of disability studies (Oliver and Barnes, 2012). According to this model, which has its roots not coincidentally in historical materialism, the question of whether a particular individual or group is "abled" or "disabled" is situational and contingent. The degree of fit between embodied capabilities or incapabilities and the physical, cognitive, emotional and social environments within which we move – the degree of what Ahmed calls "comfort" (Ahmed, 2006, 134–135) – is dependent upon both the variable biological features of bodies and the social norms according to which environments are constructed. Bodies whose capabilities are not adequately served by "normal" environments are thereby disabled. There are clearly differences among embodied individuals and social groups as to how susceptible they are to which kinds of disablement. As feminist care ethics makes clear, there are also different phases or episodes in life during which *all* individuals are more disabled in relation to normal environments (Tronto, 1993). Seeing "ability" and "disability" in this contingent, relational way has a crucial implication I want to highlight here: there is no guarantee of *general* adequacy in the relation between typical embodied capabilities and normal environments. It is possible to imagine phases of crisis in which a larger-than-normal proportion of a given population finds itself unable adequately to cope with the formerly normal environments of everyday life. This may arise because of uncoordinated increases in demands upon our different capabilities that together result in a more general disablement. It is at least possible that we are now seeing this kind of situation emerging with respect to the finite capabilities of directed practice even of the privileged denizens of the 21st-century Global North.

Social dark matter and reproduction by neglect

The foregoing sections have elaborated that part of the political economy of oriented practice that builds upon and contextualizes the analysis of alienation begun in Chapter 5. This final section expands – though not at such length – upon the account of reification given in Chapter 6, and in so doing, completes the outline of a political economy. I would like to suggest that the countless profiles we trail out behind us, individually and collectively, in the course of turning away from a succession of matters of concern and editing them into a montage, can be thought of metaphorically as helping to compose a vast but hitherto neglected realm of "social dark matter". In a manner roughly analogous to the role cosmologists attribute to physical dark matter in holding galaxies together, my contention is that the mass of (re-reified) matters we *have* turned away from – the clips lying on the cutting floor – together with the vast realm of matters we *are* turned away from in any instance, comprise a tremendously important source of the "inertia" of social relations. This inertia derives not from the specific content or meaning of that with which we have never been or are no longer engaged, but with the "weighty" fact of our *actual* non-engagement with it. "The field of positive action, of what this or that body does do, also defines a field of inaction, of actions that are possible but that are not taken up, or even actions that are not possible because of what has been taken up" (Ahmed, 2006, 58). One absolutely central aim of the present book is to insist that the things we are not doing are important to a very significant extent *because we are not doing them at this moment.*

The standard line taken in a number of strands of social theory drawing upon the "phenomenology of the 'I can'" (Ahmed, 2006, 138) – that we could be doing other things or were doing them at some time in the past – is, to be sure, still important. It would be folly to deny the role of temporal ekstases of memory and anticipation, or of retention and protention, in the flow of social practice. Likewise, it is necessary to acknowledge, as noted in Chapter 6, that repeated engagement with a matter of concern can and often does alter our habitual relations with the world in permanent ways. Further, distance and geographical extent as factors in ballasting social relations continue to be important. As Giddens notes, "the greater the time-space distanciation of social systems – the more their institutions bite into time and space – the more resistant they are to manipulation or change by any individual agent" (Giddens, 1984, 171). In part because of the time-space distanciation of social systems, it is also still the case that social reproduction occurs in part through "unintended consequences" of action. But the exclusive focus on these factors illegitimately neglects the central importance of the here-and-now-moment in practices of all kinds. Social dark matter is the weighty mass of what we are not doing, not engaging with actively, critically or creatively, *at any and every moment*. Social dark matter is at least partly indifferent to the political valence of what comprises it: it is composed just as much of instances of social "transformation" as of social "reproduction". As something we have turned away from, though, even a transformative action or engagement is inert, unless and until we ourselves or someone else actively take it up and reanimate it with critical, transformative or creative potential.

My proposal here is that focusing upon the social dark matter in back spaces highlights a second form of reproduction encompassing the much larger realm of non-engagement, which we might term "reproduction by neglect". Reproduction by neglect can be defined as the aggregate effect of patterns of collective non-engagement in allowing that which is not engaged to persist. Thus, for example, "capitalism" in the sense that this term is understood in critical social science inhabits the collective social dark matter of large swathes of the populations of the Global North. This is not just because large numbers of actors themselves explicitly assume the term refers to something real (that is, reify it in the familiar sense) and act accordingly (Gibson-Graham, 1996). Indeed, despite periodic revivals of the term in times of crisis, its use is probably far less widespread than alternative terms such as "market economy" or "global economy". Even more important is the fact that the vast majority of actors, whether individuals, groups or institutions, leave a relatively stable suite of political-economic matters critically unengaged and unattended. This systematic lack of attention and engagement cannot be chalked up entirely to the effects of ideological misrecognition. More fundamentally, many people have never understood key "capitalist" phenomena "as" anything at all, whether rightly or wrongly. Similarly, to return again to Ahmed's point, "race becomes given insofar as it does not have our attention. If race is behind what we do, then it is what we do" (Ahmed, 2006, 131). It is hard to imagine a pithier expression of the logic of reproduction by neglect I seek to emphasize here: "If X is behind what we do, then X is what we do". This implies that "what we do" has two parts: what we are actively doing, and what we are reproducing by being turned away from it.

The concepts of social dark matter and reproduction by neglect fill in the "backside" of the political economy of oriented practice, and thus bring this initial sketch to a close. They suggest a different gloss on Marx's phrase about social processes taking place "behind the backs of" producers, consumers, subjects in general (Marx, 1967, 51–52). One implication of this directional way of seeing things is that political and ethical questions of what is to be done necessarily become more complex. Such questions will be the subject of the concluding chapter, which offers some ideas for a directional approach to ethics. Before that, however, Chapter 8 brings graphic depictions of social dark matter, of the directional subject and of turning together in order to summarize important parts of the argument in an updated version of time geography.

References

Ahmed, S. (2006). *Queer Phenomenology: Orientations, Objects, Others*. Durham, NC: Duke University Press.

Althusser, L. (1971). Ideology and ideological state apparatuses. In: L. Althusser, *Lenin and Philosophy and Other Essays*. Trans. B. Brewster. London: New Left Books, pp. 127–186.

Barrett, M. (2014). *Women's Oppression Today: The Marxist/Feminist Encounter*, 3rd ed. London: Verso.

Beller, J. (2006). *The Cinematic Mode of Production: Attention Economy and the Society of the Spectacle*. Dartmouth, NH: Dartmouth College Press.

Benjamin, W. (2008). *The Work of Art in the Age of Mechanical Reproduction*. Trans. J. Underwood. London: Penguin.

Brown, W. (2015). *Undoing the Demos: Neoliberalism's Stealth Revolution*. Brooklyn, NY: Zone Books.

Dardot, P. and Laval, C. (2014). *The New Way of the World: On Neoliberal Society*. Trans. G. Elliott. London: Verso.

Davies, K. (2001). Responsibility and daily life: reflections over time-space. In: J. May and N. Thrift, eds, *TimeSpace:Geographies of Temporality*. London: Routledge, pp. 133–148.

Domosh, M. (1998). Those "Gorgeous Incongruities": Polite Politics and Public Space on the Streets of Nineteenth-Century New York City. *Annals of the Association of American Geographers* 88(2), pp. 209–226.

Domosh, M. and Seager, J. (2001). *Putting Women in Place: Feminist Geographers Make Sense of the World*. New York: Guilford Press.

Fleck, L. (1981). *Genesis and Development of a Scientific Fact*. Trans. F. Bradley. Chicago, IL: University of Chicago Press.

Foucault, M. (2005). *The Hermeneutics of the Subject: Lectures at the Collège de France, 1981–1982*. Trans. G. Burchell. New York: Palgrave Macmillan.

Fracchia, J. (2005). Beyond the human-nature debate: human corporeal organization as the 'first fact' of historical materialism. *Historical Materialism*, 13, pp. 33–61.

Gazzaley, A. and Rosen, L. (2016). *The Distracted Mind: Ancient Brains in a High-Tech World*. Cambridge, MA: MIT Press.

Gibson-Graham, J.-K. (1996). *The End of Capitalism (As We Knew It)*. Oxford: Blackwell.

Giddens, A. (1984). *The Constitution of Society*. London: Polity Press.

Goodley, D. (2014). *Dis/Ability Studies: Theorising Disablism and Ableism*. New York: Routledge.

Guthman, J. and DePuis, M. (2006). Embodying neoliberalism: economy, culture and the politics of fat. *Environment and Planning D: Society and Space*, 24, pp. 427–448.

Han, B.-C. (2014): *Psychopolitik: Neoliberalismus und die neuen Machttechniken*. Frankfurt am Main: Fischer Verlag.

Han, B.-C. (2015). *The Burnout Society*. Trans. E. Butler. Palo Alto, CA: Stanford University Press.

Hanson, S. and Pratt, G. (1988). Reconceptualizing the links between home and work in urban geography. *Economic Geography*, 64(4), pp. 299–321.

Harvey, D. (1982). *The Limits to Capital*. Chicago, IL: University of Chicago Press.

Harvey, D. (1990). Between space and time: reflections on the geographical imagination. *Annals of the Association of American Geographers*, 80(3), pp. 418–434.

Harvey, D. (1998). The body as an accumulation strategy. *Environment and Planning D: Society and Space*, 16(4), pp. 401–421.

Harvey, D. (2014). *Seventeen Contradictions and the End of Capitalism*. Oxford: Oxford University Press.

Held, V. (2006). *The Ethics of Care: Personal, Political and Global*. Oxford: Oxford University Press.

Herman, E. and Chomsky, N. (1988). *Manufacturing Consent: The Political Economy of the Mass Media.* New York: Pantheon.

Jackson, M. (2009). *Distracted: The Erosion of Attention and the Coming Dark Age.* New York: Prometheus Books.

Jaeggi, R. (2014). *Alienation.* Trans. A. Smith. New York: Columbia University Press.

James, W. (1950). *The Principles of Psychology.* 2 Volumes. New York: Dover.

Kirsch, S. and Mitchell, D. (2004). The nature of things: dead labor, non-human actors, and the persistence of Marxism. *Antipode,* 36(4): 687–705.

Leroi-Gourhan, A. (1993). *Gesture and Speech.* Trans. A. Bostock Berger. Cambridge, MA: MIT Press.

Lukács, G. (1971). *History and Class Consciousness: Studies in Marxist Dialectics.* Trans. R. Livingstone. Cambridge, MA: MIT Press.

Marx, K. (1967). *Capital,* Vol. 1. Trans. S. Moore, E. Aveling. New York: International Publishers.

Mészáros, I. (2006). *Marx's Theory of Alienation.* Delhi: Aakar Books.

Mészáros, I. (2008). *The Challenge and Burden of Historical Time: Socialism in the Twenty-First Century.* New York: Monthly Review Press.

Noddings, N. (2013). *Caring: A Feminine Approach to Ethics and Moral Education.* 2nd ed. Berkele, CAy: University of California Press.

Ojakangas, M. (2005). Impossible dialogue on bio-power: Agamben and Foucault. *Foucault Studies,* 2, pp. 5–28.

Oliver, M. and Barnes, C. (2012). *The New Politics of Disablement.* London: Palgrave Macmillan.

Orzeck, R. (2007). What does not kill you: historical materialism and the body. *Environment and Planning D: Society and Space,* 25, pp. 496–514.

Palm, R. and Pred, A. (1978). A time-geographic perspective on problems of inequality for women. In: D.A. Lanegran and R. Palm, eds., *An Invitation to Geography.* New York: McGraw-Hill.

Peck, J. (2010). *Constructions of Neoliberal Reason.* Oxford: Oxford University Press.

Postone, M. (1993). *Time, Labor, and Social Domination: A Reinterpretation of Marx's Critical Theory.* Cambridge: Cambridge University Press.

Rau, A. (2010). *Psychopolitik: Macht Subjekt und Arbeit in der Neoliberalen Gesellschaft.* Frankfurt am Main: Campus Verlag.

Rosa, H. (2015). *Social Acceleration: A New Theory of Modernity.* Trans. J. Trejo-Mathys. New York: Columbia University Press.

Rose, N. (1999). *Powers of Freedom: Reframing Political Thought.* Cambridge: Cambridge University Press.

Schatzki, T. (2010). *The Timespace of Human Activity: On Performance, Society, and History as Indeterminate Teleological Events.* Lanham, MD: Lexington Books.

Schwartz, B. (2005). *The Paradox of Choice: Why More is Less.* New York: Harper Perennial.

Shove, E., Pantzar, M., and Watson, M. (2012). *The Dynamics of Social Practice: Everyday Life and How It Changes.* London: Sage.

Srnicek, N. (2016). *Platform Capitalism.* Cambridge: Polity Press.

Stiegler, B. (2010a). *Taking Care of Youth and the Generations.* Trans. S. Barker. Stanford, CA: Stanford University Press.

Stiegler, B. (2010b). *For a New Critique of Political Economy.* Trans. D. Ross. London: Polity.

Styles, E. (2006). *The Psychology of Attention.* 2nd ed. New York: Psychology Press.

Tronto, J. (1993). *Moral Boundaries: A Political Argument for an Ethic of Care.* New York: Routledge.

Türcke, C. (2016). Aufmerksamkeitsdefizitkultur. In: J. Müller, A. Nießeler and A. Rauh, eds., *Aufmerksamkeit: Neue Humanwissenschaftliche Perspektiven.* Bielefeld: Transcript, pp. 101–114.

Waldenfels, B. (2004). *Phänomenologie der Aufmerksamkeit.* Frankfurt am Main: Suhrkamp.

8   Visualizing directed social practice

In this chapter the graphic depictions accompanying the argument through most of the book will be brought together in a kind of visual summary. This will help consolidate the directional sensibility it has been my intent throughout to develop. It will also provide opportunities for further sharpening some of the insights that have remained inchoate or under-developed until now. Sybille Krämer argues that through techniques of visualization, ways of thinking can become possible "that could not be realized, or only with difficulty, without the operational space of the surface. Inscribed surfaces open spaces of thought, they enhance cognitive creativity and mobility" (Krämer, 2016, 18). This is the hope of the present chapter. It starts with a speculative graphical exploration of configurations of social dark matter, following up on the last section of the previous chapter. These diagrams are then integrated into the graphical symbolism of time-geography. A brief history of time-geography and its symbolism is offered in the second section, followed by some graphical innovations building upon the work of Paul Channing Adams and Helen Couclelis. The result is not a complete graphical language for depicting directed practice, but rather an initial set of elements that might be elaborated and integrated further.

Picturing constellations of social dark matter

To specify in more detail how social dark matter plays a role in reproducing socio-spatial relations, it may be helpful to identify a handful of paradigmatic, broad-brush configurations of interpersonal and collective social engagement and social dark matter, each an abstract and simplified graphic representation of a distribution of engagement and non-engagement among a group of people. This typology is merely illustrative, and in real life many situations involve much more complex combinations of the configurations presented here. Also, each diagram is essentially a momentary, static snapshot. As we all move between different engagements in the course of a day, week, year or lifetime, we necessarily also co-produce shifting patterns of social dark matter as well. The point here is merely, once again, to cultivate a *sensibility* for directional aspects of practice. Figure 8.1 is a graphic representation of a generic interpersonal engagement.

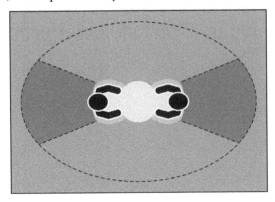

Figure 8.1 Basic interpersonal engagement

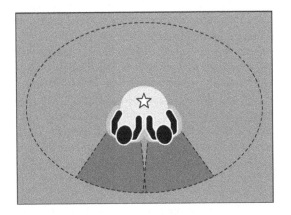

Figure 8.2 Joint engagement with a shared theme

This could be thought of as the most basic "donut" scenario: two people have each other as their theme, perhaps as friends, as lovers, in a heated conflict, or simply as temporary conversational partners over lunch. I call it a donut scenario because, in being so focused, the participants are at the same time not engaged with everything outside the topic of their joint attention. The oval-shaped region demarcated by the dashed line indicates that the dorsal spaces of the two individuals extend around the entire scene. A second basic donut scenario is that of joint engagement with a shared theme (Figure 8.2). In this scenario, the relation between participants' orientations is depicted as an acute angle. Here it is not the individuals who are each others' foci but they are still partially turned toward each other because they are doing or attending to something together. Again, their joint dorsal spaces should be understood to surround the scene.

Both of these basic donut scenarios can also involve larger groups. For example, Figure 8.3 might represent a situation of group therapy or a family dinner in which the primary focus of participants is upon each other.

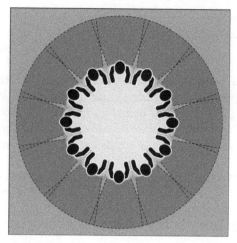

Figure 8.3 Group engagement

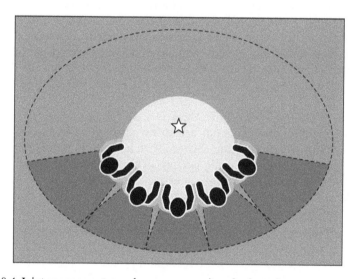

Figure 8.4 Joint engagement as a larger community of orientation

Figure 8.4 depicts a larger version of the basic joint attention scenario, what Sara Ahmed, drawing upon Benedict Anderson, calls a community of orientation:

> When citizens read a given paper, they are not necessarily reading the same thing […], let alone reading the same thing in the same way. Yet the

very act of reading means that citizens are directing their attention toward a shared object.

Ahmed, 2006, 119

This configuration could also apply to some cooperative forms of labor, or to games. In a less optimistic register, it could represent the kind of collective, passive distraction diagnosed by Benjamin (2008) or Debord (2009). In this case the donut of social dark matter would encompass (among other things) the real capitalist social relations to which the spellbound working class is not attending.

Figure 8.5 shows the most basic configuration of non-engagement: two people turned away from each other. Regardless of what the two are respectively engaged with, they are mutually unengaged with each other. If we expand this configuration to depict a larger group, it is more easily described as a "donut-hole" scenario, suggested by the dashed circle drawn in the shared dorsal space (Figure 8.6).

The donut-hole scenario can be taken as an image of the kind of atomization of social relations some theorists of alienation have diagnosed, or, to take another example, of an excessive focus on the pursuit of self-interest. Finally, it could represent people pointed away from each other absorbed in their smartphones. In all cases, mutual non-engagement is represented geometrically by the obtuse angles between all the individuals involved. The social dark matter comprising the collectively non-engaged can be seen as the arena of potential collective engagement itself, whether interpersonal or larger in scope.

In each of these ideal scenarios there is a distribution of engagement and non-engagement in which it is not necessarily clear whether the combination of what is and what is not being engaged with adds up to a desirable politics. For example, the more optimistic reading of the scenario of shared focus in Figure 8.4 seems from a critical-progressive perspective preferable to that of the circle of isolated individuals each with their back turned to the arena of

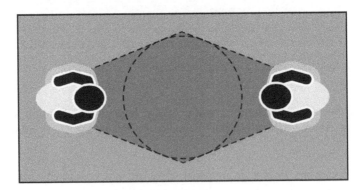

Figure 8.5 Basic interpersonal non-engagement

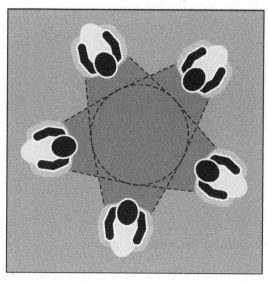

Figure 8.6 Shared non-engagement of a larger group

common interest. But a common project may leave crucial issues in the outer donut of social dark matter. This is more or less the critique of local, communitarian approaches to social politics as provincialist. The overall point of presenting these diagrams is, again, to cultivate a sense for the double character of everything we do in engaging in directed social practices of whatever sort. To paraphrase Sara Ahmed again: in doing what we actively do, we are also "doing" (directionally reifying, "reproducing by neglect") whatever we are *not* engaged with.

A final diagram can be proposed here on the basis of the visual logic outlined in the foregoing diagrams. This logic has been presented thus far in binary terms of either shared engagement or shared non-engagement. There is a third possibility, namely non-reciprocated and unshared, that is, one-way, engagement. In this constellation, one or more parties are engaged in some way with another individual or group, while the second party is not engaged with the first. This could be thought of as the most basic configuration underlying solidarity, active discrimination or oppression, or the wide range of other one-way social relations between these two ends of the spectrum (Figure 8.7).

The individuals directed toward the others are themselves in the social dark matter of those with whom they are concerned. Formally speaking, this is a special case of the joint-attention scenario depicted in Figure 8.2. But since the "objects" of joint attention are themselves subjects who could in principle turn toward those attending to or engaging with them, this scenario represents an especially significant range of possibilities for social connection. My suggestion is that if a larger, more complex web of social engagements and

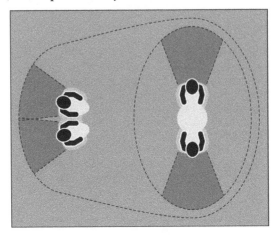

Figure 8.7 Unreciprocated or transversal engagement

non-engagements generally lacks this kind of transverse connection between different groups and individuals, it is in danger of the kind of atomization Margaret Thatcher captured in her claim that "there is no such thing as society". On the other hand, to the extent that this kind of transverse linkage between strangers takes more negative than positive forms, it can support internal fragmentation or tribalism. It is thus best thought of as a necessary but not a sufficient condition for relations of solidarity.

These schematic diagrams must remain vague and speculative. There is a great deal they are not capable of representing, for example the nesting of different scales of neglect within the realm of social dark matter. Nevertheless, they suggest some of the complexity of reproduction by neglect. In the second main section of this chapter, these diagrams will be integrated into a reworked graphical vocabulary of time-geography.

Time-geography

The scaffolding for the graphic constructions presented here will be the daily-path and life-path diagrams central to early work in time-geography (Hägerstrand, 1967, 1996; Parkes and Thrift, 1980; Pred, 1977, 1981, 1984; Thrift and Pred, 1981). Time-geographic diagrams and analysis have repeatedly been revived, critiqued, adapted and further developed in the decades since the first generation of researchers inspired by Torsten Hägerstrand. The somewhat vague geometrical and mathematical assumptions of its early iterations have been rendered more precise and analytically flexible (Miller, 2005; Miller and Bridwell, 2009). The limitations of time-geography in the face of recent developments in information and communications technology have been addressed with newly expanded conceptions of space and representational forms (Adams, 1995; Couclelis, 2009; Kwan, 2000, 2002).

The conception of human life and social reproduction transported by time geography and its visualization techniques has also been critiqued (e.g., Baker, 1979; Buttimer, 1976; Gregson, 1986; Rose, 1993). In response to critical reflections, researchers have supplemented time geographic analytical tools with greater attention to how political, cultural, experiential and bodily considerations shape social life (Kwan, 2000; McQuoid and Dijst, 2012; Scholten, Friberg, and Sandén, 2012).

The representational notation of time-geography is compatible with the diagrams I have developed in this book in the basic sense that both are geometrical constructions set in a Euclidean time-space framework. As Helen Couclelis notes, approaches like these that seek to bring together "a descriptive model of individual movement [...] with an explanatory concept that may extend into psychology, qualitative social science, and the humanities" are characterized by inner tensions (Couclelis, 2009, 1561). "Because the language of geometry is so fundamentally different from that of social science, these two pieces fit together only imperfectly" (Couclelis, 2009, 1563). The link I have sought to establish between these two registers is rooted in the argument of Chapter 4, where the experience of directed engagement as it is manifested in the lived body (*Leib*) is integrated with the physical context of corporeal (*körperliche*) organization. Corporeal organization, understood, following Leroi-Gourhan, in terms of the anterior relational field in which our sensory, manipulative, communicative and expressive capabilities are most effectively bundled, forms the basis for a zonation of lived embodiment into anterior/frontal, lateral and dorsal spaces that can be represented in geometrical terms. Corporeal organization provides the "backbone" to the more labile and fluid lived body. It is the physical body as well through which what I have called directed time forms the context in which the temporal retentions and protentions of Edmund Husserl, as well as the temporal ekstases of Martin Heidegger, are lived out. The geometrical framework of embodied directionality is, finally, at the root of the notion of occupation as a formal way of understanding power relations. In short, while the tension Couclelis identifies cannot and should not be overcome or denied, the present argument does explicitly ground this tension in the relation between corporeal and lived (*leibliche*) features of embodied life. It is this grounding that in turn makes the use of time-geographic notation compatible with the larger argument.

A good starting point for the representative strategies proposed below is the relatively basic graphical language of time-geography's early heyday. A full account of the graphical repertoire developed by Hägerstrand and others to represent the temporal and spatial tissues of social life, along with the range of analyses this graphic system has supported, is unnecessary. But a brief overview in the first section will set the stage for the enhancements offered later in the chapter. An important point that emerges from the overview of the time-geographic perspective is that it is heavily focused upon distance, with no correspondingly developed account of the directed nature of practice.

The following section draws upon the more recent work of Adams (1995) and Helen Couclelis (2000, 2009) to argue that accelerated, technologically mediated life under neoliberal capitalism is in the process of fundamentally altering the temporal and spatial presuppositions of time-geography. The graphical innovations of Adams and some of the arguments of Couclelis provide helpful tools with which to accommodate these changes. However, even these more recent analyses, like the older versions of time-geography they seek to improve, remain one-sidedly focused upon the issue of distance. They thus do not fully appreciate a major implication of their own arguments, namely, that direction, and especially *turning*, must become more central to our understanding of how social life is organized in temporal-spatial terms. To remedy this one-sidedness, the diagrams of both early and more recent time-geography are enhanced by building in some of the graphic elements developed in the foregoing chapters. The result is a visual overview of how a directional sensibility allows a more complete picture of social practice, and of the political economy of oriented practice.

The two foundational concepts of time-geography are "path" and "project". Figure 8.8 illustrates the most basic features of early daily-path and life-path diagrams.

Space is represented by the two horizontal axes, time by the vertical axis – a reduced Newtonian conception. The daily-paths are the two lines moving through space and time. When we are stationary (at work, at home, etc.), our paths take the form of vertical line segments: we are moving through time but not through space. Movements from one place to another are diagonal lines, because we are moving in both space and time. Slower movements trace steeper lines (less space is traversed for each unit of time); more rapid

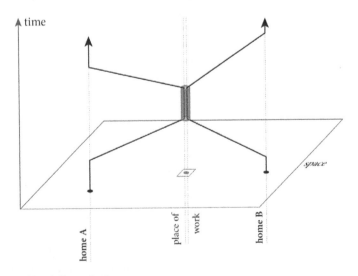

Figure 8.8 The daily-path diagram

movements are closer to horizontal, as we cover more ground in a given amount of time. These diagrams, sometimes referred to as "dioramas", can depict different temporal-spatial scales. Thus, for example, the distinction between daily-path and life-path diagrams, the latter depicting the sequence of places one has lived or traveled over many years or an entire lifetime. The diagrams are most often used, as above, to represent what Pred calls the "choreography of existence" at the scale of daily life (Pred, 1977).

One of the overarching questions addressed by time geography is how the geographies of individual and collective life are shaped by distances between places where different social interactions and processes happen, and by the fact that these interactions and processes require the presence or co-presence of people. In Figure 8.8, the cylinder where the two life-paths run together for a period of time is a situation of co-presence. These basic spatial and temporal parameters set limits either upon individuals in terms of how many and which activities within what distances they can integrate into their life paths, or alternatively, upon social activities and processes in terms of which people can be involved in them. The simplest version of these limits are represented as time-space "prisms", that is, as abstract envelopes tracing the maximum distance over which it is possible to travel and return to a starting point within a given amount of time and given a particular mode of movement (Figure 8.9).

The second basic concept of time-geography, "project", signifies the fact that daily-paths and life-paths are often composed of goal-directed practices that can involve sequences of different tasks performed in the same or in different places. Our movements through different place-based activities are neither random nor merely constrained by spatial and temporal conditions but also positively shaped and specified by practical logics. This attention to projects is one of the senses in which time geography is not merely a notational system but a way of analysing social practices (Thrift and Pred, 1981, 278–280). The conception of projects suggests one important point of overlap with the account of directed practice developed here, in particular with Schatzki's practice theory. In language very similar to Schatzki's description of "teleoaffective structure", Pred notes that "the tasks associated with a

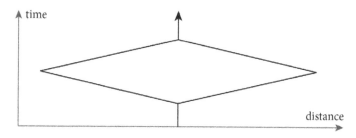

Figure 8.9 The time-space prism

project almost always possess an internal logic of their own which requires that they be sequenced in a more or less specific order" (Pred, 1981, 10).

Central to time-geographic studies is the fact that paths and projects are subject to considerations of temporal-spatial constraint. Pred pithily summarizes three main kinds of constraint people may face in pursuing projects:

- Capability constraints "circumscribe activity participation by demanding that large chunks of time be allocated to physiological necessities (sleeping, eating, and personal care) and by limiting the distance an individual can cover within a given time-span in accord with the transportation technology available".
- Coupling constraints "pinpoint where, when, and for how long the individual must join other individuals (or objects) in order to form production, consumption, social, and miscellaneous activity bundles".
- Authority constraints "in some measure spring from the simple fact that space-occupation is exclusive and that all spaces have a limited packing capacity. Authority constraints subsume those general rules, laws, economic barriers, and power relationships which determine who does or does not have access to specific domains at specific times to do specific things". Pred, 1977, 208

Pred goes on to identify further general or underlying constraints, including the indivisibility of human bodies, making it impossible for someone to be in two places at once; the path-dependency of situations; and, most significantly for the present argument, "the limited ability of any human being to undertake more than one task at a time" (Pred, 1977, 208).

Even in many of its recent iterations and adaptations, time-geography and its path diagrams have remained heavily focused upon issues of distance, co-presence, and "presence availability" (Giddens, 1984, 122), or the proximity of potential partners in interaction. In all of this, scant attention is paid to the phenomena of direction at issue in the present book. Direction is certainly depicted in daily-path and life-path diagrams in a basic sense, but is not a core analytical theme. Thus, for example, time-space prisms depicting the envelope of maximum travel distance within a given time (see Figure 8.9 above) are usually drawn as indifferent to direction. Travel times are assumed to be the same in all directions. These prisms could indeed be seen as particularly clear visual expressions of the "petri-dish" model of human agency critiqued in earlier chapters, or as visualizations of "the phenomenology of the 'I can'" (Ahmed, 2006, 138). This is in effect the underlying sense of "capability constraints": they define the temporal and spatial limits of the "I can" to the extent that capability requires physical presence. "Coupling constraints", the limitations imposed by the need to be in specific places at specific times, necessarily involve direction as well as distance in every concrete instance. To take an example from feminist geographical research, where one works in relation to the home neighborhood as this relates to the need to pick up children after school is not just a question of "how far away" (Hanson and Pratt, 1988), but always also of "in which direction". The specifics of direction become decisive as soon as any other coupling constraint comes into play. For example, in the triangle formed by home, children's school and shopping that must be negotiated by a parent, what matters is not just how far school and shopping are from home but also in which direction they lie relative to each other. A shopping center close to home but in the opposite direction from the school is quite possibly less helpful to the parent than one further from home but closer to the school. Despite the central importance of such issues in time-geographic studies, direction remains a marginal or only implicit theme.

From distance to direction in time-geography

The enhancements of time-geographic notation I will introduce below are intended to remedy this oversight, and to improve time-geography's analytical potential. However, the heightened focus upon the directedness of practice I propose to introduce is not just a matter of improving a model; it is also intended as an acknowledgment of ongoing changes to socio-spatial life in the Global North, specifically, the dialectical process identified in the previous chapter, through which the decreasing importance of distance has led to an increase in the importance of turning. Again, this is the result of the "time-space compression" identified by Donald Janelle and given theoretical depth by David Harvey's integration of the concept into his historical-geographical materialist account of the spatio-temporalities of capitalism (Harvey, 1990). More recently, the accelerating influence of electronic information technologies has been seen to intensify time-space compression and to pose a fundamental challenge to the time-geographic approach (Rosa, 2015). Capability, coupling and authority constraints have all been to some extent weakened by electronic information and communication technologies (Couclelis, 2009, 1559). As a result, the underlying time-geographic assumption of "a strong correspondence between a person's movement across space and time and that person's activity schedule over the same period" is being weakened for ever-larger numbers of people (Couclelis, 2009, 1559). No longer is it the case that location can be used straightforwardly as an indicator of activity. People "can shop from their home or workplace, carry on business transactions from their car, socialize while walking alone down the street, engage in high-tech forms of entertainment while sitting in a classroom, or work for a living while sipping cappuccinos at the corner cafe" (Couclelis, 2009, 1559).

If we can do a wider range of things from wherever we happen to be, it is also to be expected that, as Couclelis argues, a general "fragmentation of activity" will tend to occur (Couclelis, 2000). "Instead of occupying compact chunks inside the daily prism, ICT (Information and Communication Technologies)-aided activities tend to disintegrate into sets of discrete tasks which get spread out across places and over time" (Couclelis, 2009, 1560). This echoes the hypothesis of fragmentation discussed in Chapters 5 and 6, and the suggestion that what Schatzki calls "integrated practices" are increasingly broken down into disconnected, modularized pieces more akin to "dispersed practices" (Schatzki, 1996). A direct corollary of this development is that the co-presence of individuals in particular settings – even in settings configured for shared tasks – has become less likely to mean that they are engaged with each other, or in related activities. Again, the loosening of temporal and spatial constraints based on distance suggest a general increase in the significance of direction. If the range of things we can be doing from any one place increases, moving between activities becomes less a matter of covering distance and more a matter of turning. To repeat the slogan suggested in Chapter 7, turning is the new moving. But again, our capacity for active, directed engagement is limited. Precisely as the once-reliable correlation between specific places and corresponding activities weakens, the "limited ability of any human being to undertake more than one task at a time", and the fact that all activities have durations, become more central and significant constraints (Pred, 1977, 208).

Despite these new developments, daily-path and life-path diagrams remain a tremendously helpful way of representing the weave of social relations. This is because it is still the case that, in Pred's words, "each of the actions and events consecutively occurring between the birth and death of an individual has both temporal and spatial attributes" (Pred, 1981, 9). Notwithstanding the increasing complexity of some of these attributes, and even with all the new technological enhancements available especially to privileged denizens of the Global North, our lives and experiences, as well as our actions, are still centered upon finite human bodies in particular time-space contexts. These bodies still have specific spatial and temporal characteristics that both enable and constrain what it is possible for us to do at any given moment. To try to accommodate the new insights about the decoupling of place and activity while retaining the focus on temporal and spatial contexts of embodiment, Adams has sought to incorporate technologically heightened connectivity – "human extensibility" – across great distances and the accompanying relaxation of requirements for co-presence into time-geographic path diagrams (Adams, 1995). Adams's diagrams are an intuitive and continuous development of the earlier path diagrams, and provide some graphic elements that can be of use in the present argument.

Figure 8.10 captures Adams's chief additional innovation (modified after Adams, 1995, 273). The possibility of connections and joint actions over larger distances raised by electronic information technologies is depicted as bands or ribbons emanating from daily-paths. The thickness of these bands shows the duration of the distant connection (phone call, skype, e-mail, etc.). When such connections are effectively instantaneous, they are depicted as fully horizontal relative to the plane surface of space below. The ribbons do incorporate a directional element: each ribbon emanating from a particular daily-path points in a different direction. Yet the specific directions depicted

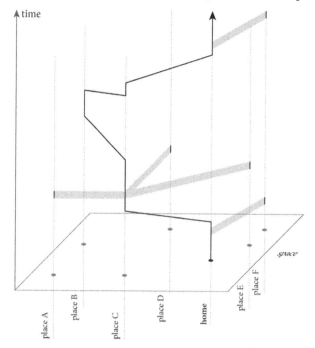

Figure 8.10 Daily-path with extensibility

in the ribbons are arbitrary and merely illustrative. To this extent the graphic innovation remains compatible with the petri-dish model of human agency: a loosening of distance constraints is pictured as a loosening in all directions. Indeed, the very concept of "extensibility" connotes a general possibility. Thus, direction is secondary. Nevertheless, if each ribbon – or multiple ribbon, as in Adams's example of an e-mail that goes to multiple destinations – shooting off from the daily-path is understood to be exclusive of other activities, Figure 8.10 can be seen to illustrate the directional exclusivity of focused engagements.

Adams's innovation provides a good starting point, but it needs to be supplemented with more prominent directional features if daily-path diagrams are to be made fit for illustrating important parts of the argument in the present book. The diagrams to follow will be built up successively from components. The first set of changes relative to earlier diagrams is shown in Figure 8.11.

This is a stretch of time an individual spends in the same place. The depictions of an individual zoned into frontal, lateral and dorsal fields developed in previous chapters is placed at the tip of a daily-path line. Trailing out behind the now-moment are a series of directed engagements, one of them, as in Adams's diagrams, involves a connection to a remote place, the others do not. In both cases, retentional triangles growing off of the daily-path depict

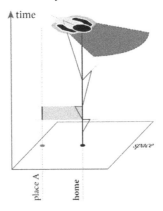

Figure 8.11 Segment of a daily-path with turnings

the segments of continuous experience accompanying each engagement, as in Chapter 6. The ribbon from Adams is superimposed upon the experiential retention in the one case of engagement over extended distances. The fact that the stretch of time depicted is completely taken up with a series of directed engagement captures better than traditional diagrams the way days tend to be occupied. The general increase in the importance and centrality of turning as hypothesized here can be pictured by juxtaposing two dioramas as in Figure 8.12 and Figure 8.13 (here with the representations of bodies left out again for simplicity).

The diorama in Figure 8.12 involves more physical movement, with only one focused engagement in each location; the one in Figure 8.13 involves less physical movement but more turning, in the form of many engagements in the same place. The two diagrams can be thought of as the extreme ends of a spectrum, and the juxtaposition is exaggerated in order to make a visual point. Matters are more complicated in reality because, among other things, time-space compression is linked not only with easier communication but with easier physical travel. Thus, there is no reason to expect that the life-paths of denizens of the Global North would generally become less structured by movement. Increasing long-distance travel and tourism numbers make this clear enough. However, the focus here is upon the relatively routine realm of everyday activities undertaken in the course of a daily-path, not so much upon longer-term (yearly or life-) paths. At this everyday level, it makes more sense to expect that the historical dialectic driven by time-space compression under recent stages of capitalism in the Global North promotes a general shift from moving to turning as the medium for the segmentation of everyday practices. Secondly, the new prominence of turning does not presuppose a spatially stationary state: the increased prominence of turning is often felt even while moving, most paradigmatically in the problematic of cell-phone use while driving.

Insofar as turning is becoming the new moving, co-location or what Giddens calls "presence-availability" is tendentially decoupled from joint attention or joint activity, and is thus ceding importance to what I termed "engagement

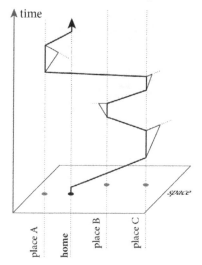

Figure 8.12 Traditional motion-intensive daily-path

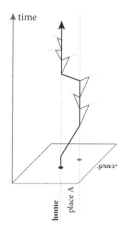

Figure 8.13 A more turning-intensive daily-path

availability". Figure 8.14 depicts this issue in a simplified way with reference to two co-present people who are nevertheless unavailable to each other for engagement at the moment.

These images could be elaborated further, scaled up and tied together into graphic representations of complex scenarios of interaction. However, I will not attempt to carry out this development here. The fundamental advantage these diagrams offer in comparison with the more traditional time-geographical images should be clear enough: by building into the picture the directional con-stellations of engagement and non-engagement, as well as a depiction of the

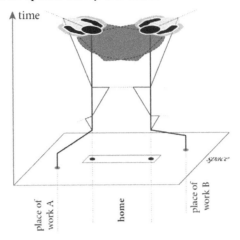

Figure 8.14 Presence-availability without engagement-availability

turnings making up the segmentation of the daily path, they balance the traditional focus upon distance with a complementary focus on the orientation of practice and thus provide an overall view of key aspects of practical life that is clearly more complete. The imagery of direction also allows such issues as deep attention, fragmentation and alienation to be represented at least in schematic form. To the extent that a larger historical dialectic is in the process of partially supplanting distance with direction as a fundamental organizing principle of social life, this change, too, can be readily illustrated. That said, the directional innovations offered here are largely restricted in their application to the micro-scale of the sequence of activities in everyday life. It would not make much sense in my view to try to enhance "life-path" – as opposed to "daily-path" – diagrams in a similar way.

This chapter has attempted to crystalize diagrammatically the sensibility developed throughout the book. The point is emphatically not to assert that the entire reality of practical life can be adequately represented in the forms presented here. Rather the idea is that such graphics can heighten our sensibility for the fact that much of our activity – however qualitatively rich and difficult to pin down in its ontological fullness – is fundamentally framed by turnings of attention and practice. The concluding chapter seeks to build upon this sensibility by asking ethical and political questions about what is to be done.

References

Adams, P.C. (1995). A reconsideration of personal boundaries in space-time. *Annals of the Association of American Geographers*, 85(2), pp. 267–285.

Ahmed, S. (2006). *Queer Phenomenology: Orientations, Objects, Others*. Durham, NC: Duke University Press.

Baker, A.R.H. (1979). Historical geography: a new beginning? *Progress in Human Geography*, 3, pp. 560–570.

Benjamin, W. (2008). *The Work of Art in the Age of Mechanical Reproduction*. Trans. J. Underwood. London: Penguin.

Buttimer, A. (1976). Grasping the dimensions of the life-world. *Annals of the Association of American Geographers*, 66, pp. 277–292.

Couclelis, H. (2000). From sustainable transportation to sustainable accessibility: can we avoid a new tragedy of the commons? In: D. Janelle and D. Hodge, eds., *Information, Place and Cyberspace: Issues in Accessibility*. Berlin: Springer, pp. 342–356.

Couclelis, H. (2009). Rethinking time geography in the information age. *Environment and Planning A*, 41, pp. 1556–1575.

Debord, G. (2009). *Society of the Spectacle*. Trans. K. Knabb. Eastbourne: Soul Bay Press.

Giddens, A. (1984). *The Constitution of Society*. London: Polity Press.

Gregson, N. (1986). On duality and dualism: the case of structuration and time geography. *Progress in Human Geography*, 10(2), pp. 184–205.

Hanson, S. and Pratt, G. (1988). Reconceptualizing the links between home and work in urban geography. *Economic Geography*, 64(4), pp. 299–321.

Harvey, D. (1990). Between space and time: reflections on the geographical imagination. *Annals of the Association of American Geographers*, 80(3), pp. 418–434.

Hägerstrand, T. (1967). *Innovation Diffusion as a Spatial Process*. Chicago, IL: University of Chicago Press.

Hägerstrand, T. (1996). Diorama, path and project. In: J. Agnew, D. Livingstone and A. Rodgers, eds., *Human Geography: An Essential Anthology*. Oxford: Blackwell, pp. 650–674.

Krämer, S. (2016). *Figuration, Anschauung, Erkenntnis: Grundlinien einer Diagrammatologie*. Frankfurt am Main: Suhrkamp.

Kwan, M.-P. (2000). Gender differences in space-time constraints. *Area*, 32(2), pp. 145–156.

Kwan, M.-P. (2002). Progress Report: Time, information technologies, and the geography of everyday life. *Urban Geography*, 23(5), pp. 471–482.

McQuoid, J. and Dijst, M. (2012). Bringing emotions to time geography: the case of mobilities of poverty. *Journal of Transport Geography*, 23, pp. 26–34.

Miller, H. (2005). A measurement theory for time geography. *Geographical Analysis*, 37, pp. 17–45.

Miller, H. and Bridwell, S. (2009). A field-based theory for time geography. *Annals of the Association of American Geographers*, 99(1), pp. 49–75.

Parkes, D. and Thrift, N. (1980). *Times, Spaces and Places: A Chronogeographic Perspective*. Oxford: John Wiley.

Pred, A. (1977). The choreography of existence: comments on Hägerstrand's time-geography and its usefulness. *Economic Geography*, 53(2), pp. 207–221.

Pred, A. (1981). Social reproduction and the time-geography of everyday life. *Geografiska Annaler Series B: Human Geography*, 63(1), pp. 5–22.

Pred, A. (1984). Place as a historically contingent process: structuration and the time-geography of becoming places. *Annals of the Association of American Geographers*, 74(2), pp. 279–297.

Rosa, H. (2015). *Social Acceleration: A New Theory of Modernity.* Trans. J. Trejo-Mathys. New York: Columbia University Press.

Rose, G. (1993). *Feminism & Geography: The Limits of Geographical Knowledge.* Cambridge: Polity Press.

Schatzki, T. (1996). *Social Practices: A Wittgensteinian Approach to Human Activity and the Social.* Cambridge: Cambridge University Press.

Scholten, C., Friberg, T. and Sandén, A. (2012). Re-Reading Time-Geography From A Gender Perspective: Examples From Gendered Mobility. *Tijdschrift voor Economische en Sociale Geografie*, 103(5), pp. 584–600.

Thrift, N. and Pred, A. (1981). Time-geography: a new beginning. *Progress in Human Geography*, 5(2), pp. 277–286.

Conclusion
Ethics and directional responsibility

If, as argued in Chapter 7, an historical-geographical dialectic is at work in which time-space compression has heightened the importance of turning and direction in step with the diminishing importance of distance and separation, it makes sense to rethink the question of "what is to be done" in directional terms. "What is to be done" has become less and less a matter of "where to be" but rather "where to turn". The concluding chapter will shift to a language of ethics. Following the fundamental feminist insight that the personal is always also the political, I understand ethics and politics to be closely intertwined. The vocabulary of ethics is intended here to accent the personal level of decision-making about how to lead one's life. The idiom of ethics also makes it possible to demonstrate once more how the style of thought typical of socio-spatial theory is one-sidedly organized around notions of distance at the expense of direction.

In the first section the stage is set for addressing these questions by a review of some general features of the geographical engagement with ethics, which has been strongly focused upon distance. The following section will begin to outline an alternative, more directional approach to ethics. Here the central ethical question emerges from the discussion of social dark matter and reproduction by neglect. In what sense can individuals be held or hold ourselves ethically responsible for the various configurations of social dark matter always behind us? How can we adequately respond to the provocative assertion that "if X is behind what we are doing, then X is what we are doing"? I suggest a differentiated understanding of responsibility that draws in part on the feminist ethics of care, and introduce the concepts of "organic composition of responsibility", "directional justice" and "directional privilege". The third section asks what happens to different kinds of responsibility when advancing time-space compression "collapses" them into the surfaces and features of our immediate bodily environments. The final part links the directional perspective to more familiar strands of progressive politics, showing how this perspective does not so much offer a new politics as a new inflection of politics based on the insistence upon the ever-present "OR" of directed engagement. To return to a point made at the very beginning of the book, the final section will illustrate the fact that thinking through the lenses of direction, an exercise that has been "discouragingly complex", also partakes of the "terrifyingly banal" (Freytag, 2015, 253).

Ethics and distance

A long-standing problem in ethics has been the question of how to behave toward distant others. Under the traditional principles of modern ethical theory, whether Kantian or utilitarian, distance is not a major difficulty. Since these theories abstract from the specific characteristics of individuals and their situations in the interest of impartiality, they can establish the presence or absence of obligations toward others without regard to distance or proximity. Traditional ethical theories, as Virginia Held, notes, are centered upon the question of how to act toward relative strangers (Held, 2006, 24). Virtue theories, such as that of Alasdair MacIntyre (1981, 1990), begin to suggest that ethics is not indifferent to distance. Individual virtues, according to MacIntyre, presuppose membership in a specific community. Although communities need be neither small-scale nor based primarily upon people who know each other personally, in many cases they are. Geographers have focused upon basic assumptions about distance and the scope of ethical responsibility in different ethical theories. In an important article in the geographical discussion of ethics, David Smith asks, "How far should we care?", or in other words, "whether geographical proximity is a relevant difference with the moral force to temper wider and perhaps universal humanitarian sentiments based on the recognition that all persons are in some significant way the same or at least very similar" (Smith, 1998, 16). One among many strands of discussion in this vein has been a critical questioning of the relation between Kant's particularist anthropology and the supposed universalism of his ethical philosophy (Harvey, 2009, 33–36; Popke, 2007; Elden and Mendieta, 2011).

In this context it is not surprising that some writers on ethics in geography have engaged with the ethics of care developed by feminist thinkers (Nelson, 1999; Smith, 1998, 2001; Smith, 2009; McEwan and Goodman, 2010). The feminist ethics of care, as noted in Chapter 7, starts with the basic fact that practices of care are experienced by every human being at different times, and that caring relationships are an integral part of human life (Tronto, 1993). Feminist care ethics, especially in earlier iterations, has thus tended to focus on small-scale, face-to-face relationships with particular persons, especially in domestic settings (Held, 2006, 18). Thus, they involve a very different picture of ethical situations than the varieties of justice ethics oriented toward impartiality and relations between strangers. A similar association with particular, interpersonal interactions can be seen in geographical approaches to ethical questions that draw upon Levinas's conception of the foundational ethical appeal of the other (Popke, 2003; Harrison, 2008).

Despite this initial association with the local, feminist care ethics and other non-traditional approaches have more recently sought to relate ethical perspectives based on caring, empathy, emotional responsiveness and relationality to broader social problems. In so doing, they have asserted that care as both attitude and practice is just as relevant to public economic and political spheres as to the household. Caring relations "even in the political and legal domain will share some of the features of caring relations in the family or among friends", such as valuing persons as distinct individuals and being attentive to their needs (Held, 2006, 130). In other words, at larger geographical scales, caring is intimately related to solidarity. "Assuring that care is available to those who need it should be a central political concern, not one imagined to be a solely private responsibility of families and charities" (Held, 2006, 69). This "scaling up" of care ethics has gone hand-in-hand with elaborations of sources of universal or global responsibility not based in abstract relations of equivalence and impartiality. In care ethics, responsibility is understood to be "located not in the abstract universals of justice, but rather in the recognition of our intersubjective being" (Popke, 2006, 507). Distant others are thus not ethical concerns because they are interchangeable with ourselves or with people closer by, but because we are all interconnected. Understanding far-reaching responsibilities is a chief concern of Jeff Popke's critical reassessment of Kant's cosmopolitan global ethics (Popke, 2007). Taking a related but differently inflected tack, Raghuram, Madge and Noxolo tie ethics explicitly to the postcolonial legacy and seek to infuse the wider awareness of interdependency with a sense of the inequalities and power-relations that have shaped the modern world (Raghuram, Madge and Noxolo, 2009).

All of these discussions continue to revolve around distance, although they have complicated David Smith's initial question of "how far we should care" with a more differentiated sense of what it is that makes distance relevant. The issue of direction, and the ethical implications of directed practice, have, by contrast, received far less attention. Some approaches do connect with the position I would like to take here. Non-representational writings that either implicitly or explicitly take up ethical themes have focused upon what Popke calls an "affective ethics of encounter" (Popke, 2009, 83). This ethics emphasizes openness to new possibilities, though there are marked differences between the more affirmative, Deleuzian version of openness associated with the writings of Thrift and Dewsbury (Thrift, 2007; Thrift and Dewsbury, 2000; Dewsbury, 2015) and the more passive-vulnerable version Paul Harrison explores on the basis of his reading of Levinas and others (Harrison, 2008, 2015). This work can be related to the model of the directionally asymmetrical human being introduced in Chapter 4. Openness to encounters is omnidirectional. On the other hand, responding actively to any particular encounter temporarily closes off others. An ethics of encounter, that is, is just as caught up in directional asymmetry as is any other account of how best to act in a given context.

Another important angle from which the initial focus on distance has been questioned is that of Doreen Massey in her consideration of responsibility in the context of a relational view of space (Massey, 2004, 2005). Massey directly challenges the dualism of "local" place versus "distant" space, and the associated "Russian doll" model according to which care is assumed to diminish with distance (Massey, 2004, 8–9). She seeks to open up "a politics of place which does not deprive of meaning those lines of connections, relations and practices, that construct place, but that also go beyond it" (Massey, 2004, 9). If the local is seen not only as inextricably co-composed with wider scales but also as potentially active in having effects at wider scales, new possibilities arise for taking responsibility for what we are used to thinking of as "space", not just for "place". Compelling as her critique of the local-global binary is, however, Massey, too, still couches her argument exclusively within the problematic of distance and proximity: the network-nodal perspective on connectivity is aimed at complicating and reconfiguring notions of distance and proximity, but it says nothing about direction.

Toward a directional ethics

How can we get a handle on this problem? How can we think ethical responsibility in a way not centered upon distance? The goal here is not to replace distance-based ethical thinking but to complement it. The question of "how far we should care" remains important, but a second question, "in which direction(s) we should care", or better, "in which direction(s) of care we should act", is recognized as equally important. The first question has long been answered in a global sense by rationalist justice ethics, but is increasingly also receiving a different global answer from ethical approaches associated earlier with interpersonal or local relations. However, none of these perspectives eliminates the directional selectivity of embodied human engagement. The fundamental starting point for thinking about directional ethics is, again, the principle adapted from Sara Ahmed, according to which "what we do" has two parts: what we are actively doing, and what we are reproducing by being turned away from it. The petri-dish "phenomenology of the 'I can'" (Ahmed, 2006, 138) clearly cannot form the basis for a directional ethics. Such an ethics cannot ignore the social dark matter behind our backs – even dark matter we have never been directed toward and have no conception of. But just as little can it condone a view in which every individual is uniformly ethically accountable to the entire world. How can we discern an ethics in the zone in between these two extremes?

To try to reflect more adequately on this issue, I would propose that ethical responsibility be differentiated into three forms corresponding to three basic directional relations we may have with ethical matters:

- Potential or merely causal responsibility, that is, the baseline responsibility we all share, if perhaps only in an infinitesimally small degree, for that part of our social dark matter made up of the situations of people (perhaps also other beings or states of affairs) toward whom we have never been directed and of whom we are not aware but could be made aware. We are responsible for these matters simply by virtue of the global interconnectedness of social life as this is theorized in a range of different ethical positions.

- Latent or "cosmopolitan" responsibility, responsibility toward matters of concern we have actually been directed toward at one time or another in the past and of which we are thus aware. This is responsibility toward what we have "re-reified". Latent responsibility, like potential responsibility, may be relatively infinitesimal or more substantial in scope according to the specific situation.
- Immediate, directed responsiveness, that is, our experience of commitment (however weak or strong) to meeting the exigencies and needs of ourselves and others in the embodied situation in which we are currently involved.

Adapting a concept from Marx, we could ask, first, about different "organic compositions" of responsibility. Generally speaking, people whose jobs involve needing to know about events beyond their immediate everyday environments – for example, social scientists and humanities scholars, journalists, activists, but also military planners or stock traders – can be seen to have a higher proportion of latent or cosmopolitan responsibility (regardless of whether we recognize or act upon it) relative to the other types. The same would be true of individuals in other socio-economic positions – for example, "news junkies" – who for other reasons regularly inform themselves about events beyond their immediate life-contexts. Being aware of a larger number of specific possible claims upon our solidarity or care may bring with it a more acute sense of the directional finitude of our active engagements. At the same time, though, this broader awareness affords more epistemic resources with which to be deliberate about the particular mix of activities with which we occupy ourselves. All of this should be understood in formal, directional terms, quite apart from the qualitative question of whether or how individuals or groups will tend to recognize or respond to different combinations of causal, latent and immediate responsibility. Systematic, positional differences in how different groups tend to relate to such constellations of responsibility is another topic that would connect the arguments made here with critical genealogies of difference and identity.

It is possible in this context to think, on the one hand, of a kind of second-order "directional justice" that asks whether the mix or sequence of directions in which we occupy ourselves through active engagement with some subset of the range of possible ethical engagements is acceptable. Justice in this sense is a matter of comparative prioritization, and is linked to our directionally finite active engagements. Here the fact that transversal relations with others who are not directed toward us are the condition of possibility of solidarity is relevant: ideally we should be directed with some degree of regularity toward others in this way. But on the other hand, as a kind of counterbalance to considerations of directional justice, there is a presumption in favor of immediate appeals that has to do with our fundamental openness and answerability, and that Held suggests it is difficult for us as embodied humans to ignore (Held, 2006, 71). "Immediacy" here need not imply geographical proximity but rather urgency. Urgency of need seems to me to be a value we often spontaneously respect, even where we do not respond to it for whatever reason. The most obvious examples of the presumption in favor of urgent need come out of care ethics: someone feels compelled to skip a protest against gun violence because her parents are ill. In this case the point is not that the ill parents are ethically more important than the protest in a comparative sense; it is just that the felt immediacy of their need pre-empts attending the protest (or doing anything else). Similarly, we might become aware through the media of an outrageous violation of the rights or welfare of distant others in a way that resonates strongly. This could lead to dropping other competing responsibilities in the conviction that one must try to do something about the injustice. I agree with Held and Noddings that responding to this kind of appeal does not involve impartially weighing alternative scenarios in order to decide which is the more just way to proceed (Held, 2006; Noddings, 2013). This is a case of directional pre-emption, and cannot be corralled within the precepts of justice ethics.

The concept of directional justice refers us back to the figure of thought borrowed from Rahel Jaeggi in Chapter 5. Again, Jaeggi argues that whether a person has an alienated relation to their life is not a question of whether they themselves are the autonomous sources of what makes up their lives but rather whether they are able to appropriate the mix of life-experiences originating both within and outside of their own activities (Jaeggi, 2014). Translating this issue into the context of our directional asymmetry, and taking account of the principles of care ethics suggests a further ethically relevant differentiation. A directional ethics would involve two nested ideals of balance. First, we should seek an acceptable balance between control and lack of control of what occupies us. Put differently, we need to balance our commitments to addressing chosen and unchosen appeals. But second, on the side of our answerability to unchosen appeals, we also need to differentiate between those appeals we don't control to which we want to be open and available, and those to which we do not want to be available. We should look for ways in which to remain open to the kinds of appeals and address that belong to leading an ethical life we can accept, while at the same time seeking to reduce the possibility of interruption by the kinds of manipulative appeals involved in capitalist value production and realization. Again, this is a formal way of approaching directional ethics.

The idea of directional justice in turn suggests a notion of "directional privilege" that begins to lead us back out toward the realm of larger-scale politics. Directional privilege in this view could be defined as *having the possibility to reflect upon and influence these nested forms of balance*. This definition does not require that the directionally privileged actually take the opportunity to act in solidarity with distant others. The category of the directionally privileged would also include many people, such as overworked executives, who might feel they cannot establish such a balance but are only in this situation because of circumstances they have chosen. The directionally underprivileged would generally be those whose answerability to exigencies (whether their own or others') is called out so continuously and with such urgency that considerations beyond the world of relatively immediate need rarely have space to develop, or can only be developed with more effort than is required for the directionally privileged. The lack of autonomy experienced by the directionally underprivileged would not only involve being unable to control what occupies them, as in the traditional notion of autonomy, but also not being involved in establishing what Virginia Held terms "mutual autonomy", that is, agreements about how much traditional autonomy to trade off against answerability to the needs of others (Held, 2006, 48–49, 55). This notion of directional privilege is clearly a matter of infinitely fine and various gradations, and should not be thought of as composing class differentiations in the more robust sense of structural positions. However, it can help illuminate some broader political questions.

Ethical implications of the shift from distance to direction

A fundamental point any directional ethics has to insist upon is that these forms of responsibility only exist *within* the lived context of the ongoing series of turnings toward and away from different matters of concern that structure our lives and in turn *may impact* the series of our engagements from that point onward. These matters of concern, again, are often set within the teleoaffective structures of integrated practices (Schatzki, 1996). As it arises within the sequence of practices, ethical responsibility engages our answerability. A new external matter of which we become aware for the first time, the recollection of a matter we were already aware of, or an immediate appeal from our current surroundings – all of these are made possible by our omnidirectional vulnerability and constitutive openness toward the world. Receiving an impulse or appeal involves the possibility – within the ongoing flow of practice – of either continuing to be turned toward that with which one is occupied or turning toward a different matter of concern. Either way, our directedness will be exclusive. Secondly, depending upon how we respond, it may or may not result in future alterations of the series of turnings. The question of which matters of concern gain or retain directional priority for us is not necessarily related to how near or distant the others are whose situation has animated our sense of responsibility. Having become aware for the first time of a situation of injustice in a different part of the world, say, through media reporting, we may shift our relation to this situation from "potential responsibility" either to "latent" or to "immediate" responsibility.

To the extent that direction gains in importance with the waning significance of distance, to the extent that turning is in the process of becoming the new moving, the different forms of responsibility laid out above will tend to be collapsed into the immediate vicinity of our embodied lives. Here the technological process of bringing ever more activities onto the small screens we have at home or carry around with us is especially significant. How we first learn about distant others and the responsibilities we may have toward them, and how we are reminded of the "latent" responsibilities of which we were already aware, become more and more similar to the way urgent appeals engage our answerability. In the not-so-distant past, most denizens of the Global North came into contact with less immediate ethical and political issues through qualitatively different processes (public broadcasting, print media, education), some of which were quite time-consuming. In the less desynchronized and fragmented knowledge-environments of previous decades, reflection upon the appropriate balance between different kinds of responsibility, and associated processes of recollection, would likewise have been a more deliberate process for many people. The collapse of the presence of all matters of concern onto the surfaces and devices around us have, I suggest, tended to undermine the ability of many people to engage in both the taking of distance and the turning involved in reflection. Deliberate reflection is of course still possible, and all of us engage with it every day. However, the relation between two possible activities to be weighed for their ethical merits against each other is encountered more and more often in the form of *an appeal to turn to a new activity intruding upon the ongoing pursuit of a current activity*. More and more such intrusions, whether we ultimately consider them legitimate or not, appear to us through the medium of carefully calibrated attention-capture technologies that draw upon psychological research to maximize the chances of inducing us to turn. "Urgency" is becoming more and more generic and ubiquitous, and the burden of distinguishing between the "truly" and the only "apparently" urgent is thus tendentially intensifying.

From OR to AND

One increasingly prominent response to this situation is the fast-growing demand for training in mindfulness, specifically as a counter-measure against stress. Mindfulness training has as one of its chief goals reflective control over the attentional dynamics of our answerability to appeals (Waldenfels, 2004). Thus, it is significant that geographers and other academics have begun to engage with mindfulness as a potential resource both for research methods and for coping more generally with the heightened demands upon individual awareness posed by accelerated, neoliberal capitalism (Whitehead, Lilley, Howell, Jones and Pykett, 2016). In a sense, mindfulness training builds directly upon the recognition of William James over a century ago of how central attentional control is to the possibility of autonomy in the traditional sense (James, 1950, 447–448). As Whitehead and his co-authors put it, however, "[m]indfulness is often categorised alongside other therapeutic forms of social intervention condemned for supporting the production of highly individualised, and politically passive subjects that are ideally suited to neoliberal hegemony". (Whitehead, Lilley, Howell, Jones and Pykett, 2016, 568).

Further, even highly trained, "mindful" individuals are not able in an absolute sense to increase the stock of directed time at their disposal available for possible directed engagements.

Thus, without denying the real benefits of mindfulness and other individual-level strategies, it is necessary to move the focus back out to larger political questions. At the most basic level, an awareness of the directedness of practice does not necessarily lead to a drastically different set of ethical positions from those that we would expect to emerge from a leftist-progressive politics. The difference a directional approach can make in many cases is chiefly in deepening or supplementing our sense of why particular issues are important to address. Again, I leave aside in this book much of the genealogy of hierarchical difference and focus chiefly on issues related to the outline of political economy presented in foregoing chapters. Within this purview, the clearest examples of reinforcement of existing critical politics have to do with the politico-ethical condemnation of and struggle against neoliberal capitalism at both a general societal and an institutional level. The politics of occupation and the political economy of oriented practice outlined in foregoing chapters deepen or extend our sense of what is meant by the capitalist exploitation of human bodies and by neoliberal programs of privatization of public goods and precarization of work. The body as an accumulation strategy can be mobilized not only in the familiar physical senses but across the entire range of its cognitive, affective and emotional registers, with corresponding damage resulting from increasingly excessive and contradictory demands placed upon it.

One thing that comes out more clearly in a directional approach is the way in which absorption in neoliberal capitalist social life tends to thwart directional justice, in the sense that it means being turned away from projects of solidarity premised upon transversal directedness toward others who are not directed toward us, as well as from relations of care associated with mutual direction of people toward each other. The heightened pressure upon directional engagements characterizing technologically mediated neoliberal capitalist life may be an important part of the explanation for why more denizens of the Global North are not actively engaged in projects of solidarity with less privileged others. It is not so much a matter of excessive distance as of intensifying directional distraction. Given the leading role attention often takes in steering our practices, part of the opposition to these features of neoliberal capitalist life must also involve the positive preservation or expansion of non-commercial sources of information on distant others and social needs. Public goods such as not-for-profit broadcasting systems and other public media, official statistics on social injustices and inequalities, and independent social scientific scholarship are necessary in order for us to continue to be made aware of appeals for care and solidarity. A related argument about heightened pressures on finite directed engagement applies to crises of care (whether childcare, healthcare or elder care): exploitative conditions of employment for care workers as well as intensifying directional pressures upon family members and friends – as producers, as consumers and as culti-vators of ourselves – conspire to place growing numbers of people needing care in situations where their need for care is not met. In a related way, a directional perspective does not suggest a new politics relative to the problem of the "double career" with which many women still grapple; it merely adds to the underlying analysis of the problem.

At the level of institutional governance, a political economy of orientation deepens critiques of neoliberal management techniques as these intensify demands on time. A directional approach argues that it is more specifically the *directed* time of *directed* practice, in the context of human *directional* asymmetry, that lies at the core of the issue. This perspective sharpens the need to insist that *human beings cannot be forced, cajoled, incentivized, induced or seduced to keep doing ever more* – apart from extremely modest prospects for improving the efficiency of our practices – without paying an ever-larger price. This price takes the form of increasing frequency of mental and physical health problems (Han, 2015; Ehrenberg, 2016), deterioration of capabilities for sustained attention (Stiegler, 2010), and deterioration of the quality of practices for which sustained attention and engagement remains essential (Gazzaley and Rosen, 2016). Here the analyses in Chapters 5 and 6 can help anchor critiques of fragmentation in our embodied relation to the world. They also implicitly support movements for "slow science" (Berg and Seeber, 2016; Mountz et al., 2015; Stengers, 2018). It is not just in the occu-pation of time but in the occupation of *directed* time that a politics of exclu-sivity is at work. At the smallest scale, a directional perspective makes clearer what it is about computer screens and smartphones that makes them such a dangerous platform for struggles over exploitation and control of our atten-tion and directed practice. All of these heightened pressures contribute to the sharpening of the contradiction discerned in Chapter 7, whereby the increas-ing demands on directed attention and practice characteristic of neoliberal capitalism in the 21st-century Global North, the shift from "moving" to "turning", may now be running up against the physical limitations of our embodied directional asymmetry. If this is indeed a (potential) contradiction, how might it be exploited in the interest of emancipation?

On this how question as well, the directional perspective amplifies existing principles. This book has argued the entire time that the directional asym-metry of embodied human practice needs to be taken more seriously. Doing so in the register of political strategy almost automatically strengthens the emphasis on the need for divisions of labor and collective *organization*. If we see more clearly that our directed engagements must always be limited in scope as compared with the range of possible directed engagements, it stands to reason that the necessity for *organized* politics also becomes more obvious. The capitalist firms, states and other large and powerful actors that partially structure our life-environments can be understood not merely as "large phe-nomena" (Nicolini, 2017) but as entities (or assemblages) that are *not limited by the directional finitude of their active engagements*, or at least not even remotely as limited as individual human beings. This is one very important implication of the historical development of "corporate human rights" (Barkan, 2013). Large organizations are the only real multi-taskers of the social world. To pursue a politics against the interests of such actors capable of multiple directional engagements, it is absolutely necessary to organize into larger movements and institutions characterized by divisions of labor. The model of the scholar-activist cannot be restricted to that of the individual heroine or hero but must very clearly include a sense of playing a necessarily limited and specific role within larger projects. This is of course a point long recognized by radical scholars, and may appear "terrifyingly banal" (Freytag, 2015, 253). But a directional perspective can add depth to the insight that "what is to be done" must and can only be done through complexly intertwined directed practices. In this way, what takes place "behind the backs" of some will be squarely in front of others acting in collaboration and solidarity with them (Marx, 1967, 51–52).

Critical socio-spatial theory has long urged taking *critical distance* from the *status quo* of life under capitalism, patriarchy, racism, and other forms of injustice and exploitation. What the argument of this book has sought to add is a sense for the importance of taking a *critical angle* on the world. Taking a critical angle is not the same as taking critical distance, in the sense that turning to a new orientation does not expand the scope of what can be critically engaged, it only changes the specific sliver of the world toward which we are pointed. In general, Ahmed's exhortation to investigate what is behind the usual assumptions of socio-spatial theory makes great sense. But we should be clear about the fact that bringing the backside of any particular discourse or activity into our frontside necessarily puts other things behind us for the moment. Socio-spatial theory would do well to face this fact more often, both in seeking to grasp the world and in seeking to understand its own actual and potential role in it.

References

Ahmed, S. (2006). *Queer Phenomenology: Orientations, Objects, Others*. Durham, NC: Duke University Press.

Barkan, J. (2013). *Corporate Sovereignty: Law and Government Under Capitalism*. Minneapolis, MN: University of Minnesota Press.

Berg, M. and Seeber, B. (2016). *The Slow Professor: Challenging the Culture of Speed in the Academy*. Toronto: University of Toronto Press.

Dewsbury, J.D. (2015). Non-representation landscapes and the performative affective forces of habit: from 'Live' to 'Blank'. *Cultural Geographies*, 22(1), pp. 29–47.

Ehrenberg, A. (2016). *The Weariness of the Self: Diagnosing the History of Depression in the Contemporary Age*. Trans. E. Caouette, J. Homel, D. Homel, D. Winkler. Montreal: McGill-Queens University Press.

Elden, S. and Mendieta, E., eds. (2011). *Reading Kant's Geography*. Albany, NY: State University of New York Press.

Freytag, T. (2015). Überlegungen zu einer geographische Praxis (auch jenseits) der Aufmerksamkeit. *Geographische Zeitschrift*, 103(4), pp. 252–254.

Gazzaley, A. and Rosen, L. (2016). *The Distracted Mind: Ancient Brains in a High-Tech World*. Cambridge, MA: MIT Press.

Han, B.-C. (2015). *The Burnout Society*. Trans. E. Butler. Palo Alto, CA: Stanford University Press.

Harrison, P. (2008). Corporeal remains: vulnerability, proximity, and living on after the end of the world. *Environment and Planning A*, 40(2), pp. 423–445.

Harrison, P. (2015). After affirmation, or, being a loser: on vitalism, sacrifice and cinders. *GeoHumanities*, 1(2), pp. 285–306.

Harvey, D. (2009). *Cosmopolitanism and the Geographies of Freedom*. New York: Columbia University Press.

Held, V. (2006). *The Ethics of Care: Personal, Political and Global*. Oxford: Oxford University Press.

Jaeggi, R. (2014). *Alienation*. Trans. A. Smith. New York: Columbia University Press.

James, W. (1950). *The Principles of Psychology*. 2 Volumes. New York: Dover.

MacIntyre, A. (1981). *After Virtue: A Study in Moral Theory*. South Bend, IN: University of Notre Dame Press.

MacIntyre, A. (1990). *Three Rival Versions of Moral Enquiry: Encyclopaedia, Genealogy and Tradition*. South Bend, IN: University of Notre Dame Press.

Marx, K. (1967). *Capital*, Vol. 1. Trans. S. Moore, E. Aveling. New York: International Publishers.

Massey, D. (2004). Geographies of responsibility. *Geografiska Annaler, Series B*, 86(1), pp. 5–18.

Massey, D. (2005). *For Space*. London: Sage.

McEwan, C. and Goodman, M. (2010). Place geography and the ethics of care: introductory remarks on the geographies of ethics, responsibility and care. *Ethics, Place and Environment*, 13(2), pp. 103–112.

Mountz, A., Bonds, A., Mansfield, B., Loyd, J., Hyndman, J. and Walton-Roberts, M. (2015). For slow scholarship: a feminist politics of resistance through collective action in the neoliberal university. *ACME: An International E-Journal for Critical Geographies*, 14(4), pp. 1235–1259.

Nelson, L. (1999). Bodies (and spaces) do matter: the limits of performativity. *Gender, Place and Culture*, 6, pp. 331–353.

Nicolini, D. (2017). Is small the only beautiful? Making sense of 'large phenomena' from a practice-based perspective. In: A. Hui, T. Schatzki and E. Shove, *The Nexus of Practices: Connections, Constellations and Practitioners*. London: Routledge, pp. 98–113.

Noddings, N. (2013). *Caring: A Feminine Approach to Ethics and Moral Education*. 2nd ed. Berkeley, CA: University of California Press.

Popke, E.J. (2003). Poststructuralist ethics: subjectivity, responsibility and the space of community. *Progress in Human Geography*, 27(3), pp. 298–316.

Popke, J. (2006). Geography and ethics: everyday mediations through care and consumption. *Progress in Human Geography*, 30(4), pp. 504–512.

Popke, J. (2007). Geography and ethics: spaces of cosmopolitan responsibility. *Progress in Human Geography*, 31(4), pp. 509–518.

Popke, J. (2009). Geography and ethics: non-representational encounters, collective responsibility and economic difference. *Progress in Human Geography*, 33(1), pp. 81–90.

Raghuram, P., Madge, C. and Noxolo, P. (2009). Rethinking responsibility and care for a postcolonial world. *Geoforum*, 40(1), pp. 5–13.

Schatzki, T. (1996). *Social Practices: A Wittgensteinian Approach to Human Activity and the Social.* Cambridge: Cambridge University Press.

Smith, D. (1998). How far should we care? On the spatial scope of beneficence. *Progress in Human Geography*, 22(1), pp. 15–38.

Smith, D. (2001). Geography and ethics: progress, or more of the same? *Progress in Human Geography*, 25(2), pp. 261–268.

Smith, S. (2009). Everyday morality: where radical geography meets normative theory. *Antipode*, 41(1), pp. 206–209.

Stengers, I. (2018). *Another Science is Possible: A Manifesto for Slow Science.* Trans. S. Muecke. Cambridge: Polity.

Stiegler, B. (2010). *Taking Care of Youth and the Generations.* Trans. S. Barker. Stanford, CA: Stanford University Press.

Thrift, N. (2007). *Non-Representational Theory: Space | Politics | Affect.* London: Routledge.

Thrift, N. and Dewsbury, J.D. (2000). Dead geographies - and how to make them live. *Environment and Planning D: Society and Space*, 18(4), pp. 411–432.

Tronto, J. (1993). *Moral Boundaries: A Political Argument for an Ethic of Care.* New York: Routledge.

Waldenfels, B. (2004). *Phänomenologie der Aufmerksamkeit.* Frankfurt am Main: Suhrkamp.

Whitehead, M., Lilley, R., Howell, R., Jones, R. and Pykett, J. (2016). (Re)inhabiting awareness: geography and mindfulness. *Social & Cultural Geography*, 17(4), pp. 553–573.

Index

acceleration 38, 121–122, 132, 173–174
activity–place space 68, 73, 76, 79, 112
actome 33, 59
Adams, Paul C. 186, 192–193
adoption 126–127
Adorno, Theodor 145
affect 3, 15, 30, 33, 34, 51, 59, 60, 71,
  78, 79, 81, 94, 96, 101, 103, 109, 121,
  122–123, 124, 144, 201, 207
agency 5, 72–73, 74, 82–84, 97–99, 139;
  intentional vs. mental 41, 153–155;
  petri-dish model of 2, 90, 106–107,
  163, 190, 193
Ahmed, Sara xi, 2, 9, 98, 110, 128, 130,
  131, 132, 143–144, 149, 162–163, 175,
  176, 177, 183–184, 185, 190, 202, 209
Akoff, Linda 144
alienation 15, 113–114; and turning 127,
  132–133; and willing 121; as distance
  or separation 118–119; Jaeggi on
  118–120; Rosa on 122, 123
Althusser, Louis 3, 163
analytic of finitude 4–8, 13, 28, 35, 42, 95
anterior (relational) field 105–106,
  107, 109, 110, 111, 124, 136, 137, 139,
  161, 187
anthropological perspective 7, 14, 36,
  41, 96
appropriation 119–120, 122, 126,
  132–133
as-structure 141, 149; weak 149, 155
Ash, James 34, 39, 40
attention: and autonomy 39, 47,
  100, 117, 161–162, 168, 206;
  and human evolution 35–38; and
  practice 2, 32, 76–79, 80, 82, 94,
  107, 108, 109, 113, 117, 153, 174,
  196, 208; as a commodity 26–28; as a
  field of subjectivation 31–35; as a

vehicle of value-creation 28–31; as
  grasping 52–53, 129–131; complexity
  of 13, 46, 77, 117; crisis of 38,
  40, 42, 66, 127, 174; deep 39,
  40, 82, 95, 127, 134; definition
  of 48; Dewsbury on 59; directedness
  of 1, 69, 110; embodied character
  of 42, 94, 107, 108; finitude of 1,
  25, 31, 40, 42, 163, 165; genealogy
  of 28–29, 42; Gurwitsch on 53,
  54–56; Heidegger on 53–54;
  Husserl on 50–53, 143–144;
  hyper 39; in human geography 25;
  integrative function of 48; James
  on 46–48; joint 41, 153–154, 182,
  183, 185, 195; Merleau-Ponty on 53,
  56–59, 108; movement of 112; passive
  vs. active 59, 60–63; phenomenology
  of 13–14, 46–65; (political) economies
  of 13, 25–45, 125; psychological
  research on 13, 39, 48, 100, 104,
  134–136, 175; saturation of 31;
  Seamon on 59–60; selective function
  of 1, 25, 48, 101; solicitation of 38,
  43, 46, 60, 63, 77; Waldenfels on
  60–63, 99
attention deficit disorders 33–34,
  136; cultural 34; global 33,
  35, 174
attentional style 61, 62, 81, 82
autonomy: attentional 39, 47, 100, 117,
  161–162, 168, 206; individual 169;
  mutual 169

back region 11, 107; *see also* dorsal space
background 48, 50, 57, 58, 59, 61, 75,
  108, 140, 143
Badiou, Alain 7
Barad, Karen 6–7

216 *Index*

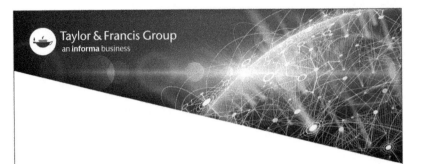

For Product Safety Concerns and Information please contact our EU
representative GPSR@taylorandfrancis.com
Taylor & Francis Verlag GmbH, Kaufingerstraße 24, 80331 München, Germany

www.ingramcontent.com/pod-product-compliance
Ingram Content Group UK Ltd.
Pitfield, Milton Keynes, MK11 3LW, UK
UKHW021613240425
457818UK00018B/539